THE PILGRIM'S PROGRESS
IN MODERN ENGLISH

D0483281

THE PILGRIM'S PROGRESS

IN MODERN ENGLISH

JOHN BUNYAN

COMPLETE AND UNABRIDGED EDITION
TRANSLATED FROM THE ORIGINAL
17TH CENTURY TEXT AND FURTHER ANNOTATED BY
L. EDWARD HAZELBAKER

Bridge-Logos

Gainesville, Florida 32614 USA

John Bunyan
THE PILGRIM'S PROGRESS IN MODERN ENGLISH
Copyright © 1998 by L. Edward Hazelbaker
Library of Congress Catalog Card Number: 98-72704
International Standard Book Number: 0-88270-757-4

09 08 07 06 05 7 6 5 4 3

Published by **Bridge-Logos**
Gainesville, FL 32614
www.bridgelogos.com

DEDICATION

To trav'lers of the past, their mem'ry to secure,
That cloud of witnesses, alive in Heaven pure.
For travelers today, to aid them in their trip;
To help them follow on, in Christ's directorship.
And future trav'lers, too, to help them run the race;
To heighten their resolve, their foes to all out-pace.
To my wife, who paid a price—putting up with me,
While I dwelt with Christian, and all his company.
To my children, each unique; help them hear a call
From the Lord of Glory, to give to Him their all.
And to the task ahead, in Bunyan's type of rhyme,
We send you, Pilgrim, out—again another time.

—LEH

And they admitted that they were aliens and strangers on earth. People who say such things show that they are looking for a country of their own. If they had been thinking of the country they had left, they would have had opportunity to return. Instead, they were longing for a better country—a heavenly one. Therefore God is not ashamed to be called their God, for he has prepared a city for them. (Hebrews 11:13-16)

ACKNOWLEDGEMENTS

I would like to acknowledge several individuals who played an important role in preparing me for Christian service and, therefore, the work involved in this translation. My heartfelt thanks and appreciation go to the following:

My Lord and Savior for granting me the privilege of translating John Bunyan's greatest work, the book I believe to be one of the most powerful works of Christian literature of all time.

My mother Irene—she prayed for my future before I was born. My Dad, Paul, would not go on Pilgrimage with her. We are satisfied that Dad made his peace with God before passing into eternity in 1982; but it was Mom who traveled in "the Way" year after year and showed the route to me, the youngest of five children. In her late 80's at the time of this writing, my mother still prays and looks forward to the day when all her children will make Celestial City their home.

My pastors, from birth to now, each one a "Great Heart" to me—Sister Marion Plies, my first pastor in Harbor City, California; and Jack T. Baron, Jimmie Ledgerwood, W.R. Redout, Otto L. Goins, Sr., and David L. Raines, respectively, all of whom have pastored in Perkins, Oklahoma.

Bob Burke, Oklahoma City attorney and author—it was Bob's enthusiasm for the idea of doing this translation that finally turned my contemplation into action.

Dr. Robert Kamm and his wife Maxine, of Stillwater, Oklahoma—they brought great encouragement to me in bringing this work to completion. The world would be a much better place if all those who dedicate their lives to teaching and academic administration were to share in their genuine love and concern for people and their dedication to God and spiritual values.

And finally, Reverend David Womack, former missionary, now an evangelist, and author of several books—his efforts during the early editing process are deeply appreciated. Without a doubt, this work is stronger because of his involvement.

—LEH

TABLE OF CONTENTS

Artwork featured on pages listed in italic typeface.

PART 2

THE PILGRIMAGE OF CHRISTIANA,
HER CHILDREN, AND HER FRIENDS

PREFACE

Since its publication in 1678, *The Pilgrim's Progress* has gone through thousands of editions and versions. Bunyan himself revised his book several times, changing some passages and adding others, including the entire second part. Because of the value placed on the book from the beginning, copies of Bunyan's early editions have been preserved in personal and public library collections throughout much of the world. In some libraries, you can even make copies of his original edition.

That edition, and most of those that followed, was, of course, written in the language of seventeenth century England, which is the language of the King James Version of the Bible. It's a delightful, musical language of the slower-paced time of yesterday. But it's also a language that is increasingly difficult to read today. For that reason, I worked for several years to produce a complete and unabridged version of *The Pilgrim's Progress* in modern English keeping in mind always that although my translation must be understandable to readers today, it must remain true to Bunyan's purpose in writing his allegorical novel. Since it is my belief that Bunyan was concerned mostly with spiritual meanings and applications, I worked carefully to retain these elements and the Christian message that he so eloquently expressed in his allegory.

To help the allegory flow easier than it previously did, I converted Bunyan's biblical quotations from the King James Version (KJV) of the Bible to the New International Version (NIV). Where this wasn't possible, I left the Scripture quotation in the language of the KJV. After translating as much as possible of *The Pilgrim's Progress* from seventeen century English into modern English, I hope this new version of Bunyan's book will be easy to read and fit in well with common speech for a long time to come.

In his book, Bunyan gave side notes with his scriptural references, and yet often made biblical allusions without telling where to find the passage in the Bible. Few of his partial and full scriptural quotations had reference marks within the text. In this new version, reference marks were put at each quotation, and the Scripture references and other notations were put at the end of the appropriate chapter. In the chapter endnotes, Bunyan's original Scripture verses or passages, some of which I corrected, and his explanatory statements are boldfaced so that you can distinguish them from the notations and Scripture references that I added.

In writing his allegory, Bunyan drew deeply from the Scriptures. In that spirit, this modern English edition has approximately five hundred Scripture references from Bunyan's original side notes, and more than eight hundred additional Scripture references. Of these, approximately sixty-six are direct Scripture quotations that Bunyan included but did not reference.

Bunyan put into his allegory some two hundred direct quotations from the Scriptures, making *The Pilgrim's Progress* one of the most scripturally based novels ever published. After researching and verifying each of the Scripture verses he used in his side notes or alluded to by context or allegory, I am awed by the scriptural depth of John Bunyan's book. It is truly a monument to the heart of the man, and to his God and Savior.

—L. Edward Hazelbaker

FOREWORD

John Bunyan's *The Pilgrim's Progress*, first published in 1678, is acknowledged by many to be second only to the Bible as a Christian publication. A religious allegory, it is regarded as a "classic among classics," with appeal to the learned and the unlearned, and to the young and old.

The book depicts, in Part 1, the life of "Pilgrim," the central figure, as he makes his Christian journey—a journey similar to that experienced by others for nearly 2000 years. Jesus foretold how difficult it would be; and His disciples, the apostle Paul, and other Christians have found that the journey is one of hardships and sacrifices, although there are great joys along the way. Part 2 of *The Pilgrim's Progress*, published six years after Part 1 relates the journey of Pilgrim's wife "Christiana," her children, and friends.

Although he wasn't formally educated, Bunyan's creative, imaginative writing impressed many of his contemporaries, as well as critics in later decades and centuries. His more than 60 published works are regarded by many to be at the same high level as those of such other great English writers as William Shakespeare and John Milton.

I became acquainted with *The Pilgrim's Progress* early in my life, as the volume was in the library of my parents' home. The original version of this book was in the language and style of the late 17th Century, and for two centuries it was widely read. Subsequently, *The Pilgrim's Progress* (as well as other literature of that period) experienced reduced readership, due mostly to changes in our English language.

Noting that Bible scholars and translators were producing more readable translations of the Bible to reach more people of all age groups and nationalities, other translators went to work to make The Pilgrim's Progress more readable. Recently, L. Edward Hazelbaker committed himself to translating The Pilgrim's Progress to modern English without losing the flavor and the power of John Bunyan's original volume.

In the words of the title sheet, the present version is a "Complete and Unabridged Edition Translated from the Original 17th Century English Text." To acquaint readers with the language used by John Bunyan, however, Hazelbaker begins his work by providing readers with Bunyan's own poetic defense of his book, as originally written. There then follows the translation with occasional words of explanation.

L. Edward Hazelbaker has brought a high Christian commitment and a deep sense of integrity to his translation efforts, striving always to preserve the volume as Bunyan's work, and not that of a translator. He has sought the reactions and the counsel of able, trusted friends and colleagues in an effort to assure both quality and validity in his translation. Also, Hazelbaker's work of further annotating Bunyan's classic is commendable.

—Robert B. Kamm
President Emeritus
Professor Emeritus
Oklahoma State University

JOHN BUNYAN'S ORIGINAL APOLOGY FOR HIS BOOK

WHEN AT THE FIRST I took my Pen in hand,
Thus for to write; I did not understand
That I at all should make a little Book
In such a mode: Nay, I had undertook
To make another; which, when almost done,
Before I was aware, I this begun.

    And thus it was: I writing of the Way
And Race of Saints in this our Gospel-day,
Fell suddenly into an Allegory
About their Journey, and the Way to Glory,
In more than twenty things, which I set down;
This done, I twenty more had in my crown,
And they again began to multiply,
Like sparks that from the coals of fire do fly.
Nay then, thought I, if that you breed so fast,
I'll put you by yourselves, lest you at last
Should prove ad infinitum, and eat out
The Book that I already am about.

Well, so I did; but yet I did not think
To show to all the World my Pen and Ink
In such a mode; I only thought to make
I knew not what: nor did I undertake
Thereby to please my Neighbour; no not I,
I did it mine ownself to gratifie.

Neither did I but vacant seasons spend
In this my scribble; nor did I intend
But to divert my self in doing this,
From worser thoughts, which make me do amiss.

Thus I set Pen to Paper with delight,
And quickly had my thoughts in black and white.
For having now my Method by the end,
Still as I pull'd, it came; and so I penn'd
It down; until it came at last to be
For length and breadth, the bigness which you see.

Well, when I had thus put mine ends together,
I shew'd them others, that I might see whether
They would condemn them, or them justify:
And some said, let them live; some, let them die;
Some said, John, print it; others said, Not so.
Some said, It might do good, others said, No.

Now was I in a straight, and did not see
Which was the best thing to be done by me:
At last I thought, Since ye are thus divided,
I print it will; and so the case decided.

For, thought I, Some, I see, would have it done,
Though others in that Channel do not run:
To prove then who advised for the best,
Thus I thought fit to put it to the test.

I further thought, if now I did deny
Those that would have it thus, to gratifie;
I did not know but hinder them I might
Of that which would to them be great delight.
For those that were not for its coming forth,
I said to them, Offend you, I am loth;
Yet since your Brethren pleased with it be,
Forbear to judge, till you do further see.

If that thou wilt not read, let it alone;
Some love the meat, some love to pick the bone:
Yea, that I might them better palliate,
I did too with them thus Expostulate:

May I not write in such a stile as this?
In such a method too, and yet not miss
Mine end, thy good? why may it not be done?
Dark Clouds bring Waters, when the bright bring none,
Yea, dark or bright, if they their Silver drops
Cause to descend; the Earth, by yielding Crops,
Gives praise to both, and carpeth not at either,
But treasures up the Fruit they yield together;
Yea, so commixes both, that in her Fruit
None can distinguish this from that; they suit
Her well, when hungry: but if she be full,
She spues out both, and makes their blessings null.

You see the ways the Fisher-man doth take
To catch the Fish; what Engines doth he make?
Behold how he engageth all his Wits;
Also his Snares, Lines, Angles, Hooks, and Nets:
Yet Fish there be, that neither Hook, nor Line,
Nor Snare, nor Net, nor Engine can make thine;
They must be grop't for, and be tickled too,
Or they will not be catch't, what e're you do.

How doth the Fowler seek to catch his Game
By divers means, all which one cannot name?
His Gun, his Nets, his Lime-twigs, light and bell:
He creeps, he goes, he stands; yea, who can tell
Of all his postures, Yet there's none of these
Will make him master of what Fowls he please.
Yea, he must Pipe and Whistle, to catch this,
Yet if he does so, that Bird he will miss.
If that a Pearl may in a Toad's head dwell,
And may be found too in an Oyster-shell;
If things that promise nothing, do contain
What better is than Gold; who will disdain,
(That have an Inkling of it,) there to look,
That they may find it? Now my little Book,

xvii

(Though void of all those paintings that may make
It with this or the other Man to take)
Is not without those things that do excel
What do in brave, but empty, notions dwell.

Well, yet I am not fully satisfied,
That this your Book will stand when soundly try'd.

Why, what's the matter! it is dark, what tho'?
But it is feigned: What of that I tro?
Some men by feigning words, as dark as mine,
Make truth to spangle, and its rayes to shine.
But they want solidness: Speak man thy mind:
They drownd the weak; Metaphors make us blind.

Solidity, indeed, becomes the Pen
Of him that writeth things Divine to men:
But must I needs want solidness, because
By Metaphors I speak; Was not God's Laws,
His Gospel-Laws, in older time held forth
By Types, Shadows and Metaphors? Yet loth
Will any sober man be to find fault
With them, lest he be found for to assault
The highest Wisdom: No, he rather stoops,
And seeks to find out what by pins and loops,
By Calves; and Sheep; by Heifers, and by Rams,
By Birds, and Herbs, and by the blood of Lambs,
God speaketh to him: And happy is he
That finds the light, and grace that in them be.

Be not too forward therefore to conclude
That I want solidness; that I am rude:
All things solid in shew, not solid be;
All things in parables despise not we,
Lest things most hurtful lightly we receive;
And things that good are, of our souls bereave.

My dark and cloudy words they do but hold
The Truth, as Cabinets inclose the Gold.

The Prophets used much by Metaphors
To set forth Truth; Yea, whoso considers
Christ, his Apostles too, shall plainly see,
That Truths to this day in such Mantles be.

Am I afraid to say that holy Writ
Which for its Style and Phrase puts down all Wit,
Is every where so full of all these things,
(Dark Figures, Allegories) yet there springs
From that same Book, that lustre, and those rays
Of light, that turn our darkest nights to days.

Come, let my Carper, to his Life now look,
And find There darker lines than in my Book
He findeth any: Yea, and let him know,
That in his best things there are worse lines too.

May we but stand before impartial men,
To his poor One, I durst adventure Ten,
That they will take my meaning in these lines
Far better than his Lies in Silver Shrines.
Come, Truth, altho' in Swaddling-clouts, I find
Informs the Judgment, rectifies the mind;
Pleases the Understanding, makes the Will
Submit; the Memory to it doth fill
With what doth our Imagination please;
Likewise it tends our troubles to appease.

Sound words I know, Timothy is to use,
And old Wives Fables he is to refuse;
But yet grave Paul, him no where doth forbid
The use of Parables; in which lay hid
That Gold, those Pearls, and precious stones that were
Worth digging for; and that with greatest care.

Let me add one word more. O man of God!
Art thou offended? dost thou wish I had
Put forth my matter in another dress,
Or that I had in things been more express?
Three things let me propound, then I submit
To those that are my betters, (as is fit).

1. I find not that I am denied the use
Of this my method, so I no abuse
Put on the Words, Things, Readers, or be rude
In handling Figure, or Similitude,
In application; but, all that I may,
Seek the advance of Truth, this or that way:

Deny'd, did I say? Nay, I have leave,
(Example too, and that from them that have
God better pleased by their words or ways,
Than any man that breatheth now a-days)
Thus to express my mind, thus to declare
Things unto thee, that excellentest are.

2. I find that men (as high as Trees) will write
Dialogue-wise; yet no man doth them slight,
For writing so: Indeed if they abuse
Truth, cursed be they, and the craft they use
To that intent; But yet let Truth be free
To make her salleys upon Thee, and Me.
Which way it pleases God: For who knows how,
Better than he that taught us first to Plough,
To guide our Mind and Pens for his Design?
And he makes base things usher in Divine.

3. I find that holy Writ in many places
Hath semblance with this method, where the cases
Do call for one thing, to set forth another;
Use it I may then, and yet nothing smother
Truth's golden Beams; Nay, by this method may
Make it cast forth its rays as light as day.

And now, before I do put up my Pen,
I'll shew the profit of my Book, and then
Commit both thee and it unto that hand
That pulls the strong down, and makes weak ones stand.

This Book it chalketh out before thine eyes
The man that seeks the everlasting Prize;
It shews you whence he comes, whither he goes,
What he leaves undone; also what he does:
It also shews you how he runs, and runs
Till he unto the Gate of Glory comes.

It shows too, who set out for life amain,
As if the lasting Crown they would attain:
Here also you may see the reason why
They lose their labour, and like Fools do die.

This book will make a Traveller of thee,
If by its Counsel thou wilt ruled be;

It will direct thee to the Holy Land,
If thou wilt its Directions understand:
Yea, it will make the slothful, active be;
The Blind also delightful things to see.

    Art thou for something rare, and profitable?
Wouldest thou see a Truth within a Fable?
Art thou forgetful? wouldest thou remember
From New-year's-day to the last of December?
Then read my fancies, they will stick like Burs,
And may be to the Helpless, Comforters.

    This Book is writ in such a Dialect,
As may the minds of listless men affect:
It seems a Novelty, and yet contains
Nothing but sound and honest Gospel-strains.

    Would'st thou divert thyself from Melancholy?
Would'st thou be pleasant, yet be far from folly?
Would'st thou read Riddles, and their Explanation?
Or else be drownded in thy Contemplation?
Dost thou love picking meat? Or wouldst thou see
A man i' th' Clouds, and hear him speak to thee?

    Would'st thou be in a Dream, and yet not sleep?
Or, wouldest thou in a moment laugh, and weep?
Wouldest thou lose thyself, and catch no harm?
And find thyself again without a charm?
Would'st read thyself, and read thou know'st not what,
And yet know, whether thou art blest or not,
By reading the same lines? O then come hither,
And lay my Book, thy Head, and Heart together.

—John Bunyan

PART 1

THE PILGRIMAGE OF CHRISTIAN, FAITHFUL, AND HOPEFUL

John Bunyan's dream

1

THE PILGRIM BEGINS HIS JOURNEY

As I WAS WALKING through the wilderness of this world, I came to a place where there was a cave. I laid down in that place to sleep,[1] and as I slept I had a dream in which I saw a man dressed in rags[2] standing in a certain place and facing away from his own house.[3] He had a Book in his hand and a great burden on his back.[4] As I looked, I saw him open the Book[5] and read out of it, and as he read he wept and trembled. Unable to contain himself any longer, he broke out with a sorrowful cry, saying, "What shall I do?"[6]

He went home in this state of mind but restrained himself as long as he could so his wife and children would not notice his distress. Yet he could not be silent long, because his troubled feeling was getting worse. He finally revealed to his wife and children what was going on in his mind, saying, "Oh, my dear Wife and Children, I'm suffering from inner turmoil because of a burden that lays heavily upon me. And, what's worse, I've been reliably informed that our city will be burned with fire from Heaven. In that fearful disaster, I with you my Wife and you my sweet Children will come to a miserable ruin unless some way of escape—which as yet I do not see—may be found by which we may be delivered."

His family members were deeply troubled at this declaration, not because they believed what he told them but because they thought some form of insanity had gotten into his head. Therefore, since it was nearing nightfall, and hoping that sleep would settle his brain, they quickly got him to bed. But the night was as troublesome to him as the day; and, for that reason, instead of sleeping he spent it sighing and weeping.

When morning came, they wanted to know how he was; and he told them, "Worse and worse." He started talking to them again, but they began to be hardened to his words. They thought they might be able to drive away his insanity by harsh and bad-tempered behavior toward him. Sometimes they would make fun of him, at other times they would criticize him, and sometimes they would simply ignore him. Because of this, he began to withdraw from them to his bedroom to pray for them, pity them, and comfort his own misery. He would also walk by himself in the fields, sometimes reading and sometimes praying. He spent his time doing these things for several days.

Now I saw once, when he was walking in the fields, that he was (as was often the case) reading in his Book. He was greatly distressed in his mind, and as he read he burst out as he had done before, crying, "What must I do to be saved?"[7]

I also saw that he looked this way and that as if he wanted to run. Yet he stood still because (as I perceived) he could not tell which way to go. Then I looked and saw coming toward him a man named Evangelist, who asked, "Why are you crying?"

He answered, "Sir, I realize by reading the Book in my hand that I am condemned to die and after that to come to judgment.[8] I find I'm not wanting to do the first, nor am I prepared to do the second."

Then Evangelist said, "Why aren't you willing to die, since this life is accompanied by so many evil things?"

The man answered, "Because I fear this burden on my back will make me sink lower than the grave, and I'll fall into Hell.⁹ And, Sir, if I'm not fit to go to prison, then I'm not fit to go to judgment and from there to execution. Thinking about these things makes me cry."

Evangelist asked, "If this is your condition, why are you standing here?"

He replied, "Because I don't know where to go."

Then Evangelist gave him a letter in which was written: "Flee from the coming wrath."¹⁰

The man therefore read it and, looking very carefully upon Evangelist, asked, "Where must I flee?"

Then, pointing with his finger over a very wide field, Evangelist said, "Do you see that Narrow Gate over there?"¹¹

"No," replied the man.

Then the other asked, "Do you see that shining light there?"

"I think I do," answered the man.

Then Evangelist said, "Keep that light in your eye and go up directly toward it. Then you will see the Gate.¹² When you knock on the Gate, you'll be told what you must do."¹³

So in my dream I saw the man begin to run. He had not run far from his own door before his wife and children, having seen it, began to cry after him to return. But the man put his fingers in his ears and ran on,¹⁴ crying, "Life! Life! Eternal Life!" So, not turning to look behind him, he fled toward the middle of the plain.¹⁵

His neighbors also came out to see him run, and as he ran some mocked, others threatened, and some cried after him to return.¹⁶

Now among those who did so, there were two who resolved to bring him back by force. The name of one was Obstinate, and the other was named Pliable. By this time the man was a good distance ahead of them, but they were resolved to pursue him, which they did; and in a short time they caught up with him.

Then the man asked, "Neighbors, why have you come?"

"To persuade you to go back with us," they answered.

But he said, "That's quite impossible. You live in the City of Destruction, the place where I also was born. I recognize it to be just that, and dying there you will sooner or later sink lower than the grave into a place burning with fire and brimstone. Be content, Good Neighbors, and go along with me."

"What?" questioned Obstinate, "and leave our friends and our luxuries behind us?"

"Yes," said Christian (for that was his name), "because everything you would forsake is not worthy to be compared with even a little of what I'm seeking to enjoy. If you'll go along with me and obtain it also, you'll do as well as I. There's enough for everyone and more left over where I'm going.[17] Come away with me and see that I'm telling you the truth."[18]

"What are the things you seek," asked Obstinate, "since you're leaving all the world to find them?"

Christian answered, "I seek an 'inheritance that can never perish, spoil, or fade.'[19] And it's laid up safely in heaven to be given at the appropriate time to those who diligently seek it.[20] Read about it here in my Book, if you like."

"Nonsense!" said Obstinate. "Away with your book! Will you go back with us or not?"

"Not I," replied Christian, "because I've put my hand to the plow."[21]

Obstinate said, "Come then, friend Pliable, let's turn back and go home without him. There's a group of these crazed-headed fools who—when they at last accept such a frivolous idea—are wiser in their own eyes than seven men who can think reasonably."

Then Pliable said, "Don't be so critical. If what the good Christian says is true, the things he follows after are better than ours. My heart is inclined to go with him."

"What?" said Obstinate, "more fools still? Follow my advice and go back. Who knows where such a brainsick person will lead you? Go back, go back and be wise."

"No," said Christian, "but come with me, Pliable. Those things are there to be gained just as I said, and many more glorious things besides.[22] If you don't believe me, read here in this Book. Regarding the truth of what is expressed in it, all of it is confirmed by the Blood of Him who made it."[23]

"Well, Obstinate," said Pliable, "I've arrived at a crossroads. I intend to go along with this good man and unite our fates and fortune. But," he said as he turned to Christian, "do you know the way to this desired place?"

To which Christian replied, "I've been directed by a man named Evangelist to travel quickly to a small Gate in front of us. We'll receive instructions there about the Way."[24]

Pliable responded, "Come, then, let's be going." And they both traveled on together.

"And I will go back to my place," said Obstinate. "I'll be no companion of such mislead dreamers."[25]

NOTES ON CHAPTER 1

[1]   This cave represents the cell in the Bedford Gaol (jail) where John Bunyan wrote *The Pilgrim's Progress*.

[2]   **Isaiah 64:6**.

[3]   **Luke 14:33**.

[4]   **Psalm 38:4**.

[5]   Exodus 32:16, 34:27; **Habakkuk 2:2**; Jeremiah 30:2; 1 Corinthians 14:37.

[6]   **Acts 2:37-38**.

[7]   **Acts 16:30-31**.

[8]   **Hebrews 9:27**; **Ezekiel 22:14**; **Job 16:22**.

[9]   **Isaiah 30:33**.

[10]   **Matthew 3:7. Pilgrim convicted of the necessity of fleeing.**

[11]   **Matthew 7:13**.

[12]   **Psalm 119:105** and **2 Peter 1:19. Christ and the way to Him, cannot be found without the Word.** All travelers seeking to find their way in this darkened world must have a light. God's Word, the Bible, is the light that leads people to the Gate.

[13]   Consider the importance of the Gate. Every ram, ewe, and lamb in a flock of sheep must pass through a gate to enter a sheepfold. In like manner, every man, woman, and child must

enter into salvation by going through Christ, "the gate for the sheep." John 10:1-10.

14 **Luke 14:26;** Matthew 10:37.

15 **Genesis 19:17. They that flee from the wrath to come are a grazing stock to the world.**

16 **Jeremiah 20:10.**

17 **Luke 15:17.**

18 **2 Corinthians 4:18; Romans 8:18;** 1 Corinthians 2:9-10; and Hebrews 11:6.

19 **1 Peter 1:4.** 1 Peter 1:3-5.

20 **Hebrews 11:16.**

21 **Luke 9:62**

22 **Christian and Obstinate pull for Pliable's soul.** Here are two voices pulling on the heart of one man. Each voice represents an opinion regarding which path should be taken in life. Joshua 24:15

23 **Hebrews 9:15-28**

24 Deuteronomy 1:32-33; Psalm 86:11, 139:24, 143:8; Proverbs 14:12; Isaiah 30:21; and John 14:6.

25 **Obstinate goes railing back.** Obstinate lived up to his name. His obstinacy caused him to reject the Truth. He tenaciously held to his worldly concepts of reality and could not be moved from them. Before we dismiss Obstinate, though, perhaps we should contemplate how obstinacy could be turned into a positive force in our lives as we tenaciously hold to and follow after the Truth.

2

THE PILGRIM FALLS INTO THE SWAMP OF DESPONDENCE

NOW AFTER OBSTINATE HAD gone back, I saw in my dream that Christian and Pliable went over the plain, talking as they went. And so they began this discussion:

"Tell me, Pliable, how are things with you?" said Christian. "I'm glad you've been convinced to go along with me. If Obstinate himself had felt what I've felt of the powers and terrors of what's yet unseen, he wouldn't have turned his back on us so casually."

"And tell me, Christian," replied Pliable, "since there is no one here but us, explain further about the things where we're going and how they're to be enjoyed."

Christian answered, "I can better understand them with my mind than speak of them with my tongue. But still, since you're really wanting to know, I'll read of them in my Book."[1]

"And do you think the words of your Book are absolutely true?" asked Pliable.

To which Christian replied, "Yes, definitely! For it was made by Him Who Cannot Lie."[2]

"Very well stated," said Pliable. "What things are they?"

Christian began, "There is an endless kingdom to be inhabited, and we are to be given everlasting life so we may inhabit that kingdom forever."[3]

"Well spoken," said Pliable. "And what else?"

"There are crowns of glory to be given us," continued Christian, "and clothing that will make us shine like the sun in the heights of Heaven."[4]

"That sounds wonderful," said Pliable. "And what else?"

"There will be no more crying nor sorrow," Christian went on, "for He who is the Owner of the place will wipe all tears from our eyes."[5]

"And what company will we have there?" asked Pliable.

Christian replied, "There we will be with Seraphim and Cherubim—creatures that will dazzle your eyes when you look at them.[6] There also you'll meet with thousands and tens of thousands[7] who've gone before us to that place. None of them are destructive but loving and holy, every one walking in the sight of God and standing in His presence with acceptance forever. In a word, there we'll see the Elders with their golden crowns[8] and the holy virgins with their golden harps.[9] We'll see people who by the world were cut in pieces, burnt in flames, eaten by beasts, and drowned in the seas, all because of the love they possessed and delivered to the Lord of the place.[10] We'll see them all well and clothed with immortality as with a garment."[11]

Pliable then said, "Just hearing this is enough to capture one's heart; but are these things obtainable? How can we get to be sharers of them?"[12]

Christian answered, "The Lord, the Governor of the country, has recorded that in this Book. The substance of the message is: If we really intend to have it, He will give it to us freely." [13]

"Well," said Pliable, "I'm glad to hear of these things. Come on! Let's walk faster!"

"I can't go as fast as I'd like because of this burden on my back," responded Christian.[14]

The Swamp of Despondence

Now I saw in my dream that just as they had ended this conversation they came near to a very muddy swamp in the middle of the plain. Since neither was paying attention, both of them fell suddenly into the bog. The name of the swamp was Despondence. Here, therefore, they wallowed for a while, being smeared all over with mud; and Christian, because of the burden on his back, began to sink in the mire.

Pliable exclaimed, "Ah, Christian, where are you now?"

"To tell the truth," said Christian, "I don't know."

At that, Pliable began to be offended and angrily said to his companion, "Is this the happiness you've been telling me about all this time? If we make such poor progress at the beginning of our travel, what can we expect between here and our journey's end? If I get out alive, you will enter the fine country without me!" And with that he gave a desperate struggle or two and got out of the mire on the side of the swamp that was in the direction of his own house. So away he went, and Christian saw him no more.

Christian, therefore, was left to tumble in the Swamp of Despondence alone, but he continued his efforts toward the side of the swamp still farther away from his own house and in the direction of the Narrow Gate. He continued to struggle but could not get out because of the burden on his back.

Then in my dream I saw a man coming toward him. His name was Help, and the man asked him what he was doing there.

"Sir," said Christian, "I was directed to come this way by a man called Evangelist. He also directed me to the Gate over there so I could escape the wrath to come. As I was going there, I fell in here."

"But why didn't you look for the steps?" inquired Help.

Christian answered, "Fear followed me so persistently that I ran away the other direction and fell in."

"Then," said Help, "give me your hand." So, he offered his hand and pulled him out, set him on solid ground, and encouraged him to continue on his way.[15]

Then in my dream I stepped up to the one who pulled him out and asked, "Since the way from the City of Destruction to the Gate over there goes through this place, why is it that this piece of ground has not been repaired so poor travelers can go there more safely?"

And Help said to me, "This muddy swamp is the kind of place that cannot be mended. It's the low place into which the scum and filth that accompanies the conviction of sin run continually. It is therefore called the Swamp of Despondence; for commonly as the sinner is awakened about his lost condition there will rise up in his soul many fears, doubts, and discouraging apprehensions, which all flow together and settle in this place. And that's the reason for the worthlessness of this ground."[16]

"It doesn't please the King for this place to remain so bad," continued Help. "For [nearly two thousand][17] years, His workers, under the direction of His Majesty's Surveyors, have been deployed around this patch of ground trying to fix it. Furthermore, to my knowledge, at least twenty thousand truckloads—undoubtedly millions of wholesome instructions—have been swallowed up here. These instructions have been brought continually from everywhere in the King's domain in an attempt to fix it, and those knowledgeable in such things say they are the best materials to use to make good ground of the place. But it still remains the Swamp of Despondence to this day, and it will remain so after they have done everything they can."

"True," Help went on speaking, "there have been some stable and sizable steps placed through the very center of this swamp under the direction of the Lawgiver. But at times when this place greatly spews out its filth, as it does when there is a change of weather, these steps are hardly seen. Or, if they are seen, people through the dizziness of their own heads step to the side and then are stuck and hindered in their ability to proceed even though the steps are there. But the ground is good when they have once gone through the Gate."[18]

Now in my dream I saw that by this time Pliable had arrived home again at his house, and his neighbors came to visit him. Some of them called him Wise Man for coming back, and some called him Fool for endangering himself with Christian. Still others mocked at his cowardice, saying, "Surely

since you began to venture away, I would not have been
so weak as to have given out because of the few difficulties." So Pliable began sneaking around to avoid them.
But he at last gained more confidence, and then they all
changed their stories and began to criticize poor Christian
behind his back. And so I heard no more of Pliable.

NOTES ON CHAPTER 2

[1]   **God's things unspeakable**. The ministrations of God to
one's spirit and soul are experiential. They are not simply learned
accidentally. Even though salvation can be examined logically and
laid out in an academic way, it will always be an enterprise of faith.
The movement of people from being lost to being saved will
always involve personal communication between the Spirit of God
and the heart of the person. Sometimes it is hard to find words to
express adequately the feelings of the heart. See Romans 8:26.

[2]   **Titus 1:2**; Hebrews 6:18.

[3]   Daniel 7:27; John 10-27-28; Isaiah 15:17.

[4]   **2 Timothy 4:8**; Revelation 3:5, 7:9, 22:5; **Matthew 13:43**.

[5]   **Revelation 7:15-17, 21:4**; Isaiah 25.8.

[6]   **Isaiah 6:1-4**.

[7]   **Revelation 5:11**.

[8]   **Revelation 4:4**.

[9]   **Revelation 14:1-5**. This is a reference to the 144,000 out
of the tribes of Israel who are to be sealed according to the
Revelation 7:3-8. Some believe they represent all the people of
God of all ages. They are further identified as "those who did not
defile themselves with women" (Revelation 14:4). Bunyan saw
them as "holy virgins." Bunyan assumes the sound John the
Apostle heard, "like that of harpists playing their harps"
(Revelation 14:3), was coming from the 144,000 themselves as
they played their harps.

[10]   **John 12:25**. These individuals whom Christian is to
meet are they who "did not love their lives so much as to shrink
from death" (Revelation 12:11). They were willing to
suffer death rather than tarnish their testimony. They knew

what it meant to deny themselves and take up their cross daily as part of their duty to follow Christ (Luke 9:23-24, 14:27; Mark 8:34). Some of these giants of faith, as they are often referred to, are spoken of in Hebrews 11:35-40.

[11] **2 Corinthians 5:1-10;** 1 Corinthians 15:51-54; **1 Thessalonians 4:13-18.**

[12] **Isaiah 55:11-12.**

[13] **John 6:35-37, 7:37**-39; **Revelation 21:6-7, 22:17.**

[14] Hebrews 12:1.

[15] **Psalm 40:2.**

[16] **Isaiah 35:3-4**

[17] At the time Bunyan wrote his book it was "over sixteen hundred years." At the time of this edition it is nearly 2,000 years since Christians began filling in the swamp.

[18] **The promises of forgiveness and acceptance to life by faith in Christ. 1 Samuel 12:23.** Christian can look forward to a better place ahead. While providing firm footing, however, the solid ground inside the Gate will not keep his faith from being challenged in the future.

Mr. Worldly Wiseman

3

THE PILGRIM AND LEGALITY

NOW AS CHRISTIAN WAS walking alone, he caught
sight of someone in the distance crossing over the field, and by
chance they met just as they were crossing each other's path.
The name of the gentleman who met him was Mr. Worldly
Wiseman, who lived in the Town of Carnal Policy—a very
large town close by from where Christian came. The man who
met Christian had some knowledge of him, for the Pilgrim's
departure from the City of Destruction was widely publicized,
not only in the town where he lived, but also it had become the
talk of the town in other places. Mr. Worldly Wiseman, having
developed some impression of him by noticing his laborious
progress and by observing his sighs and groans and the like,
began to enter into some conversation with Christian.

Worldly Wiseman started, "Say there, good Fellow, where
are you going in this burdened manner?"

"A burdened manner for sure, as great as any poor creature
ever had," replied Christian. "Since you ask me where I'm

going, I'll tell you, Sir. I'm going to that Narrow Gate over there before me. There, as I've been told, I'll be introduced to a way to get rid of my heavy burden."

"Do you have a wife and children?" asked Worldly.

"Yes," answered Christian, "but I'm so loaded down with this burden that I can't find pleasure in them as I used to. I think I'm existing as if I had none."[1]

"Will you listen to me if I give you advice?" questioned Worldly.

"If it is good, I will," replied Christian, "for I stand in need of good counsel."

"I would advise you then," said Worldly "that you quickly get rid of your burden, for you'll never be settled in your mind till you do. Nor can you enjoy the benefits of the blessings God has bestowed upon you till you do."

Christian responded, "That's what I seek, to be free of this heavy burden, but I can't get it off myself. Nor is there anyone in our country who can take it off my shoulders. That's why I'm going this way, as I told you, so I can get rid of my burden."

"Who directed you to go this way to have your burden removed?" asked Worldly.

Christian answered, "A man who seemed to me to be a very great and honorable person. His name, as I remember, is Evangelist."

"Curse him for his advice!" Worldly retorted. "There's not a more dangerous and troublesome way in the world than the one to which he's directed you. And that's what you'll find if you allow yourself to be guided by his counsel. You have, as I perceive, already met with some trouble, for I see the dirt of the Swamp of Despondence on you. That swamp is only the beginning of the sorrows that follow after individuals traveling on that path. Hear me, because I'm older than you. In the way you're going, you're likely to meet with Wearisomeness, Painfulness, Hunger, Perils, Nakedness, Sword, Lions, Dragons, Darkness, and—in a word—Death. And you think not? These things are certainly true, having been confirmed by many testimonies. And why should a man so carelessly cast himself away by listening to a stranger?"[2]

"Why, Sir," responded Christian, "this burden upon my back is more terrible to me than all these things you've mentioned. No, I don't think I care what I meet with in the way as long as I can also find deliverance from my burden."[3]

"How did you come to get your burden in the first place?" inquired Worldly.

"By reading this Book in my hand," answered Christian.

"I thought so," said Worldly. "It has happened to you as to other weak men who suddenly fall into such distractions by meddling with things too high for them. Those distractions not only strip men of manliness, as I perceive they have done to you, but also cause them to undertake desperate ventures to obtain things they know nothing about."[4]

"I know what I desire to obtain," stated Christian. "What I desire is ease—to be eased of my heavy burden."

Worldly then responded, "But why seek for ease this way, seeing so many dangers accompany it? Especially since, if you'd just have patience to hear me, I could direct you to ways of obtaining what you desire without the dangers to which you'll expose yourself in the way you're going. Yes, and the solution is apparent. Besides, you also would then meet with much safety, friendship, and contentment."

"Please, Sir, reveal this secret to me," said Christian.[5]

Worldly began his advice. "Why, in the village over there, the one named Morality, there dwells a gentleman whose name is Legality. He's a very judicious man with a good name, an individual who has skill to help people remove from their shoulders burdens like yours. He's done a great deal of good this way. He also has the skill to cure those who are driven a little insane by their burdens. As I said, you may go to him and receive help immediately. His house is not quite a mile from here. If he isn't at home himself, he has for his son a handsome young man whose name is Civility. He can do it as well as the old gentleman himself. There, I say, you may be eased of your burden. And if you don't desire to return to your former residence—as I certainly wouldn't encourage you to do—you may send for your wife and children to come to you in this village. In Morality there are houses now standing empty, one of which you could lease at a reasonable rate. Food and supplies there are cheap and good, and to be sure, what will make your life even more happy is that you'll live by honest neighbors with favor and in style."[6]

Now Christian was in somewhat of a dilemma, but he soon concluded if what this gentleman said was true, his wisest course would be to take his advice. And with that, he spoke further, "Sir, which is the way to this honest man's house?"[7]

Worldly responded, "Do you see that high hill over there?"[8]

"Yes," said Christian, "very well."

"You must go by that hill, and the first house you come to is his," advised Worldly.

So, turning out of the way he was going, Christian went toward Mr. Legality's house for help. But when he reached the hill, it seemed so high, and the side of the hill that was next to the pathway had such a great overhang, that Christian was afraid to venture farther lest the hill should fall on his head. So, he stood still there not knowing what to do. Furthermore, his burden now seemed heavier to him than while he was in his original course of travel. Flashes of fire came out of the hill, making Christian afraid he would be burned. Here, therefore, he sweat and shook with fear; and now he began to be sorry that he had taken Mr. Worldly Wiseman's advice.[9]

He then saw Evangelist coming to meet him, and at the sight of him Christian was ashamed and began to blush. Evangelist drew nearer and nearer, and coming up to him he looked upon Christian with a severe and dreadful expression. He then began to reason with him. "What are you doing here, Christian?" he asked.

At those words, Christian did not know how to answer; so he stood speechless before him.

Then Evangelist said, "Aren't you the man I found crying outside the walls of the City of Destruction?"

"Yes, Sir, I'm the man," admitted Christian.

"Didn't I advise you of the way to the small Narrow Gate?"

Evangelist comes to Christian at the hill.

questioned Evangelist.

"Yes, Sir," said Christian.

"How is it then that you've so quickly turned aside?" asked Evangelist. "For you're now out of the Way."

Christian began to explain, "As soon as I got through the Swamp of Despondence, I met with a man who persuaded me that I could find in the village before me someone who could take off my burden."

"What was he like?" inquired Evangelist.

"He looked like a gentleman and talked at length to me," said Christian. "At last he convinced me, so I came here. But when I saw this hill and how it hangs over the pathway, I suddenly stopped because I feared it would fall on my head."

"What did that gentleman say to you?" asked Evangelist.

"He asked me where I was going," answered Christian, "and I told him."

"And what did he say then," inquired Evangelist.

Christian responded, "He asked me if I had a family, and I told him. But I said I was so loaded down with the burden on my back that I couldn't take pleasure in them as I used to."

"And what did he say then?" asked Evangelist.

"He encouraged me to get rid of my burden quickly," said Christian, "and I told him it was ease from it that I sought. Therefore, I said I was going to that Gate over there to receive further direction on how I could get to the Place of Deliverance. So he said that he would show me a better and shorter way, not so frequented with difficulties as the Way you set me in, Sir. He said that path would direct me to the house of a gentleman who has skill to take off these burdens. So, I believed him and turned out of the path I was in to go into this one hoping I could soon be eased of my burden. But when I came to this place and saw things as they really are, I stopped for fear of danger. Now I don't know what to do."

"Then stand still a little while, so I may show you the words of God," said Evangelist.

As Christian stood there trembling, Evangelist said, "'See to it that you do not refuse him who speaks. If they did not escape when they refused him who warned them on earth, how much less will we, if we turn away from him who warns us from heaven?'"[10] He also said, "'But my righteous one will live by faith. And if he shrinks back, I will not be pleased with him.'[11] 'You are the man'[12] who is running into this misery. You have begun to reject the counsel of the Most High and to draw back your foot from the Path of Peace,[13] even almost to the hazarding of your destruction."

Then Christian fell down at his feet as if he were dead, crying, "'Woe to me! [for] I am ruined!'"[14]

At the sight of that, Evangelist caught him by the right hand, saying, "'All the sins and blasphemies of men will be forgiven them.'[15] 'Stop doubting and believe.'"[16] Then Christian revived a little and, still trembling, stood up before Evangelist.

Then Evangelist proceeded, saying, "Pay more careful attention to the things I tell you. I'll now show you who deluded you and who it was also to whom he sent you. The man who met you is called Worldly Wiseman. He is rightly called that, partly because he finds only the doctrine of this world tasteful, which is why he always goes to the Town of Morality to attend church, and partly because the doctrine he loves the most is the one that saves him from the suffering associated with the Cross.[17] Because he is of this carnal make-up, he seeks, therefore, to pervert my ways, though my ways are right."[18]

"Now there are three things in this man's counsel you must absolutely despise," continued Evangelist: "First—his act of turning you out of the Way; second—his work to render the Cross offensive to you; and third—his way of setting your feet in the path that leads to the administration of death."

"First," Evangelist further explained, "you must despise his act of turning you out of the Way—yes, and your own consenting to it—because to do so is to reject the instructions of God for the sake of the advice of a worldly wiseman. The Lord says, 'Make every effort to enter through the narrow door,'[19] which is the Door I sent you to, for 'small is the gate and narrow the road that leads to life, and only a few find it.'[20] And this wicked man has turned you away from this small Narrow Gate and from the path leading to it, thus bringing you close to destruction. Hate, therefore, how he turned you out of the Way and detest yourself for listening to him.

"Second—you must despise his work to make the Cross offensive to you. You must consider the Cross 'of greater value than the treasures of Egypt.'[21] Besides, the King of Glory told you that 'whoever wants to save his life will lose it,'[22] and 'If anyone comes to me and does not hate his father and mother, his wife and children, his brothers and sisters—yes, even his own life—he cannot be my disciple.'[23] I say, therefore, when anyone works to persuade you that following God's instructions will cause your death, when the Truth has said you cannot have eternal life without doing so, you must despise that person's doctrine.

"Third—you must hate the way he set your feet in the path that leads to the dispensing of death. And for this you must consider to whom he sent you and also how unable that person was to deliver you from your burden."

Evangelist continued, saying, "He to whom you were sent to find ease is named Legality. He is the son of the 'slave woman' that now exists and who is in bondage with her children. The slave woman is symbolic of Mount Sinai—this mountain you feared would fall on your head.[24] Now, if she and her children are in bondage, how can you expect to be made free by them? Therefore, Legality is not able to set you free from your burden. No one has ever been delivered from his burden by him; no, nor is it ever likely to happen. You can't be justified by the works of the law, for no one living can be loosed from his burden by the deeds of the law."[25]

"Therefore," continued Evangelist, "Mr. Worldly Wiseman is an alien, and Mr. Legality is a cheat. And as for his son Civility, in spite of his impressive looks, he's nothing but a hypocrite and can't help you. Believe me, there's nothing in all this noise you've heard from this foolish man except a plan to cheat you of your salvation by turning you away from the Path in which I set you."

After this, Evangelist called aloud to the heavens for confirmation of what he had said; and with that there came words and fire out of the mountain under which poor Christian stood. These things made the hair on his skin stand up. The

Evangelist exposes Mr. Worldly Wiseman's deceitfulness

words were, "All who rely on observing the law are under a curse, for it is written: 'Cursed is everyone who does not continue to do everything written in the Book of the Law.'"[26]

Now Christian was expecting nothing but death and began to cry out mournfully, even cursing the time when he met Mr. Worldly Wiseman. He called himself a thousand fools for listening to his advice. He was also greatly ashamed to think that the man's arguments, flowing only from human wisdom, would have such influence with him as to cause him to forsake the right road. After this, he presented himself again to Evangelist in words and reason as follows:

"Sir, what do you think?" began Christian. "Is there hope? May I now go back and go up to the Narrow Gate? Could I not be abandoned for this and sent back from here in shame? I'm sorry I listened to this man's advice, but may my sin be forgiven?"

Then Evangelist said to him, "Your sin is very great, for because of it you have committed two evils. You have forsaken the Good Road, and you have begun to walk in forbidden paths. Yet, the man at the Gate will receive you, for he favors mankind. Only take heed that you don't turn aside again lest you perish from the Way."

Then Christian committed himself to go back, and after Evangelist had kissed him, he gave him one smile and bid him God speed.[27] So, Christian went on with haste without speaking to anyone by the road; and if anyone asked him something, he would not condescend to answer. He walked like one who was constantly treading on forbidden ground and could by no means consider himself safe until he once again got onto the road that he left in order to follow Mr. Worldly Wiseman's advice.

NOTES ON CHAPTER 3

[1]   **1 Corinthians 7:29.**

[2]   **Mr. Worldly Wiseman condemns Evangelist's counsel.**

[3]   **The condition of the heart of a young Christian.**

⁴ **Mr. Worldly Wiseman does not like people to be serious in reading the Bible.**

⁵ With this statement, Pilgrim has opened the door to deception. Worldly Wiseman has been successful in bringing him to doubt the words of Evangelist and the Scriptures. Worldly has done it through persistence in human reasoning.

⁶ **Mr. Worldly prefers Morality before the Narrow Gate.** Worldly's wisdom has made the way of Legality sound good. Worldly contends that the process he proposes of ridding Christian of his burden will be quick and lead him to a wonderful new life of plenty. This is a convincing argument if one's eyes can be focused more on worldly comfort than on eternal values.

⁷ **Christian snared by Mr. Worldly Wiseman's words.**

⁸ **Mount Sinai.**

⁹ **Exodus 19:16-19; Hebrews 12:18-21.** While the way of Legality seemed attractive at the time, it became a difficult path to follow. The way of Legality is a painful path because in it there exists a constant reminder of one's inability to do right. "Therefore, no one will be declared righteous in his sight by observing the law; rather, through the law we become conscious of sin" (Romans 3:20).

¹⁰ **Hebrews 12:25.**

¹¹ **Hebrews 10:38.**

¹² 2 Samuel 12:7.

¹³ Zechariah, the priest, prophesied of the work of his newborn son John, who would become The Baptist. He said John would prepare the way of Christ in order "to shine on those living in darkness and in the shadow of death, to guide our feet into the path of peace" (Luke 1:79). John guided people into the path of peace by pointing them to Jesus, "the way and the truth and the life" (John 14:6). Evangelist had started Christian in this same path, but the Pilgrim took a terrible detour in which he found no peace. Romans 3:10-24.

¹⁴ Isaiah 6:5.

¹⁵ **Mark 3:28; Matthew 12:31.**

¹⁶ John 20:27.

¹⁷ **Galatians 6:12.** This is tantamount to compelling an individual to seek justification through the law.

18 **1 John 4:1-5.**
19 **Luke 13:24; Matthew 7:13.**
20 **Matthew 7:14.**
21 **Hebrews 11:26.**
22 **Mark 8:35; Matthew 10:39; John 12:25.**
23 **Luke 14:26.**
24 **Galatians 4:21-31.**
25 Romans 3:20.
26 **Galatians 3:10.**
27 **Psalm 2:12.**

4

THE PILGRIM ENTERS THE GATE

IN THE PROCESS OF time Christian reached the Gate, over which was written, "Knock and the door will be opened to you."[1] So he knocked several times, saying:

> May I now enter here? Will he within
> Open to sorry me, though I have been
> An undeserving Rebel? Then shall I
> Not fail to sing his lasting Praise on high.

At last a serious looking person came to the Gate. His name was Goodwill, and he asked, "Who's there, and where have you come from? What do you want?"

Christian replied, "I'm a poor burdened sinner. I've come from the City of Destruction, but I'm going to Mount Zion[2] so I can be delivered from the wrath to come. Sir, since I've been informed the way there is through this Gate, I'd like to know if you're willing to let me in."

Goodwill at the Gate

Goodwill then said, "I'm willing with all my heart." And with that he opened the Gate.[3]

As Christian was stepping in, Goodwill reached out and pulled him inside.[4] Then Christian asked, "Why did you do that?"

Goodwill said, "A short distance from this Gate stands a strong castle of which Beelzebub is the ruler. From there, both he and those with him shoot arrows at those who come up to this Gate, hoping they'll die before they can enter in."[5]

"I rejoice and tremble," said Christian.

So after Christian entered in, the man of the Gate asked him who directed him there, and Christian answered, "Evangelist directed me to come here and knock, as I did, Sir. He said you would tell me what I must do."

"An open door has been placed before you, and no one can shut it," said Goodwill.[6]

Christian replied, "Now I'll begin to reap the benefits of the risks I've taken."

"But why did you come alone?" inquired Goodwill.

"Because none of my neighbors saw their danger as I saw mine," answered Christian.

"Did any of them know you were coming?" Goodwill asked.

"Yes," said Christian, "my wife and children saw me first and called after me to turn back. Also, some of my neighbors stood crying and calling after me to return, but I put my fingers in my ears and continued on my way."

"But didn't any of them follow you to persuade you to go back?" asked Goodwill.

"Yes," said Christian. "Both Obstinate and Pliable came after me, but when they saw they couldn't convince me, Obstinate went back scoffing. Pliable, however, traveled with me a short distance."

"But why didn't he arrive with you?" asked Goodwill.

Christian then explained, "We traveled together until we suddenly fell into the Swamp of Despondence. Then my neighbor Pliable was discouraged and wouldn't travel any farther. Therefore, after he got out again on the side closest to his own house, he told me I should enter the fine country alone. So he went his way, and I came mine. He followed after Obstinate, and I came to this Gate."[7]

Then Goodwill said, "Alas, poor man! Is the Celestial Glory of so little value to him that he doesn't count it worth running the hazard of a few difficulties to obtain?"

Christian said, "I've told the truth concerning Pliable. If I should also tell all the truth concerning myself, it seems there isn't any difference between him and me. It's true he went back to his own house, but I also turned aside to travel in the Way of Death. I was persuaded to go that way through the worldly arguments of a certain Mr. Worldly Wiseman."

"Oh!" exclaimed Goodwill. "Did he confront you? He'd have you seek for ease at the hands of Mr. Legality. They're both cheats. But did you follow his advice?"

"Yes," admitted Christian, "as far as I dared. I went to find Mr. Legality until I thought the mountain standing by his house was going to fall on my head. I was forced, therefore, to stop."[8]

"That mountain has been the death of many and will be that of many more," said Goodwill. "It's good you escaped from being smashed to pieces by it."

Christian responded, "I don't know what would've happened to me there if Evangelist hadn't fortunately met me again as I was reflecting in the middle of my gloom. But it was God's mercy that he came to me again. If he hadn't, I wouldn't have arrived here. But now here I am, an individual like me, certainly more fit for death by that mountain than to stand talking with you like this, Sir. But, oh, what a privilege this is to me to be admitted entrance here!"

Goodwill then said, "In spite of everything people have done before they come here, we make no objections against anyone. No one will ever be driven away.[9] Therefore, Christian, travel awhile with me, and I'll teach you about the way you must go. Look in front of you. Do you see that Narrow Road? That is the way you must go. It was constructed by the Patriarchs, Prophets, Christ, and His Apostles; and it is as straight as a ruler can make it. This is the way you must go."[10]

"But," asked Christian, "are there any turns or twists through which a stranger might lose his way?"

"Yes," answered Goodwill, "there are many paths adjacent to this one, and they are crooked and wide; but you can distinguish the right one from the wrong one because only the right one is straight and narrow."[11]

Then in my dream I saw that Christian asked him further if he could help him remove the burden from his back, for as yet he had not gotten rid of it, nor could he by any means get it off without help.

Goodwill told him, "Concerning your burden, be content to bear it until you come to the Place of Deliverance, for there it will fall from your back by itself."[12]

Then Christian began to prepare himself to set out on his journey. So Goodwill told him that after he had gone some distance from the Gate he would come to the house of the Interpreter—at whose door he should knock—and he would show him excellent things. Then Christian bid his friend farewell, and Goodwill bid him God speed.

NOTES ON CHAPTER 4

[1]   Luke 11:9; **Matthew 7:8.**

[2]   The "heavenly Jerusalem, the city of the living God," where God dwells. Hebrews 12:22.

[3]   **The Gate will be opened to broken-hearted sinners.**

[4]   This shows how active God is in bringing people into the safety of His care. It is the *good will* of God that causes Him to take the first step in the salvation of every soul. He seeks us before we seek Him. 1 John 4:19.

[5]   **Satan envies those who enter the Narrow Gate.** Into our story enters the Archenemy of both God and humanity. Nobody makes the Pilgrim's journey without soon meeting with a direct onslaught from this opposing force. Matthew 12:24.

[6]   Revelation 3:8.

[7]   **A man may have company when he sets out for Heaven, and yet go in that direction alone.**

[8]   Here is an honest man. It is a natural tendency to protect oneself from embarrassment. It would have been easy for Christian to be critical of the actions of Pliable while at the same time covering up his own actions. God respects such honesty. "A wicked man puts up a bold front, but an upright man gives thought to his ways" (Proverbs 21:29).

[9]   **John 6:37**.

[10]   This way is an established path. Christian could not afford to be deceived into losing his confidence in it for leading him to his proper destination. Isaiah 30:20-21; Colossians 2:6-8.

[11]   **Matthew 7:13-14**. Luke 3:4-5; Proverbs 4:25-27.

[12] **There is no deliverance from the guilt and burden of Sin, but by the death and blood of Christ.** Pilgrim has entered the way of Christianity by coming to and passing through Christ, the Gate. He has not yet, however, experienced a full personal revelation of the power of God to deliver him from the weight of sin. If we continue on the right road, deliverance is in our future. Isaiah 1:18; Luke 4:17-19; Psalm 34.

5

THE PILGRIM MEETS THE
INTERPRETER

THE PILGRIM TRAVELED ON until he came to the house
of the Interpreter, where he knocked again and again. At last,
an individual came to the door and asked, "Who's there?"

Christian answered, "Sir, I'm a traveler who was directed
by an acquaintance of the owner of this house to visit here for
my profit. I would like, therefore, to speak with the head of the
house."

The individual then called for the owner of the house,
who after a short time came to Christian and asked him what
he wanted.

"Sir," said Christian, "I'm a man who has come from the
City of Destruction, and I'm going to Mount Zion. I was told
by the man who stands at the Gate at the start of this road that
if I visited here, you would show me excellent things that would
help me on my journey."

Then the Interpreter said, "Come in. I'll show you things
that will be profitable to you." So he ordered his butler to light

Christian approaches the house of the Interpreter

the candle and asked Christian to follow him. He led him into a private room and instructed his butler to open a door. When that was done, Christian saw the picture of a very serious person hanging on the wall.

This is what it looked like: The man had eyes lifted up to Heaven, the Best of Books was in his hand, the Law of Truth was written upon his lips, the world was behind his back, he stood as if he pleaded with men, and a crown of gold hung over his head.

Christian asked, "What does this mean?"

"The man whose picture you see is one in a thousand," explained the Interpreter. "He can father children—travailing in birth with children—and nurse them himself after they are born.[1] And as you see him with eyes lifted up to Heaven, the Best of Books in his hand, and the Law of Truth written on his lips, these are meant to show you that his work is to know and reveal to sinners things hard to understand. As you see, the world is at his back and a crown hangs over his head. These are meant to show you that since he's slighting and despising the things that are present—because he loves the work given to him by his Master—he is certain to have glory for his reward in the world to follow this one."

"Now," continued the Interpreter, "I've shown you this picture first because the man whose picture you see is the only man authorized by the Lord of the place where you're going to be your guide in all the difficult places you may encounter within the Way. Remember well, therefore, what I've shown you and apply your mind seriously to what you've seen, lest in your journey you meet with individuals who pretend to lead you correctly but whose ways lead to death."

Then he took Christian by the hand and led him into a very large reception room that was full of dust because it was never swept. After he had examined the room for a little while, the Interpreter called for a man to sweep. When he began to sweep, the dust began to fly around so much that Christian was almost choked by it. Then the Interpreter said to a girl standing by, "Bring water here and sprinkle the room." And when she had done it, the room was easily swept and cleaned.

"What does this mean?" asked Christian.

The Interpreter answered, "This reception room is the heart of a man that never was sanctified by the sweet Grace of the gospel. The dust is his Original Sin and the inward corruptions that have made the whole man unclean.[2] He who began to sweep in the beginning is the law; but she who brought and sprinkled the water is the gospel."[3]

"Now," he continued, "as you saw, the dust began to fly about as soon as the first individual began to sweep so that the room could not be cleaned, but you were almost choked by it. This is meant to show you that instead of cleaning the sinful heart by its works, the law actually energizes, puts strength into, and increases sin in the soul.[4] Even though it reveals and condemns sin, it doesn't have the power to conquer it."[5]

"Then," continued the Interpreter, "you saw the girl sprinkle the room with water, which caused it to be easily cleaned. This is meant to show you that when the gospel comes in, just as the girl settled the dust by sprinkling the floor with water, in like manner the sweet and precious influences of the gospel to the heart conquer and defeat sin. The soul is made clean through the faith of the gospel,[6] and consequently the soul is fit for the King of Glory to inhabit."[7]

Besides this, I saw in my dream that the Interpreter took Christian by the hand and led him into a little room in which two boys sat; each sat in his own chair. The name of the oldest child was Passion, and the other's name was Patience. Passion seemed to be very discontented, but Patience was very quiet.

Then Christian asked, "What is the reason for Passion's discontentment?"

The Interpreter answered, "Their guardian wants them to wait until the beginning of next year to receive his best things. Passion wants to have it all now, but Patience is willing to wait."

Then I saw that someone came to Passion, bringing him a bag of treasure and pouring it down at his feet. Passion gathered it up, rejoiced in it, and laughed at Patience scornfully. But as I continued to watch, he squandered it all away and had nothing left for himself but rags.

Then Christian said to the Interpreter, "Explain this matter to me more completely."

So the Interpreter began his explanation: "These two boys are figures. Passion is figuratively the people of this world, and Patience is the people of the world to come. As you see here, just like the people of this world, Passion wants it all now, this year—that is to say, in this world. The people of this world must have all their good things now, for they can't wait for their portion of good things until next year—that is, until the next world. The proverb 'A bird in the hand is worth two in the bush' carries more weight with them than all the divine testimonies of the worth of the world to come. But as you saw, he quickly wasted it all away and soon had nothing left for himself but rags. So it will be with all such people at the end of this world."

Christian then said, "Now I see that Patience has the best wisdom, and for many reasons: One—because he waits for the best things; and two—because he will have the glory of his possessions when the other has nothing but rags."

"No," said the Interpreter, "you may add another reason—namely, the glory of the next world will never wear out, but other glories are soon gone. Passion, therefore, didn't have as much reason to laugh at Patience—because Passion had his best things first—as Patience will have to laugh at Passion—because Patience had his best things last. First must give place to last because last must have its time to come, but last gives place to nothing, for there is nothing more to follow. So he who has his portion first must of necessity have a time to spend it, but he who has his portion last must have it permanently. Therefore, it is said of Dives, 'In your lifetime you received your good things, while Lazarus received bad things, but now he is comforted here and you are in agony.'"[8]

Christian responded, "Then I understand it's not best to covet things that now exist but to wait for things yet to come."

"You speak the truth," answered the Interpreter. "'For what is seen is temporary, but what is unseen is eternal.'[9] But even though this is true, things now seen live so close together with our sinful desires that they both quickly become friends. Also, things to come are such strangers to material knowledge that they continue to be separated."

Then I saw in my dream that the Interpreter took Christian by the hand and lead him into a place where a fire was burning next to a wall. Standing by the wall was an individual who was continually throwing water on the fire to put it out. Yet, the fire just burned higher and hotter.

Christian asked, "What does this mean?"

The Interpreter answered, "This fire is the work of grace working in the heart. He who throws water on it to extinguish it and put it out is the Devil. But, as you see, the fire is burning higher and hotter in spite of it. You'll be shown the reason for that."

With that, he took Christian around to the other side of the wall. There he saw a man with a jar of oil in his hand continually and secretly pouring the oil upon the fire.

Again Christian asked, "What does this mean?"

The Interpreter explained, "This is Christ, who continually maintains the work already begun in the heart by applying the Oil of His Grace. Because of this, the souls of His people remain full of grace in spite of what the Devil can do. In that you saw the man standing behind the wall to keep the fire burning, that's meant to teach you that it's hard for those tempted to see how this work of grace is continued in the soul."[10]

I saw also that the Interpreter took Christian again by the hand and led him into a pleasant place where a stately palace had been built. It was beautiful to behold, and at the sight of it Christian was very happy. He saw people walking on the walls of the palace, and they were all dressed in gold.

"May we go inside?" asked Christian.

Then the Interpreter took him and led him up toward the door of the palace. A large group of people stood at the door wanting to go inside, but they dared not do it. There also sat a man at a table a short distance from the door. He had a book and pen before him to take the name of any individual who had intentions of going in through the door. Christian also saw that many men in armor stood in the doorway to block the entrance. He was somewhat amazed to see that they were prepared to

Armored men resist the man at the gate

inflict whatever pain or injury they could upon the people who would enter through the door.

At last, when every person there had started to go back, leaving the door because of their fear of the armed men, Christian saw a man who looked like he possessed great strength. The man came up to the one who sat there to write and said, "Write down my name, Sir."

After this, he saw the man draw his sword, put a helmet on his head, and rush toward the door to confront the armed men. The armed men attacked him with deadly force; but, not to be discouraged, the man began cutting and hacking away fiercely. After he had both received wounds and inflicted many upon them who attempted to keep him out, he cut his way through them all and pressed forward into the palace. At that, there was a pleasant voice heard from those who were inside, even those who walked upon the top of the walls; and they said, "Come in, come in! Eternal glory you will win." So he went in and was dressed with the same type of clothing as they.

Christian smiled and said, "I think I actually know the meaning of this." Then he said, "Now let me continue on my journey."

"No," said the Interpreter, "stay until I've shown you a little more, and after that you will go on your way." So he took him by the hand again and led him into a very dark room where a man was sitting in an Iron Cage. Now the man looked very sad. He sat there with his eyes looking down to the ground and his hands folded together; and he sighed as if his heart would break.

Christian asked, "What does this mean?"

At this, the Interpreter invited him to talk with the man.

Then Christian asked the man, "Who are you?"

The man answered, "I am who I once was not."

"Who were you once?" inquired Christian.

The man said, "In my own eyes and the eyes of others, I was once an honest and flourishing professor of faith. I considered myself once a good candidate for a home in Celestial

City, and at that time I even had joy at the thoughts of living there."

"Well," said Christian, "who are you now?"

"I'm now a man of despair," answered the man. "I'm shut up in despair just as I am in this Iron Cage. I can't get out—oh, now I cannot!"[11]

"But how did you come to be in this condition?" asked Christian.

"I stopped being alert and self-controlled," said the man. "I let loose the reigns of my desires.[12] I sinned against the Light of the Word and the goodness of God. I've grieved the Spirit, and He is gone.[13] I tempted the Devil, and he has come to me. I've provoked God to anger, and He has left me. I have so hardened my heart that I cannot repent."[14]

Then Christian said to the Interpreter, "But is there no hope for such a man as this?"

"Ask him," said the Interpreter.

Then Christian asked, "Is there any hope from being kept in the Iron Cage of Despair?"

"No, none at all," said the man.

"Why?" asked Christian.

"I'm guilty of crucifying Him again,"[15] answered the man. "I've despised His position,[16] I've hated His righteousness, and I've treated His blood as an unholy thing. I've insulted the Spirit of Grace.[17] So I've excluded myself from all the promises, and now there remains for me nothing but threats, dreadful threats, fearful threats of certain judgment and raging fire, which will devour me as an enemy of God."[18]

"Why did you bring yourself into this condition?" inquired Christian.

The man answered, "For the desires, pleasures, and profits of this world. I promised myself great delight in the enjoyment of them. But now every one of those things bite me and gnaw at me like burning worms"

"But can't you repent now and turn?" asked Christian.

"God has denied me repentance," said the man. "His Word gives me no encouragement to believe. He himself has shut me up in this Iron Cage, and all the men in the world can't let me out. Oh, Eternity! Eternity! How will I cope with the misery I'll meet with in Eternity!"

Then the Interpreter said to Christian, "Remember this man's misery, and let it be an everlasting caution to you."[19]

"Well," said Christian, "this is a fearful thing. May God help me to be alert and self-controlled and to pray so I may avoid the cause of this man's misery. Sir, isn't it now time for me to go on my way?"

The Interpreter answered, "Stay here till I show you one more thing. Then you may go on your way." So he took Christian by the hand again and led him into a certain room. An individual was there getting out of bed, and he shook and trembled as he put on his clothes.

Then Christian asked, "Why does this man tremble like that?"

The Interpreter asked the individual to tell Christian the reason for his actions, and the individual then began his explanation: "Tonight as I was sleeping, I dreamed and saw the sky grow extremely dark. Also, there was so much dreadful thunder and lightning that it put me in great distress. So I looked up in my dream and saw the clouds rise and stretch at an unusual rate. Then I heard a great sound of a trumpet.[20] I also saw sitting upon a cloud a Man who was accompanied by the thousands of Heaven.[21] They were all in flaming fire,[22] and the heavens also were in a burning flame.[23] Then I heard a voice, saying, 'Arise, you Dead, and come to judgment!'[24] And with that, the rocks broke apart, the graves opened, and the dead who were in them came out.[25] Some of them were very glad and looked upward,[26] and some of them searched for a place under the mountains in which to hide themselves."[27]

The individual continued, "Then I saw the Man who sat upon the cloud open a book and summon the world to draw near.[28] Yet, because of a fierce flame that flowed out before Him, there was a suitable distance between Him and them, as between the judge and the prisoners at the bench. I also heard it proclaimed to those accompanying the Man sitting on the cloud, 'Gather together the tares, chaff, and stubble and cast them into the burning lake.'[29] And with that, the Bottomless

Pit opened just about where I stood, and out of its mouth came a great deal of smoke and coals of fire with hideous noises. It was also said to the same persons, 'Gather my wheat into the barn.'[30] And with that I saw many people caught up and carried away into the clouds, but I was left behind.[31] I sought to hide myself as well, but I couldn't, for the man sitting upon the cloud continued to keep His eye on me. I remembered my sins, and my conscience constantly accused me.[32] At that time I awoke from my sleep."[33]

Christian then asked, "But what was it that made you so afraid of that sight?"

The man answered and said, "Why, I thought the Day of Judgment had come, and I wasn't ready for it. But what frightened me most was that the angels gathered up several people and left me behind. Also, the pit of Hell opened its mouth just where I stood. In addition, my conscience afflicted me; and, as I thought, the Judge kept looking at me, showing anger in His expression."

Then the Interpreter asked Christian, "Have you considered all these things?"

Christian answered, "Yes, and they cause me both to hope and to fear."

"Good," replied the Interpreter. "Keep these things in your mind so they may act as prods in your sides to poke you and cause you to go forward in the way you must go."

Christian began to prepare himself to continue his journey.

Then the Interpreter said to him, "May the Counselor[34] always be with you, good Christian, to guide you in the way that leads to the City.

So Christian went on his way, saying:

Here I have seen Things rare and profitable,
Things pleasant, dreadful, Things to make me stable
In what I have begun to take in hand;
Then let me think on them, and understand
Wherefore they showed me were, and let me be
Thankful, O good Interpreter, to thee.

NOTES ON CHAPTER 5

[1] **Galatians 4:19-20; 1 Corinthians 4:14-16.**

[2] Matthew 15:18-20.

[3] **Ephesians 5:25-27.**

[4] **1 Corinthians 15:56; Romans 5:20.**

[5] **Romans 7:6**, 8-11, 24-25; 8:1-4

[6] **John 15:3; Acts 15:9; Romans 16:25-26.**

[7] Psalm 51:9-10; 1 John 4:11-16.

[8] Luke 16:25. *Dives* is the traditional name of the rich man referred to in the Scripture. **Luke 16**:19-31.

[9] **2 Corinthians 4:18.**

[10] **2 Corinthians 12:9.** One of the great challenges in life is that of maintaining the grace of God during times of temptation and trials. The human spirit is prone to exasperation and despair. It can be difficult to see the help God provides us in times of struggle when our eyes are clouded over with the pain of the moment. It is real faith that recognizes the activity of the concerned Savior even though His work may not be seen clearly for a time and even if His presence may not be greatly felt. He is there, and in the darkest of times He is actively involved in our struggles.

[11] **Despair like an Iron Cage.**

[12] 1 Thessalonians 5:6; Ephesians 2:3; **Luke 8:13.** The man allowed himself to be lulled into complacency and eventually lost the ability to restrain the natural man from pursuing its desires. As the horse is allowed to roam at will without the application of the reins by an able rider, so the natural man is loosed to wander unguided without spiritual restraint.

[13] Ephesians 4:30.

[14] Hebrews 3:13

[15] **Hebrews 6:4-6**

[16] **Luke 19:14.**

[17] **Hebrews 10:26-31**

[18] Hebrews 10:27; Luke 19:27

[19] Hebrews 12:14-17

[20] **1 Corinthians 15:52; Isaiah 26:21; 1 Thessalonians 4:16.**

[21] **Jude 14,15; Daniel 7:9-10.**
[22] **2 Thessalonians 1:7-8.**
[23] 2 Peter 3:10-13.
[24] **1 Thessalonians 4:16.**
[25] **John 5:28-29.**
[26] **Psalm 5:1-3.**
[27] Revelation 6:15-17; **Malachi 3:2-3; Micah 7:16-17.**
[28] **Revelation 20:11-13.**
[29] **Malachi 4:1; Matthew 3:12, 13:30; Luke 3:17;** Revelation 20:15.
[30] **Matthew 3:12, 13:30.**
[31] **1 Thessalonians 4:17.**
[32] **Romans 2:12-16.**
[33] **Daniel 10:7.**
[34] Counselor in NIV, Comforter in KJV and Bunyan's original text. John 14:16-17, 26; 15:26;16:7-11.

Christian coming to the Cross

6

THE PILGRIM REACHES THE PLACE OF DELIVERANCE

NOW I SAW IN my dream that the Highway up which Christian was to go was fenced on either side with a Wall, and that wall was called Salvation.[1] Therefore, Christian ran up that way, but not without great difficulty because of the load on his back.

So he ran until he came to a place somewhat elevated. Upon that place stood a Cross, and below at the bottom there was a Tomb. I saw in my dream that just as Christian came up to the Cross, his burden came loose from his shoulders and fell off his back. It began to tumble and continued to do so until it came to the mouth of the Tomb. It then fell into the Tomb, and I saw it no more.[2]

Then Christian was glad and relieved, and he said with a joyful heart, "He has given me rest from my sorrow and life through His death."[3] Then he stood still awhile to look and wonder, for he was very surprised that the sight of the Cross should ease him of his burden in such a way. He looked, therefore, and looked again, even until the springs in his head sent their waters flowing down his cheeks.[4]

Now, as Christian stood looking and weeping, three Shining Ones[5] came to him and greeted him with, "Peace be to you!" The first said to him, "Your sins are forgiven."[6] The second one stripped him of the rags he was wearing and clothed him with rich garments.[7] The third set a mark on his forehead and gave him a Document with a seal on it.[8] He instructed Christian to look at the Document as he continued on his way and to deliver it at the Celestial Gate. This done, the three went on their way. Christian gave three leaps for joy[9] and continued on his way singing:

> Thus far did I come laden with my Sin;
> Nor could ought ease the grief that I was in,
> Till I came hither: What a place is this!
> Must here be the beginning of my bliss?
> Must here the Burden fall from off my back?
> Just here the strings that bound it to me crack?
> Blest Cross! Blest Sepulchre! Blest rather be
> The Man that there was put to Shame for me![10]

Then I saw in my dream that he went on like this until he came to the bottom of the hill. There he saw three men with shackles on their feet. They were fast asleep a little distance off the pathway. The name of one was Simple, another was Sloth, and the third was named Presumption.

Upon seeing them lie in this state, Christian went to them (if by chance he might awaken them) and cried, "You're like those who sleep on the top of the rigging, for the Dead Sea is under you, a gulf that has no bottom.[11] Wake up, then, and leave here! If you desire, I'll help you rid yourselves of your shackles." He also told them, "If he who prowls around like a roaring lion comes by, he will certainly devour you."[12]

With that, they looked up at him and began to reply in this manner:

"I see no danger," said Simple.

"Just a little more sleep," replied Sloth.[13]

Presumption ended with, "Every tub must stand upon its own bottom."

So they lay down to sleep again, and Christian continued on his way.[14]

Christian was troubled to think that men in such danger would so lightly esteem the kindness of one offering help to them so freely by awakening them, counseling them, and offering to help them remove their leg irons. As he entertained these troubling thoughts, he saw two men come tumbling over the Wall on the left side of the Narrow Way, and they quickly approached him. The name of one was Formality, and the other was Hypocrisy. As they drew near him, Christian entered into a conversation with them.

"Gentlemen, where did you come from, and where are you going?" asked Christian.

Formality and Hypocrisy together replied, "We were born in the Land of Boasting, and we're going to Mount Zion for praise."

Christian inquired further, "Why didn't you come in at the Gate that stands at the beginning of the Path? Don't you know it is written that 'the man who does not enter . . . by the gate, but climbs in by some other way, is a thief and a robber?'"[15]

Formality and Hypocrisy explained that to go to the Gate for entrance was considered by all the citizens of their country as too far to go; and that their usual way, therefore, was to find a shortcut and climb over the Wall, as they had done.[16]

Christian then asked, "But won't it be considered a trespass against the Ruler of the City where we're going to violate His revealed will in such a manner?"

The two men told him that he didn't need to worry about that matter, for they had established customs for what they did. They added that if necessary they could produce testimony that would witness to these customs for more than a thousand years.[17]

"But," asked Christian, "will your practice stand a trial by law?"

They then told him that customs so old as having been

accepted for over a thousand years would doubtless be admitted as a legal thing by an impartial judge. "And besides," they said, "if we get into the pathway, what does it matter which way we get in? If we're in, we're in. You're in the Way—as we understand—by just coming in at the Gate, and we're also in the Way by coming over the Wall. How is your condition better than ours?"

"I walk by the rule of my Master," answered Christian. "You walk by the rude working of your imaginations. The Lord of the Way already considers you to be thieves, so I doubt you'll be found worthy at the end of the Way. You came in by yourselves without His direction, and you'll go out by yourselves without His mercy."

They had little to say to him about this but only advised him to take care of himself.

Then I saw each of them go on his way without much discussion between them, except that the men told Christian that as far as laws and ordinances were concerned, they believed they were just as conscientious to keep them as he was. "Therefore, we don't see how you differ from us except for the coat on your back," they said. "It was probably given to you by some of your friends to hide the shame of your nakedness."

Christian then stated, "You'll not be saved by laws and ordinances since you didn't come in through the Door.[18] And as for this coat on my back, it was given to me by the Ruler of the place where I'm going. And, as you say, it is for the purpose of covering my nakedness. Furthermore, I take it as a token of His kindness toward me; for I had on nothing but rags before. And besides, as I go, I comfort myself with the thought that when I come to the gate of the City, the Ruler of the City will easily recognize me since I have this coat on my back—a coat He freely gave me the day He stripped me of my rags."

"In addition," continued Christian, "I have a mark in my forehead, which perhaps you haven't noticed. One of my Lord's closest associates placed it there the day my burden fell off my shoulders. Furthermore, I'll tell you I was given a sealed Document to comfort me by reading it as I travel in the Way. I was also instructed to present it at the Celestial Gate as a token of the certainty of my entrance. I doubt you even want all these things, since you didn't come in through the Gate."

They made no response to these things but just looked at each other and laughed. Then I saw they all traveled on, except that Christian walked in front. He had no more discussions except for those he had with himself. Sometimes these were accompanied by sighing and sometimes with comfort. Also, he was often found reading the Document given to him by one of the Shining Ones, and he was renewed by it.

NOTES ON CHAPTER 6
[1] **Isaiah 26:1**.
[2] Romans 6:4; Galatians 2:19-20; 2 Timothy 2:11; Galatians 3:13.
[3] Psalm 30:1-4; Romans 5:10; Hebrews 4:9-11.
[4] **Zechariah 12:10**. It is a common thing for one to weep as the Lord removes pressures from one's life and mind. Such pressure Christian had been dealing with! His burden had been heavier than even he had imagined.
[5] "Are not all angels ministering spirits sent to serve those who will inherit salvation?" Hebrews 1:14.
[6] **Mark 2:5**. The Pilgrim has finally reached the point of having a full revelation of deliverance and acceptance by God. The Cross has had a dramatic effect on his life. Colossians 2:13-15.
[7] **Zechariah 3:1-5**.
[8] **Ephesians 1:13-14**. Here Pilgrim's document must be distinguished from the Book he carried earlier. By his reference to these verses, Bunyan draws attention to the work and presence of the Holy Spirit with his reference to both the seal placed upon Christian's forehead and the sealed document given to him. In the original, the document was called a "Roll." In this passage the promised Holy Spirit is called in the NIV "a deposit guaranteeing our inheritance." In the KJV, the Holy Spirit is the "earnest of our inheritance until the redemption of the purchased possession."
[9] **When God releases us of our guilt and burden, we are as those who leap for joy.**
[10] **A Christian can sing, though alone, when God gives him the joy of his heart.**

[11] **Proverbs 23:34-35**. The context of these verses portrays an individual who has fallen asleep in a drunken stupor.

[12] **1 Peter 5:8**.

[13] Proverbs 6:9-11.

[14] **There is no persuasion will do if God opens not the eyes.**

[15] **John 10:1**.

[16] **They that come into the Way, but not by the Door, think that they can say something in vindication of their own practice.**

[17] Regardless of anyone's testimony, if God declares there is only one Way to the Celestial City, then there is only one Way. John 14:6.

[18] **Galatians 2:15-16**.

7

THE PILGRIM CLIMBS THE HILL OF DIFFICULTY

I THEN SAW THAT they all went on until they came to
the foot of the hill called Difficulty. At the bottom of the hill
was a spring, and two other paths were there at that place
besides the one that came straight from the Gate. There at the
bottom of the hill one path turned to the left hand and the other
to the right; but the narrow pathway led right up the hill, and
the name of the way up the side of the hill is called Difficulty.
Christian then went to the spring and drank from it to refresh
himself,[1] after which he began to go up the hill, saying:

> This hill, though high, I covet to ascend,
> The Difficulty will not me offend.
> For I perceive the Way to Life lies here:
> Come pluck up, Heart; let's neither faint nor fear;
> Better, though difficult, the Right Way to go,
> Than Wrong, though easy, where the End is Woe.

Formality and Hypocrisy also came to the foot of the hill, but when they saw the hill was steep and high and that there were two other ways to go (and also supposing these two paths might meet again on the other side of the hill with the one Christian had taken) they decided to travel those roads. Now the name of one of those paths was Danger, and the name of the other one was Destruction. So one took the way called Danger, which led him into a great forest. The other walked directly up the Way to Destruction, which led him into a wide area full of dark mountains where he stumbled and fell and arose no more.

Then I looked after Christian to watch him climb the hill. As he went, I noticed he changed from running to walking and from walking to crawling upon his hands and knees because of the steep grade of the hill. Now about halfway to the top of the hill there was a pleasant arbor, which had been made by the Lord of the Hill for the refreshment of weary travelers. When Christian arrived there, he sat down to rest himself. He then pulled his Document out of his coat and comforted himself by reading it. He also began again to examine the coat that had been given to him as he stood by the Cross. Pleasing himself in that way for a while, he finally began dozing and then fell fast asleep. His sleep detained him in that place until it was almost night, and in his sleep the Document fell out of his hand.

As he was sleeping, an individual approached him and woke him up, saying, "Go to the ant, you sluggard; consider its ways and be wise!"[2] And with that, Christian suddenly jumped up and ran quickly on his way. He continued that pace until he came to the top of the hill.

When he arrived at the top of the hill, two men came running toward him from the opposite direction. The name of one was Fearful, and the other's name was Mistrust.

Christian addressed them and said, "Sirs, what's the matter? You're running the wrong way."

Fearful answered and said they were going to the City of Zion and had gotten up this difficult place. "But," said Fearful, "the farther we go, the more danger we meet, and because of that we turned around and are going back."

Fearful and Mistrust run towards Christian

"Yes," said Mistrust, "for just ahead lie a couple of lions in the path. We can't tell whether they're asleep or awake, but we couldn't help but think they would quickly tear us to pieces if we came within reach."

Christian said, "You're making me afraid, but where can I run to be safe? If I go back to my own country, which is prepared for fire and brimstone, then I'll certainly die there. If I can get to Celestial City, I'm sure to live in safety there. I must continue, for to go back means nothing but death. To go forward is the fear of death, but beyond it is life everlasting. I'll keep going forward."

So Fearful and Mistrust ran down the hill, and Christian went on his way.[3]

Thinking again of what he had heard from the men, he felt in his coat for his Document so he could read it and be comforted; but he could not find it. Christian was greatly distressed and did not know what to do; but at last he remembered that he had slept in the arbor on the side of the hill. Falling down on his knees, he asked God to forgive his foolish act and went back to look for his Document. But all the way back, who can describe the sorrow of Christian's heart? Sometimes he sighed, sometimes he wept, and oftentimes he lectured himself for being so foolish as to fall asleep in that place that was erected only for a little refreshment from his weariness.

So he went back, carefully looking on this side and that side all the way. He went back in hope that he might find the Document that had been his comfort so many times in his journey. He continued until he came again within sight of the arbor where he had sat and slept, but seeing it just increased his sorrow by bringing the evil of his slumber into his mind again.

Christian continued on, therefore, lamenting his sinful sleep, saying, "What a wretched man I am![4] that I should sleep in the daytime!—that I should sleep in the middle of difficulty!—that I should so indulge the flesh to bring my flesh ease by misusing that place of rest that the Lord of the Hill constructed only for the relief of the spirits of Pilgrims! I've taken so many steps in vain!"[5]

Christian continued speaking to himself: "This is what happened to the people of Israel; for because of their sin they were sent back again by the way of the Red Sea.[6] I'm now made to walk with sorrow those steps that I might have walked with joy if it hadn't been for that sinful sleep. How far I might have been on my way by this time! I have to walk those steps three times when I should've only had to walk them once. Yes, and now I'm about to be overcome by darkness, for the Day is almost spent.[7] Oh, if only I hadn't slept!"

By this time, he had arrived back at the arbor where he sat down for a while weeping. But at last, sorrowfully looking under the seat, he saw (as he was hoping) his Document. With trembling and haste he picked it up and put it next to his heart in his coat.[8] Who can understand how joyful Christian was when he had found his Document again? For this Document provided him assurance of life and acceptance at the desired Place of Refuge. He took it up again, therefore, and, giving thanks to God for directing his eye to the place where it lay, he returned to his journey with joy and weeping. But, oh, how alertly he went up the rest of the hill.[9]

Yet, the sun went down upon Christian before he had reached the top of the hill, and this made him once again recall to his mind the foolishness of his sleeping. So Christian again began to grieve with himself. "Oh, you sinful slumber!" he began. "Because of you I could be overcome by darkness in my journey. I must now walk without the sun; darkness must cover the path of my feet; and I must listen to the noise of threatening creatures because of my sinful sleep!"

Then he remembered the story Mistrust and Fearful told him, how they were frightened by the sight of the lions. Christian said to himself again, "These beasts wander about in the night for their prey, and if they should meet with me in the darkness, how shall I evade them? How will I escape from being torn in pieces by them?"

So he went on his way, but while he was lamenting his unhappy circumstance, he lifted up his eyes and saw before him a very stately palace. The name of the palace was Beautiful, and it stood just by the side of the Highway.

NOTES ON CHAPTER 7

[1]   **Isaiah 49:10**.

[2]   **Proverbs 6:6**. The journey calls for diligence. God provides places and times for rest, but allegorically speaking, there is no time for sleep. **He that sleeps is a loser.**

[3]   Deuteronomy 20:8; Judges 7:3; Isaiah 35:4; Revelation 21:8; Psalm 112:6-8.

[4]   Romans 7:24.

[5]   **1 Thessalonians 5:4-9; Revelation 2**.

[6]   Numbers 14:21-34.

[7]   John 9:4.

[8]   The phrase "next to his heart" is not in the original but is used to enhance the context of the word "coat," which is used here and elsewhere to replace Bunyan's word "bosom." As a place where Christian could store his document, the word "bosom" is difficult to translate into modern English. In the NIV, the word "bosom"—as used in the KJV in "into my own bosom" (Psalm 35:13)—is changed to "to me." In the KJV of Psalm 74:11, God is asked to "pluck" his hand out of his bosom. This is translated in the NIV as, "Take it from the folds of your garment." In Psalm 129:7 the word is seen as referring to gathering reaped grain into one's arms. The phrase, "How I do bear in my bosom the reproach . . ." in the KJV of Psalm 89:50 is changed in the NIV to "how I bear in my heart the taunts." So, the old word "bosom" can be seen to show: simple receipt of action toward an individual, a physical location in relation to one's body or the clothing covering it, or the internalizing of action or feeling. Bunyan undoubtedly refers here and elsewhere to the internal, indwelling, document. It had been lost, forgotten, or disregarded; and he is now once again taking it up to himself.

[9]   **Christian finds his roll where he lost it.**

8

THE PILGRIM MEETS THE FAMILY

I SAW IN MY dream that Christian moved hastily toward the palace and went forward so that if possible he could get lodging there. Now before he had gone far, he entered into a very narrow passage that was about an eighth of a mile from the porter's lodge. Looking very closely as he went, he saw two lions in the way.

"Now," Christian thought, "I see the dangers that drove back Mistrust and Fearful." The lions were chained, but the Pilgrim did not see the chains, so he was afraid.

He considered going back and following Mistrust and Fearful, for he thought nothing but death was before him. But noticing that Christian paused as if he would go back, the Porter (whose name was Watchful)[1] cried out to him, saying, "Is your strength so small?[2] Don't fear the lions, for they're chained. They're placed there for the trial of faith,[3] to find out where it is and to reveal those who have none. Stay in the middle of the path, and no injury will come to you."

The path with the lions

Then I saw that Christian walked on. He trembled for fear of the lions. He heard their roar, but, heeding the directions of the Porter, they did not harm him. He clapped his hands with joy and went on until he came and stood before the gate where the Porter was.

Then Christian said to the Porter, "Sir, what is this house? May I stay here tonight?"

The Porter answered, "This house was built by the Lord of the Hill, and He built it for the relief and security of Pilgrims." The Porter also asked Christian where he came from and where he was going.

Christian answered him, "I've come from the City of Destruction, and I'm going to Mount Zion. But because the sun is now set, I desire to stay here tonight if possible."

"What is your name?" asked the Porter.

"Now my name is Christian," he told him, "but my name used to be Graceless. I descended from the race of Japheth, whom God persuades to dwell in the Tents of Shem."[4]

"But how is it that you've arrived so late?" inquired the Porter. "The sun has set."

"I would've been here sooner," explained Christian, "but— wretched man that I am!—I slept in the arbor that stands on the hillside! No, besides that, I would've been here much sooner if I hadn't lost my Evidence. I traveled without it to the top of the hill, and then feeling for it and not finding it, I was forced to go back with a sorrowful heart to where I slept. I recovered it, and now I'm here."

The Porter said, "Well, I'll call out one of the virgins of this place. According to the rules of the House, if she likes your explanation, she'll bring you into the company of the rest of the Family." So Watchful, the Porter, rang a bell; and at the sound of the bell a beautiful and serious-looking girl named Discretion came out of the door and asked why she had been called.

The Porter answered, "This man is in a journey from the City of Destruction to Mount Zion, but being weary and overtaken by the night, he asked me if he might lodge here tonight. So I told him I would call for you. After talking with him, you may do what seems fit to you according to the law of the house."

She asked Christian where he came from and where he was going, and he told her. She also asked him how he got in the Way, and he told her. Then she asked him what he had seen and met with in the Path, and he told her that also. At last she asked for his name; so he told her, "It's Christian, and I have an increasing desire to stay here tonight, since by what I observe this place was built by the Lord of the Hill for the relief and security of Pilgrims."

So she smiled, but tears stood in her eyes. And after a short pause, she said, "I will call upon two or three more of the Family." With that, she ran to the door and called out Prudence, Piety, and Charity, who after a little more discussion with him led him into the Family. Many of the members of the Family met him at the threshold of the house and said, "Come in, You who are blessed of the Lord! The Lord of the Hill built this house for the purpose of caring for such Pilgrims." Then he bowed his head and followed them into the house.[5]

When he had come in and was seated, they gave him something to drink. Then they agreed together that until supper was ready (and in order to make the best use of the time) some of them should discuss certain things with Christian. They appointed Piety, Prudence, and Charity to talk with him, and so they began:

"Come, Christian," said Piety; "since we've been so loving to you as having received you into our house tonight, let's talk with you about all the things that have happened to you in your Pilgrimage so that perhaps we may better ourselves by it."

"Gladly," said Christian. "I'm happy that you desire to do so."

Piety then asked, "What caused you at first to take upon yourself the life of a Pilgrim?"

To which Christian responded, "I was driven out of my native country by a dreadful sound in my ears—that is, news of the unavoidable destruction I was to experience if I continued living in the place where I was."

"But," continued Piety, "how is it that you came out of your country this way?"

"It was as God would have it," answered Christian, "for when I was experiencing the fears of destruction, I didn't know which way to go. But by chance a man came to me as I was trembling and weeping. His name is Evangelist, and he directed me to the Narrow Gate, which I wouldn't ever have found otherwise. Anyway, he set me into the path that has led me directly to this house."

"But didn't you come by the house of the Interpreter?" asked Piety.

"Yes," said Christian, "and I saw such things there that the memory of them will stick with me as long as I live. This is especially true of three things: First—how Christ, in spite of Satan, maintains His work of grace in the heart; Second—how the man had sinned himself quite out of the hope of obtaining God's mercy; and Third—the dream of him who thought in his sleep the day of judgment had come."

"Why, did you hear him tell his dream?" inquired Piety.

"Yes," answered Christian, "and I thought it was a dreadful one. It made my heart ache as he was telling about it, but I'm still glad I heard it."

"Was that all you saw at the house of the Interpreter?" asked Piety.

"No," said Christian, "he took me and led me to a place where he showed me a stately palace and how the people in it were dressed in gold. I saw there an adventurous man who came and cut his way through the armed men who stood in the doorway to keep him out. I was also shown how he was invited to come in and win eternal glory. These things carried away my heart! I could've stayed at that good man's house for a year, but I knew I had farther to travel."

Then Piety asked, "And what else did you see in your journey?"

"Saw!" exclaimed Christian. "Why, I went just a little farther and saw—as I thought in my mind—a Man hung bleeding upon a tree. The very sight of Him made my burden fall off my back. I had groaned under a weary burden, but then it fell down from off me. It was a strange thing to me, for I never saw such a thing before. And while I stood looking up—and I couldn't keep from doing so—three shining individuals came to me. One of them declared that my sins were forgiven; another stripped me of my rags and gave me this embroidered coat, which you see; and the third set upon me the mark you see in my forehead and gave me this sealed Document." With that, he removed it out of his coat.

"But you saw more than this, didn't you?" inquired Piety further.

Christian continued, "The things I've told you were the best; yet I saw some other lesser matters. As I traveled, I saw three men wearing leg irons. Their names were Simple, Sloth, and Presumption, and they lay asleep a little out of the Path. But do you think I could wake them up? I also saw Formality and Hypocrisy come climbing over the Wall to go, as they pretended, to Zion. But they were quickly lost, even as I warned them. They wouldn't believe me though. But above all, I found it hard work to get up this hill, and just as hard to pass by the mouths of the lions. Really, if it hadn't been for the Porter— the good man who stands at the gate—I might've gone back again. But now I thank God I'm here, and I thank you for accepting me."

Then Prudence thought it good to ask him a few questions and desired to hear his answer to them. She asked, "Don't you sometimes think of the country you came from?"

Christian answered her, "Yes, but with feelings of shame and abhorrence, for if I had been thinking of the country I had left, I would have had opportunity to return. Instead, I am longing for a better country—a heavenly one."[6]

"Don't you still carry with you some of the things that you were acquainted with there?" continued Prudence.

"Yes," admitted Christian, "but much against my will, especially my inward and worldly thoughts. All my fellow countrymen, as well as I myself, were delighted in them, but now all those things are my grief. If I could have my own way, I would choose never to think of those things again, but when I want to do good, evil is right there with me."[7]

Prudence responded, "But don't you find that at times it is as if those things were conquered that at other times cause you confusion?"

"Yes," said Christian, "but seldom. Those times, however, are golden hours to me in which such things happen."

Prudence continued her questioning, "Can you remember what causes your annoyances to be as if they were conquered?"

"Yes," answered Christian, "when I think about what I saw at the Cross, that will do it; and when I look upon my embroidered coat, that will do it. Also, when I look into the Document I carry next to my heart in my coat, that will do it; and when my thoughts are warmed about where I'm going, that will do it."[8]

Prudence then asked, "And what is it that makes you want so much to go to Mount Zion?"

"Why, I hope to see alive there the One who hung dead on the Cross," said Christian, "for to tell you the truth, I love Him because my burden was eased by Him. And there I hope to get rid of all those things that to this day are in me and that are an annoyance to me, for I'm weary of my inward sickness. They say there is no death there,[9] and that I'll dwell there with such company as I like best; I desire to be where I shall die no more and with the company that shall cry continually, 'Holy, holy, holy!'"[10]

Then Charity said to Christian, "Do you have a family? Are you a married man?"

"Yes," answered Christian, "I have a wife and four small children."

"And why didn't you bring them along with you?" inquired Charity.

Christian then began to weep and said, "Oh, how willingly I would have done it! But all of them were absolutely opposed to my leaving on the Pilgrimage."

"But you should've talked to them and tried to show them the danger of being left behind," counseled Charity.

"I did," said Christian, "and I also told them what God had shown me concerning the destruction of our city. But I appeared to them to be like a mocker, and they didn't believe me."

"And did you pray to God that He would bless your witnessing to them?" asked Charity further.

"Yes, and I did so with much passion," answered Christian, "for you must know that my wife and poor children were very dear to me."

Then Charity asked, "But did you tell them of your own sorrow and fear of destruction? For I suppose that destruction was visible enough to you."

"Yes," said Christian, "over, and over, and over. They could also see my concern in my expression, in my tears, and also in my trembling due to my understanding of the judgment hanging over our heads. But all of that was not sufficient to cause them to come with me."

"But what could they say for themselves as an excuse for not coming?" asked Charity.

Christian explained, "Why, my wife was afraid of losing this world, and my children were carried away with the foolish delights of youth. So, because of one thing or another, they left me to wander like this alone."

"But didn't you make the words you used to persuade them ineffective by your vain life?" asked Charity.

"True, I can't commend my life," answered Christian, "for I'm fully conscious of my many failings. I also know that by the life he lives a man can quickly destroy what he by reasoning and through persuasion has worked to give to others for their good. Yet, I can say this: that I was very wary of giving them an occasion to make themselves opposed to going on the Pilgrimage based upon any improper action on my part. And because of that, they would tell me I was too righteous and that I denied myself things—for their sakes—in which they saw no evil. No, I think I can say that if they saw anything in me that hindered them, it was my great sensitivity toward sinning against God or toward doing any wrong to my neighbor."

Charity then stated, "Yes, Cain hated his brother because his own actions were evil, and his brother's were righteous.[11] Now if your wife and children have been offended by you for this, then they have shown themselves by that to be merciless toward good, and you have delivered your soul from responsibility for their end."[12]

Now I saw in my dream that they sat talking together like that until supper was ready. When they had made ready, they sat down to eat. The table was furnished with "the best of meats and the finest of wines."[13] All their conversation at the table was about the Lord of the Hill: such as what He had done, why He did what He did, and why He had built that house. From what they said, I perceived that He had been a great warrior and had fought with and slain the one who had the power of death,[14] but that He hadn't done it without great danger to himself, and this made me love Him all the more. For as they said (and as I believe Christian said) He did it by shedding a great deal of blood.[15]

But what put the glory of grace into all He did was that He did it out of pure love for His country. And besides, there were some of those in the Household who said they had seen and spoken with Him since He died on the Cross.[16] They affirmed they heard from His own lips that He loves poor Pilgrims so much that there isn't anyone like Him to be found from the East to the West.

Beyond that, they gave an example of what they declared, and that was: He had stripped himself of His glory in order to do this work for the Poor.[17] And in addition, they heard Him say and affirm that He would not live in the Mountain of Zion alone.[18] In addition, they said He had made many Pilgrims into princes even though they were born needy and though they were originally from the ash heap.[19]

They talked together this way until late at night, and after they had committed themselves to their Lord for protection, they retired for the night. They gave the Pilgrim a large room upstairs in which to sleep. The room had a window which opened toward the East to catch the sunrise. The name of the bedroom was Peace, and Christian slept there until the break of day, when he awoke and sang:

> Where am I now! Is this the Love and Care
> Of Jesus; for the men that Pilgrims are,
> Thus to provide! That I should be forgiven,
> And dwell already the next door to Heaven!

They all got up in the morning; and after more conversation they told him that he should not leave until they had shown him the excellence of that place. First, they led him into the study where they showed him records of the greatest antiquity. As I remember in my dream, they first showed him the lineage of the Lord of the Hill, how He was the Son[20] of the Ancient of Days[21] and came by an eternal generation.[22] The acts He had done were also more fully recorded here along with the names of many hundreds whom He had taken into His service and how He had placed them in dwelling places that could not be dissolved by either length of days[23] or decays of nature.[24]

Then they read to him some of the worthy acts of some of His Servants, such as how they had conquered kingdoms, administered justice, gained what was promised, shut the mouths of lions, quenched the fury of the flames, escaped the edge of the sword, had their weakness turned to strength, became powerful in battle, and routed foreign armies.[25]

Then they read again in another part of the records of the house where it was shown how willing their Lord was to receive anyone into His Favor, even though in time past they had shown great disrespect for His character and actions.[26] There were historical accounts here of many other honored things, and Christian looked at them all. These were things both ancient and modern, together with prophecies and predictions of things that are certain to be fulfilled to both the dread and alarm of enemies and the comfort and cheer of Pilgrims.[27]

The next day, they took Christian and led him into the Armory where they showed him all kinds of equipment that their Lord had provided for Pilgrims. This equipment included the Sword, Shield, Helmet, Breastplate, Prayers, and Shoes that will not wear out.[28] There was enough of all this there to equip for the service of their Lord as many people as there are stars in the sky for multitude.[29]

They also showed him some of the weapons with which some of His servants had done amazing things. They showed him Moses' Staff,[30] the hammer and tent peg with which Jael killed Sisera,[31] and also the jars, trumpets, and torches that Gideon used to vanquish the armies of Midian.[32] Then they showed him the oxgoad that Shamgar used to slay six hundred men.[33] They also showed him the jawbone that Samson used to do such mighty deeds.[34] Besides that, they showed him the sling and stone that David used to slay Goliath of Gath[35] and the Sword that their Lord will use to kill the man of Lawlessness in the day when He will confront His prey.[36] They showed him many other excellent things that delighted Christian. With this done, they retired again to sleep.

Then I saw in my dream that he got up the next day to travel on, but they desired to have him stay for yet another day. "Then," they said, "if the day is clear we will show you the Delightful Mountains." They said it would further add to his comfort because the mountains were nearer to the desired sanctuary than where he presently was. So, he agreed and stayed.

When morning came they led him to the top of the house and asked him to look south. So he did, and there at a great distance he saw a very pleasant looking mountainous country made beautiful with woods, vineyards, fruits of all kinds, flowers, springs, and fountains.[37] They were delightful to behold. Then he asked the name of the country, and they told him it was Immanuel's Land.[38] "It's just as common," they said, "for Pilgrims to walk through and experience that land as it is for them to experience this hill. And when you arrive there, you'll be able to see the gate of Celestial City, as the Shepherds who live there will reveal."

Now Christian reminded himself of traveling on, and they were willing that he should. "But first," they said, "let's go into the armory again." So they did, and when he got there they fitted him from head to foot with equipment that had proven effective. This was done for the event he might be assaulted in the Way.

Being prepared then, he walked out with his friends to the gate and asked the Porter if he had seen any other Pilgrim pass by.

Christian showed Immanuel's Land

The Porter answered, "Yes."

"Tell me," said Christian, "did you know him?"

"I asked for his name," answered the Porter, "and he told me it was Faithful."

"Oh," said Christian, "I know him. He's from my town, a close neighbor of mine. He comes from the place where I was born. How far do you think he is ahead of me?"

"By this time he has reached the bottom of the hill," said the Porter.

"Well, Porter," said Christian, "may the Lord be with you and increase all your blessings for the kindness you have shown to me."

Then he began to journey on. Discretion, Piety, Charity, and Prudence decided to accompany him down to the foot of the hill. So they went on together, restating their earlier discussions until they came to the start of the descent down the hill.

Then Christian stated, "As far as I can see, it's just as dangerous going down the hill as it was coming up."

"Yes, it is," responded Prudence, "for it's a difficult matter for a man to go down into the Valley of Humiliation, as you are doing, without losing his footing along the way. Therefore," she said, "we've come out to accompany you down the hill." And so, they began the descent very carefully, but even then he lost his footing a time or two.

Then I saw in my dream that when Christian got down to the bottom of the hill, these good companions gave to him a loaf of bread, a bottle of wine, and a cluster of raisins. Then Christian went his way.

Notes on Chapter 8

[1] **Mark 13:34**

[2] Proverbs 24:10.

[3] 1 Peter 1:7

[4] A tent is a dwelling place and refuge. Japheth and Shem were both sons of Noah (Genesis 6:10). The Israelites and,

therefore, Jesus descended from Shem. Bunyan alludes to **Genesis 9:27,** inferring the fulfillment of Noah's prophecy in being drawn to Christ, our refuge.

[5] The Family is a place of refuge. This family is the Church, the body of Christ—Ephesians 5:22-30. No one but God cares more than the Family for the welfare of a new Christian. Note that prior to this event, Christian had not directly identified with or been taken into the body of believers, the Church. At this time of need, the Family is there to minister to and encourage the weary traveler. But though the Family has no greater earthly concern than that of ministering to others, Bunyan points out that it is the way of discretion for the Family to examine the sincerity of the traveler before he is to be entrusted with the full rights and privileges of family membership. The apostle Paul even faced discretion after his conversion—Acts 9:1-31. For the body of Christ to function correctly in receiving and authorizing workers among them, more than charity (unconditional love) is required; It also calls for prudence (wisdom, care, caution) and piety (devoutness, allegiance, holiness, godliness)—1 Timothy 5:22.

[6] **Hebrews 11:15,16**; Hebrews 11:13-16.

[7] Romans 7:21. **Romans 7**.

[8] Philippians 4:4-9.

[9] **Revelation 21:4; Isaiah 25:8.**

[10] Isaiah 6:1-3; Revelation 4:8.

[11] **1 John 3:12**; Genesis 4:1-8.

[12] **Ezekiel 3:19**.

[13] Isaiah 25:6.

[14] **Hebrews 2:14-15**.

[15] Mark 14:64-65; John 19:1-3, 33-34; Hebrews 9:11-14, 22, 10:8-10.

[16] Acts 1:3; 1 Corinthians 15:3-8.

[17] Philippians 2:5-8

[18] Zechariah 2:10-11; John 14:1-3.

[19] **Christ makes princes of beggars. Psalm 113:7; 1 Samuel 2:8.**

[20] Matthew 3:16-17.

[21] Daniel 7:9-14.

22 John 1:1, 14.

23 Psalm 21:4.

24 Matthew 6:20.

25 **Hebrews 11:33-34.**

26 John 3:16-17

27 Luke 21:25-28.

28 Ephesians 6:10-18.

29 Genesis 15:4-6; Romans 9:6-8; Galatians 3:26-29; Hebrews 11:11-12.

30 Exodus 4:1-5, 14:13-22.

31 Judges 4:21.

32 Judges 7.

33 Judges 3:31.

34 Judges 15:15-17.

35 1 Samuel 17:40-51

36 2 Thessalonians 2:3; Revelation 19:11-21

37 **Isaiah 33:15-17.**

38 Matthew 1:23-25.

9

THE PILGRIM GOES THROUGH VALLEYS

NOW IN THIS VALLEY of Humiliation, poor Christian was severely challenged. He had gone only a short distance when he saw coming over the field toward him a disgusting fiend named Apollyon.[1] Christian then began to fear and consider in his mind whether to go back or stand his ground. He considered again that he had no armor for his back, and he thought, therefore, that turning his back to him might give Apollyon a greater advantage and allow the fiend to pierce him with his arrows. So he resolved to go on and stand his ground, thinking, "If I only plan to save my life, it will still be the best way to stand."

So he went on, and Apollyon met him. That monster was hideous to look at. He was covered with scales like a fish (these are his pride). He had wings like a dragon and feet like a bear, and out of his belly came fire and smoke; and his mouth was as the mouth of a lion.[2] When he came up to Christian, he looked upon him with disdain and then began to question him.

"Where did you come from," asked Apollyon, "and where are you going?"

Christian answered him, "I've come from the City of Destruction, which is the Place of all Evil, and I'm going to the City of Zion."

Apollyon responded, "By this, I perceive you're one of my subjects, for all that country is mine, and I am the prince and god of it.[3] How is it then that you've run away from your king? If it were not for my desire to have you serve me longer, I would now strike you down to the ground with one blow."

"True," said Christian, "I was born in your empire. Yet serving you was hard, and the wages you paid were such that a man couldn't live on them, 'for the wages of sin is death.'[4] When I reached maturity, therefore, I did as other concerned people do: I searched for a way to renew myself."

Apollyon then replied, "There is no prince who will lose his subjects so lightly, and I don't intend to lose you. But, since you complain about your work and wages, be content to go back. What our country yields, I now promise to give to you."

"But I've given my service to another, even to the King of Princes,"[5] replied Christian. "How can I, in all fairness, go back with you?"

Then Apollyon said, "In this you have, according to the proverb, exchanged bad for worse, but it's common for those who've professed themselves his servants to slip away from him after a while and return again to me. Do the same thing, and all will be well."

Christian said, "I've given Him my faith and have sworn allegiance to Him. How can I then go back from this and not be hanged as a traitor?"

"You did the same to me," replied Apollyon, "and yet I'm willing to let it pass if you'll now turn around and go back."[6]

"What I promised you was in my adolescence," said Christian, "and besides, I believe the Prince, under whose flag I now serve, is able to forgive me, yes, and even pardon what I did as to my agreement with you. In addition—Oh, you destroying Apollyon!—to speak the truth, I like His Work, His Wages, His Servants, His Government, His Company, and His Country better than yours. Therefore, quit trying to persuade me; for I am His servant, and I will follow Him."

Apollyon countered, "Consider again, when you cool down,what you're likely to meet with in the way you're going. You know that for the most part his servants come to an ill end because they are transgressors against me and my ways. Think of how many of them have been put to shameful deaths! And besides, you count his service better than mine even though he has never yet come from the place where he is to deliver out of our hands any who served him. But as for me, how many times—as the whole world knows very well—have I delivered from him and his, either by power or fraud, those who have faithfully served me, even though they were taken by them. And I'll deliver you in the same way."

Christian then said, "His forbearance at that time from delivering them is on purpose, to try their love, to see whether they'll serve Him to the end. And as for the bad end you say they come to, that is most glorious to their credit. But as for present deliverance, they don't much expect it, for they remain faithful in order to obtain glory, and they'll have it when their Prince comes in His glory and the glory of the angels."

"You've already been unfaithful in your service to him," accused Apollyon, "and how do you expect to receive wages from him?"

"And how, oh Apollyon, have I been unfaithful to Him?" questioned Christian.

Apollyon quickly answered,"You fainted at the beginning of your journey when you were almost choked in the Gulf of Despondence. You attempted to rid yourself of your burden in the wrong way when you should've waited until your prince had taken it off. You sinfully slept and lost your valuable things. Also, you were almost persuaded to go back at the sight of the lions. And when you talk about your journey and what you've heard and seen, you are inwardly boastful in everything you say and do."[7]

"All this is true," admitted Christian, "and much more

that you've left out, but the Prince whom I serve and honor is merciful and ready to forgive. These infirmities controlled me in your country, for there I sucked them in; and I've groaned under them and been sorry for them, but I've obtained pardon for them from my Prince."[8]

Then Apollyon broke out into a tremendous rage, saying, "I'm an enemy of this prince! I hate his person, his laws, and his people. I've come here to oppose you!"

"Beware of what you do, Apollyon," said Christian, "for I'm in the King's Highway, the Way of Holiness. Therefore, take heed to yourself."

Then Apollyon straddled over the whole breadth of the Path, and said, "I'm void of fear in this matter. Prepare yourself to die, for I swear by my infernal abode that you will go no farther. I will spill your soul here!"

And with that, he shot a flaming arrow at Christian's chest!

But Christian had the Shield in his hand, and with it he intercepted the arrow and averted its danger.[9]

Then Christian drew his Sword, for he recognized it was time to arouse himself. And, just as quickly, Apollyon charged him, shooting arrows as thick as hail.

Despite all that Christian could do to avoid it, Apollyon wounded him with arrows in his head, his hand, and his foot.[10] This caused Christian to fall back a little. Apollyon, therefore, followed with another sudden and forceful attack. Christian took courage again and resisted as bravely as he could. This severe combat lasted for over half a day, even until Christian was almost worn out; for you must realize that Christian had to have grown weaker and weaker because of his wounds.

Then, seeing his opportunity, Apollyon began to draw close to Christian and, wrestling with him, gave him a dreadful fall. With that, Christian's Sword flew out of his hand. Then Apollyon exclaimed, "I have you beaten now!" With that, he almost crushed him to death, and Christian began to despair of life.

But, as God would have it, while Apollyon was preparing for his last blow, which he would use to bring an end to this

Christian's victory over Apollyon

good man, Christian skillfully reached out his hand for his Sword and grasped it, saying, "'Do not gloat over me, my enemy! Though I have fallen, I will rise.'"[11]

Then Christian gave him a deadly thrust, which made Apollyon back away as if he had received a mortal wound. Recognizing it, Christian attacked him again, saying, "'No, in all these things we are more than conquerors through him who loved us.'"[12] With that, Apollyon spread out his dragon's wings and quickly sped away, so that Christian saw him no more.[13]

During this fight, no one can imagine (unless he had seen and heard as I did) what yelling and hideous roaring Apollyon made all the time of the fight; for he spoke as a dragon.[14] And on the other side, what sighing and groaning burst from Christian's heart. All the while, I never saw him give as much as one pleasant look until he perceived he had wounded Apollyon with his Double-edged Sword.[15] Then, yes, he did smile and look upward. But it was the most dreadful fight I ever saw.

So when the battle was over, Christian said, "I'll give thanks here to Him who has delivered me out of the mouth of the lions, to Him who helped me against Apollyon."

And he did, saying:

Great Beelzebub, the Captain of this Fiend,
Design'd my Ruin; therefore to this end
He sent him harness'd out; and he with rage,
That hellish was, did fiercely me engage:
But blessed Michael helped me, and I,
By dint of Sword, did quickly make him fly:
Therefore to Him let me give lasting Praise,
And Thank, and bless His holy Name always.[16]

Then a Hand holding some of the leaves of the Tree of Life came to him. Christian took them, and applying them to the wounds he had received in the battle, he was immediately healed.[17] He also sat down in that place to eat bread and to drink from the bottle that had been given to him a little earlier. So, feeling refreshed, he began his journey again with his Sword drawn in his hand, for he said, "I don't know but what some other enemy may be close by." But he didn't meet with another insulting challenge from Apollyon throughout this valley.

Now at the end of this valley was another one called the Valley of the Shadow of Death,[18] and Christian had to go through it. This was because the road to Celestial City ran right through the middle of it. This valley is a very lonely place. The prophet Jeremiah described it as a "wilderness . . . a land of deserts and rifts, a land of drought and darkness, a land where no one (except a Christian) passes through, and where no one lives."[19] Here, Christian was subjected to more hardship than in his fight with Apollyon, as you will see in what followed.

I saw then in my dream that when Christian arrived at the edge of the Shadow of Death, two men met him. They were descendants of those who brought back a bad report of the good land.[20] These two men were hurriedly going back, and they spoke to Christian as follows:

"Where are you going?" asked Christian.

"Back! Back!" they exclaimed. "And we would advise you to do the same thing, that is if you prize either life or peace."

"Why?" questioned Christian. "What's the matter?"

"Matter!" they exclaimed again. "We were going that way, as you are going. We went as far as we dared, and we were really very close to the point of no return, for if we had gone a little farther we wouldn't have been here to bring the news to you."

"But with what did you meet?" asked Christian.

"Why, we were almost in the Valley of the Shadow of Death," they said, "but by good chance we looked before us and saw the danger before we came to it."

"And what did you see?" asked Christian.

"See!" they exclaimed. "Why, the valley itself, which is as dark as pitch. We also saw there the Hobgoblins, Satyrs, and Dragons of the pit. We also heard in that valley a continual howling and yelling, as of people under unutterable misery sitting there in affliction and irons.[21] Over that valley hang the discouraging clouds of confusion, and death also spreads his wings over it. In a word, it's completely dreadful, being utterly without order."[22]

Then Christian said, "In spite of what you've said, I still see this as my path to the desired refuge."

"Let it be your way," they replied. "We'll not choose it for ours."[23]

So they parted, and Christian went on his way with his Sword drawn in his hand for fear of being assaulted.

I saw then in my dream that a very deep ditch lay on the right hand for the full length of the valley. It is the Ditch into which the blind have led the blind throughout the ages and where both have miserably perished.[24] Also, on the left hand was a very dangerous quagmire into which, if a good man falls, he finds no bottom for his foot to stand on. This is the Quagmire into which King David once fell, and in which he would have been smothered if He Who is Able had not pulled him out.[25]

The pathway was also extremely narrow here. Good Christian, therefore, was seriously challenged, for when he sought in the dark to avoid the Ditch on one hand, he was close to tipping over into the mire on the other. Also, when he sought to escape the mire, without great care he would be ready to fall into the Ditch. He went on like this, and I heard him sigh bitterly; for beside the dangers mentioned above, the pathway was so dark here that often, when he lifted up his foot to go forward, he did not know where or upon what he would set it down next.[26]

I perceived the Mouth of Hell to be about in the middle of this valley, and it also stood close to the side of the Path.

"Now," thought Christian, "what shall I do?"

Again and again the flame and smoke would come out of it in such abundance and with sparks and hideous noises—things not moved by Christian's Sword as Apollyon was before—that he was forced to put up his Sword and resort to take up another weapon called All-Prayer.[27]

I heard Christian cry out, "O Lord, save me!"[28]

He went on like this for a great while, but the flames were still reaching toward him. He heard threatening voices and rushings about, so that sometimes he thought he would be torn in pieces or trodden down like mud in the roads. For several miles altogether he saw these frightening sights and heard these dreadful noises; and coming to a place where he thought he heard a gang of fiends coming toward him, he stopped and began to consider what would be the best thing to do. Sometimes he had half a mind to go back; then he thought again that he might be halfway through the valley. Also, he remembered how he had already vanquished many a danger and that the risk of going back might be much more than going forward. So he resolved to go on, yet the fiends seemed to come nearer and nearer.

When they had almost reached him, Christian cried out with a most earnest voice, "'I will go in the strength of the Lord God.'"[29]

So they backed off and came no farther.

One thing I would not forget to tell: I took notice that now poor Christian was so confounded that he did not know his own voice, and this is how I observed it: Just when he had come close to the mouth of the burning pit, one of the Wicked Ones[30] got behind him, stepping up softly to him and whispering suggestions of deplorable blasphemies to him. He actually thought these had originated in his own mind. To think that he should now blaspheme the one he loved so much before challenged Christian more than anything he had met with. Yet, if he could have helped it, he would not have done it; but he did not have the freedom to either stop his ears or to know where the blasphemies came from.

After Christian had traveled in this sad condition for a considerable time, he thought he heard the voice of a man as if he were going before him, saying, "'Even though I walk through the valley of the shadow of death, I will fear no evil, for you are with me.'"[31]

Then he was glad, and these are the reasons: First—because he gathered by it that others who feared God were in this valley as well as himself. Second—he perceived God was with them even in that dark and dismal condition. "And why wouldn't He be with me?" he thought, "even though I can't feel it because of the hindrances associated with this place."[32] Third—if he could catch up with them, he hoped to eventually have fellowship with them.

He went on then and called out to him who was ahead, but the one ahead did not know what to answer because he also considered himself to be alone.

In time the Day broke, and Christian then said, "He has turned blackness into dawn."[33] Now, morning having arrived, he looked back, not out of a desire to return but to see by the Light of the Day what hazards he had gone through in the dark. So he saw more clearly the Ditch that was on one hand and the Quagmire that was on the other. He saw how narrow the Path was that led between them both. And he also saw the Hobgoblins, Satyrs, and Dragons of the pit, but from a distance; for after the break of day they did not come near him but were revealed to him according to that which is written, "He reveals the deep things of darkness and brings deep shadows into the light."[34]

Now Christian was much affected by his deliverance from all the dangers of his solitary path. Yet he feared those dangers more before—even though he saw them more clearly now, since the light of day made them conspicuous to him. The sun was rising about this time, and this was another mercy to Christian, for you must note that though the first part of the Valley of the Shadow of Death was dangerous, yet the second part—which he was yet to experience—was (if possible) far more dangerous. From the place where he now stood, even to the end of the valley, the Pathway was set so full of snares, traps, and nets up here and so full of pits, pitfalls, deep holes, and ledges down there that had it now been dark (as it was when he came the first part of the way), and had he possessed a thousand souls, they would have been lost. But as I said, the sun was now rising.[35]

Then Christian said, "His lamp shines upon my head, and by His Light I go through darkness."[36]

In this light, therefore, he came to the end of the valley.

Now I saw in my dream that at the end of this valley lay the blood, bones, ashes, and mangled bodies of Pilgrims who had gone this way earlier. While I was reflecting on what the reason for this might be, I spotted a short distance before me a cave where two giants lived in days past. Their names were Pope and Pagan, and by their power and tyranny, those whose bones, blood, ashes, and other remains lay there had been put to death. Christian went by this place without much danger, at which I was somewhat amazed, but I have learned since that Pagan has been dead a long time. As for the other one, though he is still alive, yet because of his age and the many clever brushes he met with in his younger days, he has grown so senile and stiff in his joints that he can now do little more than sit in the mouth of his cave, grinning at Pilgrims as they go by, and biting his nails because he cannot confront them.

So I saw that Christian went on his way. He did not know what to think of the sight of the old man who sat in the mouth of the cave, especially since (though he could not go after him) the man spoke to him, saying, "You'll never be restored until more of you are burnt." But Christian held his peace and kept his composure, and so he passed by and was not harmed. Then Christian sang:

> O World of Wonders! (I can say no less)
> That I should be preserv'd in that Distress
> That I have met with here! O blessed be
> That Hand that from it hath deliver'd me!
> Dangers in darkness, Devils, Hell, and Sin,
> Did compass me, while I this Vale was in:
> Yea Snares, and Pits, and Traps, and Nets did lie
> My Path about, that worthless, silly I
> Might have been catch'd, entangled, and cast down:
> But since I live, let JESUS wear the Crown.

NOTES ON CHAPTER 9

[1]   The angel of the Abyss. Revelation 9:11.
[2]   Revelation 13:2.
[3]   John 12:31, 16:11; Ephesians 2:1-2.
[4]   **Romans 6:23**.
[5]   1 Timothy 6:15
[6]   **Apollyon pretends to be merciful.**
[7]   Revelation 12:10
[8]   Romans 8:1
[9]   Ephesians 6:16.

10   **Christian wounded in his understanding, faith, and Christian walk.**

11   **Micah 7:8.**

12   **Romans 8:37.**

13   **James 4:7.**

14   Revelation 13:11.

15   Psalm 149; Hebrews 4:12.

16   Fighting this "fiend" is like fighting the devil himself because Apollyon shares in his power and intentions. The name "Beelzebub" is applied to Satan in Matthew 10:25; 12:24-28; Mark 3:22-30; Luke 11:15-20. Michael is one of God's chief angels—Daniel 10:13-21; 12:1; Jude 9; Revelation 12:7.

17   Genesis 2,8-9, 3:22; Revelation 22:1-2, 14.

18   Psalm 23.

19   **Jeremiah 2-6.**

20   **Numbers 13.**

21   **Psalm 44:19, 107:10.**

22   **Job 3:5, 10:22.**

23   **Jeremiah 2:5.**

24   Matthew 15-14; Luke 6:39.

25   **Psalm 69-14, 40:1-2.**

26   Isaiah 50:10.

27   Mark 9:17-29; **Ephesians 6:18.** Even a thorough knowledge and use of "the Sword"—the Word of God—is not weapon enough. This is an instance when Christian must rely principally upon what only God himself can do on his behalf. Sometimes in our spiritual battles, prayer is our greatest weapon.

28   **Psalm 116:4.**

29   Psalm 71:16 (KJV).

30   Bunyan certainly refers to evil spirits as Wicked Ones, as opposed to ministering spirits; that is, Shining Ones.

31   **Psalm 23:4.**

32   **Job 9:10-11.**

33   **Amos 5:8.**

34   **Job 12:22.**

35   Malachi 4:2.

36   **Job 29:3.**

10

Two Pilgrims Meet

As HE WENT ON his way, Christian came to a little incline that was purposely built up so Pilgrims might see ahead of them. Christian, therefore, went up there and, looking forward, saw Faithful before him on his journey.

Then Christian shouted loudly, "Hey, hey! Say, hey! Wait, and I'll be your Travel Companion!"

At that, Faithful looked behind him.

And Christian cried out again, "Wait! Wait till I catch up with you!"

But Faithful answered, "No! I'm concerned for my life, and the avenger of blood is behind me."

Christian was quite moved by that. And calling upon all his strength, he quickly caught up with Faithful and even ran past him, so that the last was first.[1] Then Christian smiled smugly because he had gotten ahead of his Brother; and not paying attention to his feet, he suddenly stumbled and fell and could not rise again until Faithful came to help him.

Then I saw in my dream that they went on together with much friendship and engaged in delightful discussion of all the things that had happened to them in their Pilgrimage. And thus they began:

"My honored and well beloved brother Faithful," said Christian, "I'm glad I've overtaken you and that God has so tempered our spirits that we can walk as companions in this pleasant path."

Faithful responded, "My friend, I wanted to have your company ever since leaving our town, but you started ahead of me. I was forced, therefore, to come this much of the Way alone."

"How long did you stay in the City of Destruction before you set out after me on your Pilgrimage?" asked Christian.

"Until I could stay no longer," responded Faithful. "Immediately after you left, there was great talk that our city would soon be burned down to the ground with fire from Heaven."

"What? Did your neighbors talk like that?" questioned Christian.

"Yes," answered Faithful, "for a while it was in everybody's mouth."

"What?" questioned Christian. "Then didn't any more of them besides you come out to escape the danger?"

Faithful explained, "Though there was, as I said, great talk about it, yet I don't think they firmly believed it. For in the heat of the discussion, I heard some of them speak mockingly of you and of your desperate journey, which is what they called your Pilgrimage. But I believed then, and still do, that the end of our city will be with fire and brimstone from above.[2] Therefore, I've made my escape."

"Didn't you hear any talk of our neighbor Pliable?" asked Christian further.

"Yes, Christian," answered Faithful, "I heard that he followed you until he came to the Swamp of Despondence, where—as some said—he fell in. He wouldn't let it be known he'd done so, but I'm sure he was thoroughly covered with that kind of dirt."

"And what did the neighbors say to him?" inquired Christian.

"Since going back," responded Faithful, "he's been held in great contempt by all sorts of people. Some mock and despise him, and scarcely will anyone give him work. He's now seven times worse than if he'd never gone out of the city."

"But why should they be so set against him since they also despise the Way he deserted?" asked Christian.

"Oh," answered Faithful, "they say, 'Hang him; he's a turncoat! He wasn't true to his profession!' I think God has stirred up even his enemies to hiss at him and make him an object of ridicule because he's forsaken the Way."[3]

"Didn't you talk with him before you came out?" asked Christian.

"I met him once in the streets," said Faithful, "but he sheepishly crossed to the other side as one who was ashamed of what he'd done; so I didn't speak to him."

"Well," said Christian, "when I first set out on my journey, I had hopeful expectations of that man, but now I fear he will perish in the overthrow of the city. For it has happened to him according to the true proverb, 'A dog returns to its vomit,' and, 'A sow that is washed goes back to her wallowing in the mud.'"[4]

"Those are my fears of him, too," admitted Faithful, "but who can stop that which will be?"

"Well, Faithful," said Christian, "let's end our discussion of him and talk of things that more immediately concern ourselves. Tell me now what you've met with in the Path as you came, for I know you've met with some things, or else it would be accounted a miracle."

"I escaped the swamp, which I assume you fell into, and arrived at the Gate without that danger," said Faithful, "but I met with one whose name was Wanton, who would like to have caused me mischief."

"It's a good thing you escaped her trap," responded Christian. "Joseph was greatly challenged by her, and he escaped her as you did, but it could have cost him his life.[5] What did she do to you?"

Faithful answered, "You can't imagine, unless you have personal experience, what a flattering tongue she had. She tried her best to persuade me to turn aside with her, promising me all kinds of contentment."

"No," said Christian, "she didn't promise you the contentment of a good conscience."

"You know what I mean," said Faithful, "all worldly and fleshly contentment."

"Thank God, you've escaped her," replied Christian. "Those who are under the Lord's wrath will fall into her pit."[6]

"No," said Faithful, "I don't know whether I completely escaped her or not."

"Why, I don't suppose you yielded to her desires did you?" inquired Christian.

"No, not to pollute myself," answered Faithful, "for I remembered an old writing I had seen, which said, 'Her steps lead straight to the grave.'[7] So I shut my eyes because I would not be bewitched by her looks.[8] Then she hurled insults upon me, and I went my way."

"Did you meet with any other assault as you came?" asked Christian further.

Faithful answered, "When I came to the foot of the hill called Difficulty, I met with a very old man who asked me what I was and where I was bound. I told him I was a Pilgrim going to Celestial City. Then the old man said, 'You look like an honest fellow; will you be content to live with me in exchange for the wages I'll give you?' He said his name was Adam the First and that he lived in the Town of Deceit.[9] I asked him what his work was and what wages he would pay. He told me that his work was Many Delights and his wage was that I would become his heir in the end. I asked him further what house he owned and what other servants he had. So, he told me that his house was maintained with all the fine things of the world and that his servants were those of his own fathering. Then I asked how many children he had. He said that he had only three daughters: the Lust of the Flesh, the Lust of the Eyes, and the Pride of Life.[10] He told me I could marry all of them if I wished. Then I asked how long he desired to have me live with him, and he told me: as long as he himself lived."

"Well," said Christian, "and what conclusion did you and the old man come to?"

"Why, at first I found myself somewhat inclined to follow after the man," answered Faithful, "for I thought he spoke honestly. But looking on his forehead as I talked with him, I saw written there, 'Put off the old man with his deeds.'"[11]

"And what then?" asked Christian.

Faithful continued, "Then burning hot into my mind came the thought that whatever he said, and however he flattered, when he got me home to his house, he would sell me for a slave. So I asked him to stop talking, for I would not come near the door of his house. Then he criticized me and told me that he would send after me a certain individual who would make my journey bitter to my soul. So I turned to go away from him, but just as I turned myself to leave, I felt him take hold of my flesh and give me such a deadly jerk back, that I thought he had pulled part of me toward him. This made me cry, 'What a wretched man I am!'[12] I then went on my way up the hill."

Faithful went on, "Now when I'd gotten over halfway up the hill, I looked behind me and saw someone coming after me as swiftly as the wind. He overtook me just about the place where the bench stands."

"That's the place where I sat down to rest myself," remarked Christian, "but being overcome by sleep, I lost this Document out of my coat."

"But dear Brother, hear me out," said Faithful. "As soon as the man overtook me, he was but a word and a blow, for he knocked me down and laid me out for dead. But after I had somewhat come to my senses again, I asked him, 'Why did you do that to me?' He said it was because of my secret inclination to follow after Adam the First; and with that, he struck me another deadly blow on the chest and beat me down backward, so I lay at his foot as if I were dead like before. When I came to myself again, I cried for him to have mercy; but he said, 'I don't know how to show mercy!' And with that he knocked me down again. No doubt he would have made an end of me, except that another individual came by and caused him to stop."

"Who was it that made him stop?" asked Christian.

"I didn't know Him at first," answered Faithful, "but as He went by, I saw the holes in His hands and in His side. Then I concluded that He was our Lord. After this, I went up the Hill."[13]

"That man who overtook you was Moses," explained Christian. "He spares no one, and he doesn't know how to show mercy to those who transgress his law."

"I know it very well," replied Faithful. "It wasn't the first time he met with me. He was the one who came to me when I lived securely at home and told me he would burn my house down on my head if I stayed there."

Then Christian asked, "But didn't you see the house that stood there on the top of that hill, the hill on the side of which Moses met you?"

"Yes," answered Faithful, "and also the lions before I reached it. But as for the lions, I think they were asleep, for it was about noon; and because I had so much of the day left, I passed by the Porter and came on down the hill."

"Yes, he told me he saw you go by," said Christian, "but I wish you had called at the house, for they would have shown you so many valuable things that you would scarcely have forgotten them to the day of your death. But please, tell me, didn't you meet anyone in the Valley of Humiliation?"

"Yes," said Faithful, "I met with one named Discontent, who would've gladly persuaded me to go back again with him. The reason he used was that the valley was completely without honor. He also told me that to go there was to disobey all my friends, such as Pride, Arrogance, Self Conceit, Worldly Glory, and others, who—as he said—would be very much offended if I made such a fool of myself as to wade through this valley."[14]

"Well," said Christian, "how did you answer him?"

Faithful replied, "I told him that although all these he named might claim me as a relative—and rightly so, for they were related to me according to the flesh—yet since I became a Pilgrim, they have disowned me just as I have also rejected them. To me, therefore, they were now no more than if they had never been of my lineage. I also told him that, as for this valley, he had quite misrepresented the thing, for 'humility comes before honor,'[15] and 'a haughty spirit before a fall.'[16] So I said I'd rather go through this valley to receive honor that was accounted so by the Wisest,[17] than to choose that which Discontent considered most desirable to us."

"Did you meet with anything else in that valley?" asked Christian.

"Yes," answered Faithful, "I met with Shame, but of all the men I met with in my Pilgrimage, I think he bears the wrong name. A person shamed could be turned after a little reasoning and debate—and somewhat else—but this bold-faced Shame would never have turned."[18]

"Why?" questioned Christian. "What did he say to you?"

"What?" said Faithful excitedly. "Why he objected against religion itself. He said it was a pitifully low, deceptive business for a man to give attention to religion. He said that a tender conscience was an unmanly thing and that by watching over his words and ways—so as to keep himself from enjoying that domineering liberty the brave spirits of the times are accustomed to—a man would make himself the ridicule of the times. He also argued that only a few of those who are mighty, rich, or wise were ever of my opinion, nor of the opinion of those who were once mighty, rich, or wise before they were persuaded to become fools and desire to voluntarily lose everything they had in exchange for who knows what."[19]

"Furthermore," continued Faithful, "he objected to the inferior and low estate and condition of most of those who were the Pilgrims of the times in which they lived. He also objected to their ignorance and lack of understanding in the natural sciences.[20] In like manner he spoke critically to me about many more things than I can relate here, such as how it was a shame to sit whining and agonizing under a sermon and a shame to come home sighing and groaning. He said it was a shame to ask forgiveness of my neighbor for petty sins[21] or to make restitution if I've stolen from someone.[22] He also said

that because of a few vices—which he called by finer names—
religion made a man grow strange to those who are great and
made him possess and admire lowly things due to his religious
affiliations. And he asked me, 'Is not this a shame?'"

"And what did you say to him?" asked Christian.

"Say?" asked Faithful. "I didn't know what to say at first.
Why, he challenged me so much that my face flushed hotly.
Shame caused it to happen so. He'd almost gotten the best of
me, but finally I began to consider that those things 'highly
valued among men [are] detestable in God's sight.'[23] I thought
again that Shame tells me what men are but tells me nothing
about what God or the Word of God is. In addition, I thought
that at the Day of Doom we will not be sentenced to either
death or life according to the domineering spirits of the world
but according to the Wisdom and Law of the Highest. I thought,
therefore, that what God says is best, even though everyone in
the world may be against it. Seeing then that God prefers this
religion, that He prefers a tender conscience, and that they
who make themselves fools for the Kingdom of Heaven are
the wisest and that the poor man who loves Christ is richer
than the greatest man in the world who hates him, I said,
'Shame, go away! You are an enemy to my salvation. Shall I
consider what you say above the words of my Sovereign Lord?
How could I look Him in the face at His Coming? If I'm
ashamed of His Ways and servants now, how can I expect the
blessing then?'"[24]

Faithful continued, "But this Shame was a bold villain. I
could hardly rid myself of him. Yes, he'd be haunting me and
continually whispering in my ear about one or another of the
infirmities that accompany religion. But at last I told him it
was a waste of time for him to continue this business, for those
things which he despised were those in which I see the most
glory. So at last I got past this insistent individual, and when I
had shaken him off, then I began to sing:

The Tryals that those men do meet withal,
That are obedient to the Heavenly Call,
Are manifold and suited to the Flesh,

And come, and come, and come again afresh;
That now, or some time else, we by them may
Be taken, overcome, and cast away.
O let the Pilgrims, let the Pilgrims then
Be vigilant, and [prepare] themselves like Men.

"My Brother," said Christian, "I'm glad you withstood this villain so bravely, for finally—as you say—I think he has the wrong name. He is so bold as to follow us in the streets and attempt to put us to shame before all men—that is, to make us ashamed of that which is good. If he himself were not bold and daring, he would never attempt to do as he does. But let's continue to resist him, because in spite of all his boasting, he promotes the fool and nothing else. Solomon said, 'The wise inherit honor, but fools he holds up to shame.'"[25]

Faithful then replied, "For help against Shame, I think we must cry to Him who would have us be valiant for Truth upon the earth."

"You say the truth," said Christian, "but did you meet anybody else in that valley?"

"No, I didn't," answered Faithful, "for I had sunshine all the rest of the way through it and also through the Valley of the Shadow of Death."

"You fared well, I'm sure," said Christian, "but it was quite the opposite for me. Almost as soon as I entered that valley, I had a long period of dreadful combat with that foul fiend Apollyon. Yes, I thought he was surely going to kill me, especially when he got me down and pressed me under him as if he wanted to crush me to pieces. As he threw me, my Sword flew out of my hand. He told me he had me, but I cried to God, and He heard me and delivered me out of all my troubles.[26] Then I entered into the Valley of the Shadow of Death, and I had no light for almost half the way through it. Over and over I thought I would be killed there, but at last the Day broke and the sun arose, and I went through that which is behind with far more ease and peace."

NOTES ON CHAPTER 10

1   Matthew 19:30.

2   2 Peter 3:3-13.

3   **Jeremiah 29:18-19**; 1 Kings 9:6-9.

4   **2 Peter 2:22.**

5   **Genesis 39.**

6   **Proverbs 22:14.**

7   **Proverbs 5:5.**

8   **Job 31:1.**

9   Romans 5:14; 1 Corinthians 15:22; 15:45-49; **Ephesians 4:22.**

10   **1 John 2:16** (KJV). The NIV lists these as "the cravings of sinful man, the lust of the eyes, and the boasting of what he has and does."

11   Colossians 3:9 (KJV).

12   **Romans 7:24.**

13   Romans 7:24-25.

14   Pride, arrogance, conceit, and glorying in the accomplishments of the flesh—all of these are friends to unregenerate mankind. They go with the flesh like a well fitting glove. Proverbs 8:13, Romans 12:16, and Proverbs 26:12.

15   Proverbs 15:33, 18:12.

16   Proverbs 16:18.

17   The "Wisest" refers to Solomon, who penned the words quoted in this passage. By God's own admission, Solomon was and shall ever be the wisest man who has lived. 1 Kings 3:10-11.

18   Reason and debate is seldom enough to turn the heart. Perhaps Bunyan's "somewhat else" refers to a yielding to the Holy Spirit's conviction.

19   **+1 Corinthians 1:26; Philippians 3:7-11.**

20   **John 7:48; 1 Corinthians 3:18-21**; Romans 1:16-25.

21   James 5:16; Luke 17:3-4.

22   Exodus 22:1-15.

23   **Luke 16:15.**

24   **Mark 8:38.**

25   **Proverbs 3:35.**

26   Psalm 34:6, 17.

11

THE PILGRIMS MEET TALKATIVE

I SAW IN MY dream as they continued on that Faithful, by chance looking to one side, saw a man named Talkative walking near them (for in this place there was enough room for all of them to walk). He was a tall man and somewhat better-looking at a distance than up close. Faithful addressed himself to the man in this manner:

"Say there, Friend," said Faithful, "are you going to the Heavenly Country?"

"Yes, I'm going to that place," answered Talkative.

"That's good," said Faithful. "Then I hope we may have your good company."

"Gladly," replied Talkative. "I would be pleased to be your companion."

"Come on then," said Faithful. "Let's go together and spend our time discussing profitable things."

"Talking with you or with anyone about things that are good is very acceptable to me," said Talkative. "I'm glad to

Christian and Faithful meeting Talkative

have met with those who are inclined to do such a good work. To tell you the truth, there are only a few who care to spend their time in such a way while they're traveling. Most would much rather choose to speak of unprofitable things, and this has troubled me."

"That really is a thing to be deplored," responded Faithful. "What is more worthy of the use of the tongue and mouth of people on Earth than to speak of the things of the God of Heaven?"

"I really like the way you talk," said Talkative, "for you speak with conviction. And, in addition, what is more pleasant and more profitable than to talk of the things of God? 'What pleasantness?' someone may ask, that is if one has delight in things that are wonderful. Well, for instance, if people enjoy talking about the history or mystery of things, or if they love to talk about miracles, wonders, or signs, where shall they find things recorded so delightfully and so sweetly written as in the Holy Scripture?"

"That's true," said Faithful, "but it should be our intention to be profited by such things in our discussion."

"That's what I said," replied Talkative, "for talking of such things is most profitable. By doing so, a person may acquire knowledge of many things—in general, the meaningless nature of earthly things and the beneficial nature of things above. But more particularly, by talking like this, a person may learn the necessity of the New Birth, the insufficiency of our works, the need of Christ's righteousness, and so forth. Besides, by this a person may learn what it means to repent, believe, pray, suffer, and the like. People may also learn—for their own comfort— what the great promises and encouragements of the Gospel are. Furthermore, by this pursuit, one may learn to refute false opinions, to vindicate the truth, and learn also to instruct the ignorant."

"All this is true," said Faithful. "I'm glad to hear these things from you."

"Alas," exclaimed Talkative, "the lack of this is the reason so few understand the need of faith and the necessity of a work of grace in their soul in order to obtain eternal life. Most live ignorantly in the works of the Law, through which no one can by any means obtain the Kingdom of Heaven."

"Excuse me," said Faithful, "but heavenly knowledge of these things is a gift of God. No one attains them by human effort or by only talking about them."

"I know all this very well," remarked Talkative, "for a man can receive only what is given him from heaven.[1] All is of grace, not of works. I could give you a hundred Scriptures for the confirmation of this."[2]

"Well then," said Faithful, "what is the one thing with which we shall now begin our discussion?"

"Whatever you like," replied Talkative. "I'll talk about heavenly things or earthly things, conforming things or evangelical things,[3] sacred things or profane things, foreign things or domestic things, essential things or incidental things—as long as we can profit by all of it."[4]

Now Faithful began to wonder, and stepping over to Christian (who all this while had been walking alone), he said to him softly, "What a fine companion we've got here. This man will make an extremely good Pilgrim."

At this, Christian smiled modestly and said, "This man with whom you're so impressed will beguile with his tongue twenty people who don't know him."

"You know him then?" asked Faithful.

"Know him!" exclaimed Christian. "Yes, better than he knows himself."

"Tell me, what is he?" asked Faithful.

"His name is Talkative," answered Christian. "He lives in our town. I'm surprised you would be a stranger to him, but I realize our town is large."

"Who is his father," asked Faithful, "and where does he live?"

"He's the son of a man named Saywell," answered Christian, "and he lives on Gabby Row. He is known of all those acquainted with him by the name of Talkative on Gabby Row, and regardless of his fine tongue, he's really a sorry fellow."

"Well," said Faithful, "he seems to be a very handsome man."

"Perhaps to those who don't have a thorough knowledge of him," replied Christian, "for he's at his best away from home. Near home he's ugly enough. Your saying he's a handsome man brings to mind what I've observed in the work of the painter whose pictures show best at a distance but up close are more unpleasant."

"But I'm tempted to think you jest because you smiled," said Faithful.

Christian answered quickly, "God forbid that I should jest in this matter—though I did smile—or that I should accuse anyone falsely. I'll give you further information about him: This man is happy with any company, and he's for any conversation. Just as he talks with you now, he'll talk when he's sitting on the bar stool. And the more drink he has in his head, the more of these things he has in his mouth. Religion has no place in his heart, or house, or lifestyle. Everything he has lies in his tongue, and making a noise with it is his religion."

"You don't say!" interjected Faithful. "Then I've been greatly deceived by this man."

"Deceived?" asked Christian. "You can be sure of it. Remember the sayings, 'They do not practice what they preach,'[5] and 'For the kingdom of God is not a matter of talk but of power.'[6] He talks about prayer, repentance, faith, and the New Birth, but he only knows how to talk about them. I've been with his family and have observed him both at home and away, and I know what I say about him is the truth. His house is as empty of religion as the white of an egg is of flavor. There is neither prayer nor a sign of repentance for sin there. An animal in his way serves God far better than he. He is a veritable stain, reproach, and shame on religion to everyone who knows him. One can hardly hear a good word about him in the whole end of town where he lives. The common people who know him say he's a saint abroad and a devil at home. His poor family finds that true; he's such a rascal. He speaks to his servants with such bitterness, and he's so unreasonable with them that they know neither how to please him nor how to speak to him. Men who have any dealings with him say it's better to deal with a Turk[7] than with him, for they would have fairer dealings at their hands. Talkative will—if it's possible—surpass them in his dirty dealing through fraud and deception. Besides that, he's bringing up his sons to follow in his footsteps. And if he recognizes in any of them a foolish fearfulness—as he calls the first appearance of a tender conscience—he calls them fools and blockheads and refuses to give them much work to do nor will by any means recommend their work to others. As for me, I'm of the opinion that he has caused many to stumble and fall because of his wicked life,[8] and he will be the ruin of many more if God doesn't prevent it."

"Well, my Brother," said Faithful, "I'm bound to believe you, not only because you say you know him but also because you make your reports of men with the attitude of a Christian. I believe you speak these things because it is exactly as you say and not out of ill-will for him."

Christian replied, "Had I not known him better than you, it's possible I might have thought of him at first as you did. Yes, if he'd earned this reputation only at the hands of those who are enemies of religion, I would've thought it to have been slander. A lot of things like that fall from the mouths of bad men upon the names and professions of good men. But I can prove him guilty of all these things—yes, and a lot more just as bad from my own experiences. Besides, good men are ashamed of him and call him neither brother nor friend. If they know him, the mere mention of his name among them makes them blush."

"Well," said Faithful, "I see that talking and doing are two different things, and after this I'll pay closer attention to this distinction."

"They really are two separate things, and they're as diverse as the soul and the body," said Christian. "As the body without the soul is dead, so talking by itself is but a dead carcass. The soul of religion is the practical part. 'Religion that God our Father accepts as pure and faultless is this: to look after orphans and widows in their distress and to keep oneself from being polluted by the world.'[9] Talkative isn't aware of this. He thinks that hearing and saying will make him a good Christian, and so he deceives his own soul. Hearing is only like the sowing of seed.[10] Talking isn't sufficient to prove that fruit is truly in the heart and life,[11] and we can be assured that at the Day of Doom men will be judged according to their fruit.[12] It will not be said then, 'Did you believe?' but 'Were you doers or only talkers?'[13] And they shall be judged accordingly.[14] The end of the world is compared to our harvest,[15] and you know workers at harvest don't care about anything but fruit. Nothing will be accepted that is not of Faith. I say this to show you how insignificant the profession of Talkative will be on that day."[16]

Faithful then said, "This reminds me of the words of Moses when he described the animal that is ceremonially clean.[17] It is the animal that has a split hoof and chews its cud, not the one that has a split hoof only, or one that only chews its cud. The rabbit chews its cud, but it's still unclean because it doesn't have a split hoof. This actually resembles Talkative. He chews the cud—that is, he seeks knowledge and chews on the Word—but he doesn't have a separated hoof; he doesn't separate himself from the Way of Sinners. Like the rabbit, he retains the foot of a dog or bear, and so he's unclean."

"How well I know," said Christian. "You've spoken the true Gospel sense of those texts, and I'll add another thing. Paul calls some men—those great talkers included—resounding gongs and clanging cymbals.[18] In another place he speaks of them as, 'lifeless things that make sounds.'[19] That is, they're things without life, without the True Faith and Grace of the Gospel. Consequently, they're things that will never be placed in the Kingdom of Heaven among those who are the Children of Life, even though the sound of their speech is like the tongue or voice of an angel."

"Well," said Faithful, "I wasn't so fond of his company before, but now I'm sick of it. What should we do to get rid of him?"

"Take my advice and do as I suggest," replied Christian. "You'll find that unless God touches his heart and changes it, he'll soon be sick of your company, too."

"What do you want me to do?" asked Faithful.

"Why, just go up to him and begin some serious discussion about the power of religion," said Christian. "After he has approved of the conversation, for he surely will, then ask him plainly if this thing can be found in his heart, house, or lifestyle."

Then Faithful stepped forward again and said to Talkative, "Say, there. How are you doing?"

"Good, thank you," answered Talkative. "I thought we would've had several discussions by now."

"Well," responded Faithful, "if you want, we can talk now. Since you left it to me to choose a topic, let it be this question: How does the saving grace of God reveal itself when it is in a person's heart?"

"I perceive then that our discussion must be about the power of things," stated Talkative. "Well, that's a very good question, and I'll be more than willing to answer you. Take my answer in brief to be this: First—the grace of God in the heart causes a great outcry there against sin. Second . . ."

"No, wait!" interjected Faithful. "Let's consider them one at a time. I think you should rather say that it shows itself by inclining the soul to abhor its sin."

"Why?" asked Talkative. "What's the difference between crying out against sin and abhorring it?".

"Oh, a great deal," said Faithful. "Someone may cry out against sin as a matter of policy, but one can't abhor it except through the virtue of a godly aversion for it. I've heard many cry out against sin from the pulpit who are pleased enough to have it dwell in their own heart, house, and lifestyle. Potipher's wife cried out with a loud voice as if she had been very holy, but in spite of that she would have willingly committed adultery with Joseph.[20] Some cry out against sin like a mother cries out against her child in her lap when she calls her a dirty and a naughty girl and then begins hugging and kissing her."[21]

"I see you set a trap," said Talkative.

"No, not I! I'm only for setting things right," responded Faithful. "But what is the second thing through which you would prove the existence of a work of grace in the heart?"

"A great knowledge of Gospel Mysteries," replied Talkative.

"This sign should've been named first," said Faithful, "but first or last, it's also false. Knowledge, great knowledge, may be accumulated in the mysteries of the Gospel without a work existing in the soul. Even if a man has all knowledge, he may yet be nothing and so consequently not a child of God.[22] When Christ said, 'Have you understood all these things?' and His disciples answered 'Yes,'[23] He added later, 'You will be blessed if you do them.'[24] He doesn't place the blessing in knowing them but in doing them. There is a knowledge that isn't associated with doing. For example, a man who knows his master's will but doesn't do it.[25] A man may have knowledge like an angel and yet not be a Christian. Your sign, therefore, isn't true. Yes, knowing is a thing that pleases talkers and boasters, but doing is the thing that pleases God. That's not to say the heart can be good without knowledge, for without that the heart is nothing. There is knowledge, and then there is *knowledge*—knowledge that rests in the bare speculation of things, and knowledge that is associated with the grace of faith and love, which causes a person to begin doing the will of God from the heart. The first of these will satisfy the talker; but without the other, the true Christian is not content. Psalm one nineteen, thirty-four says, 'Give me understanding, and I will keep your law and obey it with all my heart.'"[26]

"You have set a trap again," said Talkative. "This is not for edification."

"Well, if you like, submit another sign showing how the work of grace reveals itself where it is," responded Faithful.

"Not I," answered Talkative, "for I see we won't agree."

"If you won't," said Faithful, "then will you allow me to do it?"

"Have your way," said Talkative.

Faithful began, "A work of grace in the soul reveals itself to him who has it and to those around him. To him who has it, it convicts him of sin,[27] especially the sin of defiling his own nature[28] and the sin of unbelief,[29] for which he is sure to be damned if he doesn't find mercy at God's hand through faith in Jesus Christ.[30] This struggle with conviction[31] and knowledge of things causes him to feel sorrow and shame for sin.[32] Moreover, he finds revealed in himself the 'Savior of the world'[33] and the absolute necessity of coming together with ιdim for life. And when he does, he experiences hungering and thirsting after Him. The promise is made to those hungering and thirsting. 'Blessed are those who hunger and thirst for righteousness, for they will be filled.'"[34]

"Now," Faithful went on, "he'll experience joy and peace according to the strength or weakness of his faith in his Savior.[35] His desire to know Him more and to serve Him in this world will be according to his love of holiness.[36] But, although I say it reveals itself like this to him, yet he is seldom able to conclude that this is a work of grace. That's because his existing depravity and his abused ability to reason cause his mind to misjudge the matter. Therefore, before he can conclude with confidence that this is a work of grace, the one experiencing this work must make a very sound judgment."

"To others," continued Faithful, "it is revealed like this: First—by an experiential confession of his faith in Christ,[37] and, second—by a life in agreement with that confession.[38] That is, he must have a life of holiness: heart-holiness, family-holiness if he has a family, and lifestyle-holiness[39] before the world.[40] In general, his confession teaches him to inwardly condemn his sin, and himself for doing it secretly.[41] It teaches him to suppress sin in his family and to promote holiness in the world, not by talk only, as a hypocrite or talkative person may do,[42] but by a practical subjection to the power of the Word in faith and love."

"And now, Sir," concluded Faithful, "if you have something to object to regarding this brief description of the work of grace and how it reveals itself, then do so. If not, then permit me to submit to you a second question."

"No," said Talkative, "It's not my place now to object but to hear. Let me, therefore, have your second question."

Faithful began, "It is this: Have you experienced the first part of the description of the work of grace? And do your life and lifestyle testify to it? Or does your religion exist in word or tongue and not in deed and truth? Please, if you choose to answer me in this, don't say anything except what God above will say 'Amen' to. Also, don't say anything except what your conscience can justify you in, 'For it is not the one who commends himself who is approved, but the one whom the Lord commends.'[43] Besides, it's great wickedness to say I am thus and so, when my lifestyle and all my neighbors tell me I'm lying."

Talkative at first began to blush but, regaining his composure, he replied, "You come now to experience, conscience, and God and to appeal to Him for justification of what is spoken. I didn't expect this kind of discussion. I'm not inclined to answer such questions because I don't feel obliged to do so, unless you take upon yourself to be an instructor of religion. Yet, even if you do, I may refuse to allow you to be my judge. But tell me, why do you ask me such questions?"

"Because I saw you were inclined to talk," answered Faithful, "and because I didn't know if you had anything more than mere opinions. Besides, to tell you the truth, I've heard of you: that you're a man whose religion lies in talk and that your lifestyle makes the confession of your mouth a lie. They say you're a spot among Christians and that religion fares the worse because of your ungodly lifestyle. They say that some have already stumbled due to your wicked ways and that more are in danger of being destroyed by the same. Your religion and your appearance at drinking establishments, greed, impurity, swearing, lying, the arrogant company you keep, and so forth will all stand together. The proverb that is said of a prostitute, that 'she is a shame to all women,' is true of you. In the same way, you're a shame to all those professing to know Christ."

Talkative then responded, "Since you're inclined to speak of hearsay and to judge as rashly as you do, I can only conclude that you are some fretful and depressed man who's not fit to chat with. And so, good-bye."

Christian then came up and said to Faithful, "I told you how it would happen. Your words and his desires couldn't agree. He would rather leave your company than reform his life. Now he's gone, so let him go. The loss is no one's but his own. He saved us the trouble of departing from him, for continuing as he is—as I suppose he'll do—he would've been a blotch in our fellowship. Besides, the Apostle tells us 'to keep away from

Talkative leaving Christian and Faithful

every brother who is idle and does not live according to the teaching you received from us.'"[44]

"But I'm glad we had this little discussion with him," said Faithful. "Perhaps he'll think of it again. However, I've dealt openly with him, so I'm not accountable for his blood if he perishes."[45]

"It was a good thing you talked to him plainly as you did," said Christian. "There's not much of this straight dealing with people these days, and that's what makes religion stink in the nostrils of men the way it does. For many are these talkative fools whose religion is only in word, and who are perverted and arrogant in their lifestyles. Being admitted into the fellowship of the godly, they puzzle the world, blemish Christianity, and grieve the sincere. I wish that everyone would deal with them as you've done. Then they would either be made to conform to religion, or the Fellowship of Saints would be too hot for them to remain."

Then Faithful said:

How Talkative at first lifts up his plumes!
How bravely doth he speak! How he presumes
To drive down all before him! But so soon
As Faithful talks of Heart-work, like the Moon
That's past the Full, into the Wane he goes;
And so will all, but he that Heart-work knows.

They went on talking like this about what they had seen by the way, and it made that part of the journey easy that would have otherwise no doubt been exhausting for them, because now they were going through a wilderness. When they had gotten almost completely out of this wilderness, Faithful happened to look back and see an individual coming up behind them.

Faithful recognized him and said, "Oh, look who's coming yonder, Brother!"

Then Christian looked and exclaimed, "It's my good friend Evangelist!"

"Yes," said Faithful, "and my good friend, too. He's the one who set me in the pathway to the Gate."

By that time Evangelist had caught up with them and greeted them, saying, "Peace be with you, dearly Beloved, and peace be to your helpers."

"Welcome, welcome, good Evangelist," said Christian. "The sight of your face brings to my remembrance your kindness in times past and your unwearied labor for my eternal welfare."[46]

"And welcome a thousand times over," said Faithful. "Dear Evangelist, your companionship is so desirable to us poor Pilgrims!"

Then Evangelist spoke, saying, "My friends, how has it gone with you since the time of our last parting? With what have you met, and how have you behaved yourselves?"

Then Christian and Faithful told him about all the things that had happened to them in the Way and how and with what difficulty they had arrived where they were then.

"I'm so glad," said Evangelist, "not that you met with trials, but that you've been champions and have continued in the Way to this very day regardless of your many weaknesses. I say I'm extremely glad, for your sake and mine, for I have sowed, and you have reaped. The day is coming when both he who sows and they who reap will be glad together,[47] for at the proper time, you will reap a harvest if you do not give up.[48] The Crown is in front of you, and it is one that will last forever. So run that you may win it.[49] There are some who set out after this Crown, and after they've gone a great distance to reach it, someone comes and takes it from them. 'Hold on to what you have, so that no one will take your crown.'[50] You're not yet out of gunshot range of the Devil. 'In your struggle against sin, you have not yet resisted to the point of shedding your blood.'[51] Let the Kingdom always be before you, and believe resolutely in things that are invisible.[52] Let nothing on this side of the Other World get inside of you, and above all, pay close attention to your own hearts and to the desires of it, for they're more deceitful than anything and desperately wicked.[53] Set your faces like stone. You have all power in Heaven and earth on your side."[54]

Then Christian thanked him for his words of encouragement but told him that they, nevertheless, wanted him to speak more to them for their edification the rest of the Way, and preferably—for they knew very well he was a Prophet—tell them of things that might happen to them and how they might resist and overcome them. Faithful also agreed with this.

So Evangelist began, saying, "My Sons, you've heard in the words of the truth of the Gospel that you must enter into the Kingdom of Heaven through many hardships,[55] and again that prison and hardships face you in every city.[56] You can't expect, therefore, to travel far on your Pilgrimage without them in some form or other. You've experienced something of the truth of these testimonies already, and more will immediately follow; for now, as you see, you're almost out of this wilderness. Therefore, you will soon enter into a town that you will in time see before you. In that town you'll be severely besieged by enemies who will try hard in their attempts to kill you, and you can be sure that one or both of you must seal with blood the testimony that you hold. But, 'be faithful even to the point of death, and [the King] will give you the crown of life.'[57] Even though his death will be unnatural and perhaps his pain great, yet the one who dies there will have the advantage over his partner, not only because he will have arrived in Celestial City soonest, but because he will escape many miseries that the other one will meet with during the rest of his journey. But when you arrive at the town and find fulfilled what I've told you here, then remember your friend and 'be men of courage;'[58] commit yourselves to your faithful Creator and continue to do good"[59]

NOTES ON CHAPTER 11

1   John 3:27.
2   **O brave Talkative.**
3   The original reads "moral things or evangelical

113

things." The phrase could have been translated, "conservative things or liberal things;" but its religious application would have been lost. Moral has to do with a view of justification based solely upon strict adherence to a moral code and standing traditions.

4   **O brave Talkative.**

5   **Matthew 23:3.**

6   **1 Corinthians 4:20.**

7   This statement is based upon feelings held by those in West European society for the Ottoman Empire to the East, which was ruled by Muslims from the 16th to 19th centuries and whose heartland was the area of modern Turkey. The Turks often kidnapped Christians who were foolish enough to wander into their area and then demanded ransoms for their release. After the ransoms were paid, they would sometimes release their prisoners, sometimes keep them, and sometimes mutilate or kill them. Thus they developed a reputation of having unsavory and untrustworthy characters.

8   **Romans 2:17-24.**

9   **James 1:23-27.**

10   **Matthew 13:1-23.**

11   Matthew 7:15-20, 12:33-37; Luke 6:43-45.

12   Matthew 21:19; Luke 13:6-9; John 15:1-8

13   James 2:14-26

14   Revelation 20:11-13.

15   Matthew 13:37-43; Mark 4:26-29; Revelation 14:14-16.

16   **Matthew 25.**

17   **Leviticus 11; Deuteronomy 14.**

18   **1 Corinthians 13:1.**

19   **1 Corinthians 14:7.**

20   **Genesis 39:11-18.**

21   **The crying out against sin, no sign of grace.**

22   **1 Corinthians 13:2. Great Knowledge, no sign of Grace.**

23   Matthew 13:51.

24   John 13:17.

25   Matthew 7:26; Luke 6:49.

26   **True knowledge attended with endeavors.**

27   **John 16:7-11.**

28   1 Corinthians 3:16-17.

114

[29] Revelation 21:8.
[30] **Galatians 2:16**; **Acts 4:12.**
[31] **Psalm 38:17-18**; **Romans 7:24**; **Mark 6:16,** in which Herod is convicted of past deeds when he hears of the works of Christ.
[32] **Jeremiah 31:19.**
[33] 1 John 4:14.
[34] **Matthew 5:6**, not included in Bunyan's original text. It was, however, included in his sidenotes and is added here to define the promise. **Revelation 21:6.**
[35] Psalm 4:8, 16:11, 119:165.
[36] Psalm 73:24-26, 42:1-2.
[37] **Romans 10:10.**
[38] **Philippians 1:27.**
[39] **Psalm 50:23**
[40] Romans 6:19; 2 Corinthians 7:1; Ephesians 4:17-29; Hebrews 12:14; **John 14:15.**
[41] **Job 42:5-6**; **Ezekiel 20:43.**
[42] Matthew 15:8.
[43] 2 Corinthians 10:18.
[44] 2 Thessalonians 3:6. This scripture was substituted for 1 Timothy 6:5 (KJV), "From such withdraw thyself," which was used by Bunyan in his original.
[45] Ezekiel 3:16-21
[46] Colossians 4:12-13; 1 Thessalonians 1:2-3; Hebrews 6:10.
[47] **John 4:36.**
[48] **Galatians 6:9.**
[49] **1 Corinthians 9:24-27.**
[50] **Revelation 3:11.**
[51] Hebrews 12:4.
[52] Hebrews 11:1-3, 6, 8-10, 13-16, 24-27
[53] James 1:13-15
[54] Matthew 28:18.
[55] Acts 14:22.
[56] Acts 20:23.
[57] Revelation 2:10.
[58] 1 Corinthians 16:13.
[59] 1 Peter 4:19.

12

THE PILGRIMS SUFFER AT THE VANITY FAIR

I THEN SAW IN my dream that when they had gotten out of the wilderness they saw a town before them, and the name of that town is Vanity. A fair is set up in the town, and it is called the Vanity Fair.[1] It is held there year-round, and it bears the name of the Vanity Fair because the town where it is located is "lighter than vanity,"[2] and also because everything sold there or that comes there is meaningless, as in the saying of the Wise, "Everything to come is meaningless."[3] This fair is not a recently established business but a thing of ancient standing.

I will tell you about its origin: Almost five thousand years ago there were Pilgrims walking to Celestial City, as were these two honest persons. Recognizing by the path the Pilgrims took that their way to the City went through this Town of Vanity, Beelzebub, Apollyon, and Legion,[4] with their companions, conspired to set up a fair here. According to their plan, all kinds of worthless things would be sold at this fair, and it would last all year long. At this fair, therefore, are sold such merchandise as houses, lands, businesses, places, honors, promotions, titles, countries, kingdoms, desires, pleasures, and delights of all sorts such as prostitutes, brothels, wives, husbands, children, masters, servants, lives, blood, bodies, souls, silver, gold, pearls, precious stones, and so forth.

Besides this, to be seen at all times at this fair are all kinds of jugglings, cheats, games, plays, fools, apes, rascals, and mischief makers. Also to be seen here (and at no charge) are the worst kinds of thefts, murders, adulteries, and those who perjure themselves by giving false testimony.

As in other fairs of less significance, where there are several avenues and streets under their proper names where such and such merchandise is sold, so it is here. You have here the proper places, avenues, and streets (that is countries and kingdoms) where the merchandise of this fair is most likely to be found. Here are Britain Avenue, French Avenue, Italian Avenue, Spanish Avenue, and German Avenue, where different sorts of meaningless things are to be sold. But as in other fairs, where one of the commodities is held out to be the most prominent of the whole fair, so the goods of Rome and her merchandise are greatly promoted in this fair; only our English nation, with some others, have taken a dislike of them.[5]

Now, as I said, the way to Celestial City goes right through the town where this lively fair is located, and all who desire to go to the City and yet avoid going through this town 'would have to leave this world.'[6] The Prince of princes himself, when here, went through this town to His own country, and it happened on a fair-day, too. Yes, and as I think, it was Beelzebub, the chief ruler of this fair, who invited Him to purchase his meaningless things; and he would have made Him lord of the fair if He would have only worshipped him as He went through the town.[7]

Because the Prince was such an honorable person, Beelzebub led Him from street to street and showed Him all the kingdoms of the world in just a short time so that he might (if possible) allure that Blessed One to cheapen himself and buy some of his meaningless things. Since He had no desire for the merchandise, He left the town without laying down so

The Pilgrims enter the Vanity Fair

much as one penny for these worthless things.[8] This fair, therefore, is an ancient thing of long standing and a very great fair.

As I said, these Pilgrims had to go through this fair. Well, so they did, but even as they entered into it, all the people in the fair were moved; and the town itself was in a hubbub about them. It was for several reasons:

First—the Pilgrims were dressed in a kind of clothing that was different from the clothes of any of those who traded in that fair. The people of the fair, therefore, stared at them a great deal. Some said they were fools, some that they were lunatics, and some that they were freaks.

Second—just as they wondered at their apparel, so likewise they wondered at their speech, for few could understand what they said. They naturally spoke the language of Canaan,[9] but those who kept the fair were the men of this world. So from one end of the fair to the other they seemed barbarians to each other.[10]

Third—and that which greatly amazed the merchandisers, these Pilgrims held all their wares as so unimportant. They did not care so much as even to look at them, and if they called upon them to buy, they would look upwards (signifying their trade and business was in Heaven) and put their fingers in their ears and cry, "Turn my eyes away from worthless things."[11]

One individual, seeing how the men conducted themselves, mockingly risked to say to them, "What do you intend to buy?"

They looked upon him seriously and said, "We buy the truth."[12]

At that, there was an occasion taken to despise the men even more, with some of them mocking, some taunting, some speaking slanderously, and some calling upon others to strike them. At last things came to an uproar and a great stir in the fair, so much so that everything was in a state of confusion. Word was soon taken to the great one of the fair, who quickly came down and appointed some of his most trusted friends to take and interrogate these men who were responsible for almost destroying the fair. So the men were brought to interrogation, and those who had taken them asked them where they came from, where they were going, and what they were doing there in such unusual attire.

The men told them they were pilgrims and strangers in the world, and that they were going to their own country, which was the Heavenly Jerusalem.[13] They said they had done nothing to give the men of the town or the merchandisers a reason to abuse them, except that when one asked them what they wanted to buy, they said they would buy the truth. They then asked to be allowed to continue on their journey.

But those who were appointed to examine them did not believe them to be any other than lunatics and madmen or else such who came to cause confusion in the fair. They took them, therefore, and beat them, then smeared dirt on them and put them into the cage so they might be made a spectacle to everyone of the fair. Therefore, they lay for some time there and were made the objects of anyone's mockery, hostility, or vengeance as the great one of the fair constantly laughed at all that happened to them.

But the men being patient, and not rendering insult for insult but instead blessing,[14] and giving good words for bad and kindness for injuries done, some people in the fair who were more observing and less prejudiced than the rest began to check and blame the meaner ones for continually abusing the men. Those, therefore, let fly at them again in an angry manner, accounting them to be as bad as the men in the cage and telling them they seemed to be associates and should be made partakers of their misfortunes. The others replied that for all they could see, the men were quiet and sober and intended nobody any harm. They said there were many who traded in their fair who were more worthy than the men they abused to be put into the cage and even the pillory, too.[15] So, after various words had been spoken on both sides (and with the men behaving themselves all the while very wisely and soberly before them) they began fighting among themselves and hurt one another.

Then these two poor men were again brought before their examiners and charged for being guilty of the recent hubbub that had been in the fair. So they beat them pitifully, hanged irons upon them, and led them in chains up and down the fair for an example and a terror to others in case any should speak further in their behalf or associate themselves with them. But Christian and Faithful behaved themselves even more wisely and received the contempt and shame cast upon them with so much meekness and patience that it won to their side (though few in comparison to the rest) several of the people in the fair. This put the other group into an even greater rage, so much so that they determined the death of these two men. They therefore threatened that neither cage nor irons were sufficient, but that they should die for the outrage they had done and for deluding the people of the fair. They were then remanded to the cage again until a further decision of their fate could be made. So they put them in and made their feet firmly held in the stocks.

At that time, they called again to mind what they had heard from their faithful friend Evangelist and were more encouraged in their ways and sufferings by what he had said would happen to them. They also comforted each other with the knowledge that the one whose lot it was to suffer would have the best of it. Each man, therefore, secretly wished he might be the preferred one. But committing themselves to the all-wise decision of Him Who Rules All Things, they remained with much contentment in the condition they were in until they should be otherwise disposed of.

Then with a convenient time being appointed, the authorities brought them forth to their trial and, in order, to their condemnation. When the time was come, they were brought before their enemies and arraigned. The judge's name was Judge Hate Good.[16] Their indictment was one and the same in substance, though somewhat varying in form, the contents of which was this: They were enemies of and disturbers of the town's trade; they had made commotions and caused divisions in the town, and in contempt of the law of the town's ruler they had won over a number of individuals to their own most dangerous opinions.

Then Faithful began to answer that he had only set himself against that which had set itself against Him Who is Higher Than the Highest. "And as for the disturbance," he said, "I didn't cause any, being myself a man of peace. Those who were won to us were won by acknowledging our truth and innocence, and they have only been turned from the worse to the better. And as for the king you talk of, since he is Beelzebub, the enemy of our Lord, I defy him and all his angels."

Then a proclamation was made that whoever had something to say in behalf of their lord the king against the Prisoner at the Bar should now appear and give their evidence. So three witnesses came in, named Envy, Superstition, and Gainglory. They were asked if they knew the prisoner at the bar and then instructed to say what they wanted in behalf of their lord the king against him.

Envy then stepped forward and said, "Your Honor, I have known this man a long time and will attest under oath before this honorable court that he is . . ."

"Stop!" said the judge. "Swear the witness in."

So they made him swear his oath, and Envy continued. "Your Honor, in spite of his credible name, this man is one of the vilest men in our country. He does not regard either ruler or people, or law or custom, but instead does everything he can to instill in all men certain of his disloyal notions, which he generally calls Principles of Faith and Holiness. In particular, I heard him myself once declare that Christianity and the customs of our Town of Vanity were diametrically opposite and could not be reconciled. By saying this, your Honor, he immediately not only condemns all our noble acts but also us for doing them."

Then the judge said to him, "Do you have anything else to say?"

"Your Honor I could say much more," continued Envy, "only I don't want to be wearisome to the court. Yet, if need be, after the other gentlemen have presented their evidence, if anything more is needed to dispose of him, I will enlarge my testimony against him."

So he was asked to stand by.

They called Superstition and asked what he could say against him in behalf of their lord the king. Then they swore him in, and he began his testimony.

"Your Honor," said Superstition, "I'm not closely acquainted with this man, nor do I desire to have further knowledge of him. However, this I know, that he is a very obnoxious fellow judging from a discussion I had with him the other day in this town. Talking with him then, I heard him say that our religion was nothing and was such as no man would be able to please God with. And you know very well, your Honor, what must follow his reasoning. That is, that we still worship in vain, are yet in our sins, and finally shall be damned. And that is what I have to say."

Then Gainglory was sworn in and instructed to say what he knew in behalf of their lord the king against the prisoner at the bar.

"Your Honor," started Gainglory, "and all you Gentlemen, I've known this fellow for a long time and have heard him speak things that ought not to be spoken. He has scoffed at our noble ruler Beelzebub and has spoken with contempt for his honorable friends, whose names are the honorable Mr. Old Man, the honorable Mr. Carnal Delight, the honorable Mr. Luxurious, the honorable Mr. Desire Of Glory, my old master Mr. Lechery, and Mr. Having Greedy, together with all the rest of our noble leaders.[17] Moreover, he said that if all men were like-minded as he, if possible, not one of these noblemen would have a position in this town. Besides that, he has not been afraid to speak critically of you, your Honor, who are now appointed to be his judge, calling you an ungodly villain and many other such degrading terms with which he has slandered most of the leaders of our town."

When Gainglory had told his tale, Judge Hate Good directed his speech to the prisoner at the bar, saying, "You Renegade, Heretic, and Traitor, have you heard what these honest gentlemen have testified against you?"

Faithful answered, "May I speak a few words in my own defense?"

"Shame! Shame!" said the judge. "You deserve to live no longer but to be put to death immediately right here on the spot. Yet, so that all men may see our gentleness toward you, let us hear what you have to say."

Faithful began his defense, saying, "In answer then to what Mr. Envy has said, I never said anything but this: Whatever

Gainglory testifies against Faithful

rule, or law, or custom, or people is flatly against the Word of God is also diametrically opposite to Christianity. If I have spoken wrongly in that, convince me of my error, and I'm ready to recant it here before you."

"As to the second, that is, Mr. Superstition and his charge against me," continued Faithful, "I said only this: In the worship of God there is required a divine faith; but there can be no divine faith without a divine revelation of the will of God. Whatever, therefore, is thrust into the worship of God that is not agreeable to divine revelation, it cannot be done except by human faith, and that is faith that will not gain anyone eternal life."

"As for what Mr. Gainglory has said," continued Faithful, "avoiding the arguments that I am said to scoff and the like, I say that the ruler of this town, with all the riffraff—his attendants who were named by this gentleman—are more fit for being in Hell than in this town and country. And so, the Lord have mercy on me."

Then the judge spoke to the jury (who all this while had stood by to hear and observe), "Gentlemen of the jury, you see this man about whom so great an uproar has been made in this town. You've also heard what these worthy gentlemen have testified against him. You've heard his reply and confession. It now becomes your responsibility to either hang him or save his life, but I think it necessary to instruct you in our law."

Continuing to speak, the judge said, "There was an order made in the days of Pharaoh the Great, servant to our king, that to keep those of a contrary religion from multiplying and growing too strong for him, their male children should be thrown into the river.[18] There was also a proclamation made in the days of Nebuchadnezzar the Great, another of his servants, that whoever would not fall down and worship his golden image should be thrown into a fiery furnace.[19] There was also a decree made in the days of Darius, that whoever for a time called upon any god but him should be cast into the lions' den.[20] Now the substance of these laws has been broken by this rebel, not only in thought—which is not to be accepted—but also in word and deed, which must therefore be considered intolerable."

The jury then went out. Their names were, Mr. Blindman,

Mr. Nogood, Mr. Malice, Mr. Lovelust, Mr. Liveloose, Mr. Heady, Mr. Highminded, Mr. Enmity, Mr. Liar, Mr. Cruelty, Mr. Hatelight, and Mr. Nosatisfying. Each one presented his private verdict against him among themselves, and afterwards they unanimously concluded to bring him in guilty before the judge.

The most prominent among them and the foreman, Mr. Blindman, said, "I see clearly that this man is an heretic."

Then Mr. Nogood said, "Away with such a fellow from the earth!"

"Yes," said Mr. Malice, "for I hate the very looks of him."

Then Mr. Lovelust said, "I could never endure him."

"Nor I," said Mr. Liveloose, "for he would always be condemning my way."

"Hang him! Hang him!" said Mr. Heady.

"A sorry scrub," said Mr. Highminded.

"My heart rises up against him," said Mr. Enmity.

"He's a rogue," said Mr. Liar.

"Hanging is too good for him," said Mr. Cruelty.

"Let's dispatch him out of the way," said Mr. Hatelight.

Then Mr. Nosatisfying said, "Even if I had the whole world given to me, I couldn't be reconciled to him. Therefore, let's at once bring him in guilty of death."

And so they did.

Therefore, Faithful was presently condemned to be removed from the place where he was in order to be taken to the place from where he came, and there to be put to the most cruel death that could be invented. They brought him out to do with him according to their law. First they whipped him, then they beat him, then they lanced his flesh with knives. After that, they stoned him with stones, then pricked him with their swords, and last of all, they burnt him to ashes at the stake. Thus came Faithful to his end.

Now I saw that behind the multitude there stood a chariot and a team of horses waiting for Faithful, who as soon as his adversaries had taken his life was taken up into it and immediately carried up through the clouds with the sound of a trumpet. He was taken by the nearest way to the Celestial gate.

But as for Christian, he had some rest and was remanded back to prison, where he remained for a time. But He Who Rules Over All Things, having the power of their rage in His own hand, turned things around so that Christian escaped for the moment and went his way. As he went he sang:

Well, Faithful, thou hast faithfully profest
Unto thy Lord, with Him thou shalt be blest;
When faithless ones, with all their vain delights,
Are crying out under their hellish plights:
Sing, Faithful, sing, and let thy Name survive;
For tho' they kill'd thee, thou art yet alive.

NOTES ON CHAPTER 12

[1] **Ecclesiastes 1.** The word *vanity* appears in the KJV.

[2] Psalm 62:9 (KJV); **Isaiah 40:17.**

[3] Ecclesiastes 11:8, **Ecclesiastes 2:11, 17**. In several places the words "meaningless" and "worthless" are used in place of "vanity." Both "meaningless" and "worthless" are used in the NIV to translate the word "vanity," which is from the KJV.

[4] Mark 5:1-20; Luke 8:26-39.

[5] These lines would have been very significant to the first readers of *The Pilgrim's Progress*. King Henry VIII of England had the British Parliament declare him the head of the Church of England in the year 1534. This was, in effect, a political rejection of the power of the Pope and the Church of Rome.

[6] **1 Corinthians 5:10.**

[7] **Matthew 4:1-11; Luke 4:1-13. Christ went through this fair. Christ bought nothing in this fair.**

[8] Hebrews 4:15.

[9] The language of the land of promise. The Pilgrims spoke in spiritual and heavenly terms.

[10] **1 Corinthians 2:1-8.**

[11] Psalm 119:37.

[12] **Proverbs 23:23.**

[13] Hebrews 12:22; **Hebrews 11:13-14.**

Faithful's cruel death

14   1 Peter 3:9.

15   A pillory was a structure for punishing law breakers. A post with a horizontal beam was set upon a platform and the criminal's arms were fastened to the beam. People passing by would insult and ridicule the person being punished.

16   Micah 3:1-3.

17   **Sins are all lords and great ones.** In the original text, the men were named *Lord Old-Man, Lord Carnal-Delight,* and so forth. In Great Britain, *lord,* when not referring to God, is a term historically given to aristocracy, highly positioned, or powerful men.

18   **Exodus 1**.

19   **Daniel 3**.

20   **Daniel 6**.

13

THE PILGRIMS AND THE DECEITFULNESS OF RICHES

NOW I SAW IN my dream that Christian did not travel on alone, for there was one whose name was Hopeful (becoming so by beholding the words and behavior of Christian and Faithful during their suffering at the fair) who joined him. And entering into a brotherly covenant, Hopeful told him that he desired to be his companion. So one individual died to produce testimony to the truth, and another one rose out of his ashes to be a companion of Christian in his Pilgrimage. This one named Hopeful also told Christian that there were many more people in the fair who would in time follow after his example.

So I saw that soon after they had gotten out of the fair, they caught up with a man named ByEnds,[1] who had been walking ahead of them.

They said to him, "What country are you from, and how far are you going on this Path?"

He told them he came from the Town of Fairspeech[2] and was going to Celestial City (but he did not tell them his name).

"From Fairspeech?" asked Christian. "And is there anything good that lives there?"

"Yes," said ByEnds. "I hope."

"Tell me, Sir, what may I call you?" asked Christian.

"I'm a stranger to you, and you to me," said ByEnds. "If you're going this way, I'll be glad to have your company. If not, I must be content."

"This town of Fairspeech," said Christian, "I've heard of it. As I remember, they say it's a wealthy place."

"Yes," agreed ByEnds. "I'll assure you it is, and I have very many rich relatives there."

"Tell me, who are your relatives there," asked Christian, "if I may be so bold to ask."

"Almost the whole town," answered ByEnds. "And in particular, the honorable Mr. Turn About, the honorable Mr. Time Server, and the honorable Mr. Fair Speech, from whose ancestors the town first got its name. Also Mr. Smooth Man, Mr. Facing Bothways, Mr. Anything, and the pastor of our church, Mr. Two Tongues, who was my mother's own brother on her father's side. And to tell you the truth, I have become a gentleman of fine quality even though my great grandfather was only a boat oarsman, looking one way and rowing another; and I got most of my estate by the same occupation."

Then Christian inquired, "Are you a married man?"

"Yes," responded Mr. ByEnds, "and my wife is a very virtuous woman, the daughter of a virtuous woman. She was Madam Feigning's daughter. She came, therefore, from a very honorable family. She has arrived at such a state of good breeding that she knows how to present herself socially to all, from prince to peasant. It's true, we do differ somewhat in religion from those of the stricter sort, but only in two minor points. First—we never strive against wind and tide. Second— we're always most zealous when Religion goes about wearing his silver slippers. We love to walk with him in the street if the sun shines and the people applaud him."

Then Christian stepped a little to the side and up to his companion Hopeful and said, "It crosses my mind that this is a certain Mr. ByEnds of Fairspeech. If it is him, we have as great a rascal in our company as lives in all these parts."

Then Hopeful said, "Ask him. I wouldn't think he'd be ashamed of his name."

So Christian came up to ByEnds again and said, "Sir, you talk as if you know a little more than the whole world knows. If I'm not mistaken, I believe I have half a guess of who you are. Isn't your name Mr. ByEnds of Fairspeech?"

"That's not my name," replied ByEnds, "but it is indeed a nickname given to me by some of those who can't stand me. I must be content to bear it as a reproach, as other good men have borne theirs before me."

"But didn't you ever give a reason to men to call you by that name?" inquired Christian.

"Never! Never!" exclaimed ByEnds. "The worst I ever did to give them a reason to give me this name was that I always had the luck to look ahead when making judgments regarding the state of the times—whatever the decisions—and my fate was to get wealth through them. But if things are bestowed upon me, let me count them a blessing, and don't let malicious people load me up with reproach because of it."

"I thought you were surely the man I'd heard of," said Christian. "To tell you what I think, I'm afraid this name belongs to you more properly than you would like to have us believe."

"Well," said ByEnds, "if you will imagine so, I can't help it. You'll find me a fairly good company keeper if you will still allow me to be your associate."[3]

Christian responded, "If you intend to go with us, you must go against wind and tide, which is, I believe, against your opinion. You must also accept Religion in his rags as well as when he is in his silver slippers and stand by him too when he is bound in irons as well as when he walks the streets with applause."

Then ByEnds said, "You must not impose upon nor lord it over my faith. Allow me to keep my liberty, and let me go with you."

"Not a step farther," interjected Christian, "unless you intend to do as we propose."

Mr. Holdtheworld, Mr. Moneylove, and Mr. Saveall

ByEnds responded, "I'll never desert my old principles since they are harmless and profitable. If I may not go with you, I must do as I did before you overtook me, go by myself until someone overtakes me who will be glad to have my company."

I saw in my dream that Christian and Hopeful left him and kept their distance in front of him. One of them looked back and saw three men following Mr. ByEnds; and as they came up to him he greeted them very courteously, and they also returned the compliment. The men's names were Mr. Holdtheworld, Mr. Moneylove, and Mr. Saveall. They were men with whom Mr. ByEnds had formerly been acquainted, for in their youth they were school chums and were taught by a certain Mr. Gripeman, a school teacher in Lovegain, which is a market town in the County of Coveting in the north. The school teacher taught them the Art of Getting by violence, deceit, flattery, lying, or by putting on a guise of religion; and these four gentlemen had attained much of the art of their teacher, so much so that they could have conducted such classes themselves.

Well, when they had, as I said, thus greeted each other, Mr. Moneylove said to Mr. ByEnds, "Who are those upon the road in front of us?" For Christian and Hopeful were still within view.

"They are a couple of men from a far off country, who in their own way are going on a Pilgrimage," said ByEnds.

"Alas!" said Moneylove. "Why didn't they stay, so we might have had their good company; for they and we, and you, Sir, I hope, are all going on a Pilgrimage."

"We are, to be sure," said ByEnds, "but the men ahead of us are so rigid and love their own notions so much, and so lightly esteem the opinions of others, that although a man be extremely godly, yet if he doesn't agree with them in all things, they thrust him quite out of their company."

Mr. Saveall spoke up, "That's bad, but we read of some who are much too righteous, and such men's rigidness causes them to judge and condemn everyone but themselves. But tell me, what and how many were the things you differed in."

Mr. ByEnds answered, "Why, in their belligerent manner they conclude it's their duty to rush on their journey in all kinds of weather, and I'm for waiting for the proper wind and tide. They're in favor of hazarding everything for God at any moment, and I'm in favor of taking all advantages to secure my life and estate. They're in favor of holding their notions even though all other men are against them, but I'm in favor of religion in what and for as far as the times and my safety will sustain it. They're in favor of Religion when in rags and contempt, but I'm in favor of him when he walks in his golden slippers in the sunshine and with applause."

Then Mr. Holdtheworld added, "Yes, and stick to your beliefs, good Mr. ByEnds. As for me, I can only account as a fool an individual who has had the liberty to keep what he has but then has been so unwise as to lose it. Let us be shrewd as snakes.[4] It's best to make hay while the sun shines. You see how the bee lies still all winter and wakes only when she can have profit with pleasure. God sometimes sends rain and sometimes sunshine. If those two are content to go through the first, let's just be content to take fair weather along with us. As for me, I like best the kind of religion that will believe in the security of God's good blessings unto us. For who that is ruled by his own reason could imagine that God would not want us to keep for His sake the good things of this life He has given us? Abraham and Solomon grew rich through religion, and Job says that a good man shall 'lay up gold as dust.'[5] But such a man must not be like the men in front of us, if they are as you described them."

Mr. Saveall then spoke, "I think we're all agreed in this matter, so we don't need to discuss it further."

"No," said Mr. Moneylove, "there need be no further discussion indeed, for he who believes neither Scripture nor reason—and you see we have both on our side—doesn't understand his own liberty nor does he seek his own safety."

"My Brothers," said Mr. ByEnds, "as you see, we're all going on Pilgrimage, and in order to provide us a better diversion from thinking about things that are bad, allow me to submit to you this question: Suppose a man, a minister, a tradesman, or such should see before him the favorable possibility of getting good things from this life. And suppose there is no way he can obtain them without at least in appearance becoming extraordinarily zealous in some points of religion with which he has no experience. May he not use this means to attain his end and yet remain a perfectly honest man?"

Mr. Moneylove answered him, "I see the bottom of your question, and with the permission of these gentlemen I'll endeavor to give you an answer. To speak to your question as it concerns a minister himself, suppose a minister—a worthy man but with a very small salary—has in his eye a greater one more fat and plump by far. He also takes an opportunity to get it by being more studious and by preaching more frequently and zealously, and by altering some of his principles because the temperament of the people requires it. As for me, I see no reason why a man can't do this—and even a great deal more—and still be an honest man, provided he has a calling."

"And why is this?" Moneylove went on. "First—his desire of a higher salary is lawful. This can't be contradicted, since it's set before him by providence. So then, he may get it if he can do so 'without raising questions of conscience.'[6] Second—besides, his desire for that salary makes him more studious, a more zealous preacher, and so forth; and so, it makes him a better man . . . yes, causes him to improve himself better, which is according to the mind of God. Third—now as for his complying to the wishes of his people by compromising some of his principles in order to serve them, this shows that he is apt to practice self-denial, that he is of a sweet and influential demeanor, and that he is, therefore, even more fit for the ministry. Fourth—I conclude, then, that a minister who exchanges something small for something great should not be judged as covetous for doing so, but rather—since the part he plays in his work is improved by it—he should be counted as one who pursues his calling and the opportunity to put his hand into doing good."

Mr. Moneylove continued, "And now to the second part of the question, which concerns the tradesman you mentioned. Suppose such a person has only a poor business in the world, but by becoming religious he can expand his market, perhaps get a rich wife or more and far better customers into his shop. As for me, I see no reason why this might not be lawfully done. Why is this?"

"First," said Mr. Moneylove, "becoming religious is a virtue, regardless of the means he employs to be so. Second—it's not unlawful to get a rich wife or to bring more business to his shop. Third—the man who gets these by becoming religious gets things that are good from them who are good by becoming good himself. So then, here are a good wife, good customers, and good gain; and he has gotten all these things by becoming religious, which is good. Becoming religious in order to get all these things, therefore, is a good and profitable intention."

They all highly applauded Mr. Moneylove's answer to Mr. ByEnds' question. They all concluded, therefore, that it was most wholesome and advantageous. Because they thought no man was able to contradict it, and because Christian and Hopeful who had earlier opposed Mr. ByEnds were still within hailing distance, they jointly agreed to assault them with the question as soon as they caught up with them. So they called after them, who then stopped and stood still until they came up to them. They concluded as they went that instead of Mr. ByEnds, Mr. Holdtheworld should present the question to them because, as they supposed, their answer to him would be without the heat that was kindled between Mr. ByEnds and them at their parting a short time before.

So they came up to Christian and Hopeful, and after a short salutation, Mr. Holdtheworld presented the question to Christian and his companion and asked them to answer it if they could.

Then Christian said, "Even a babe in religion may answer ten thousand such questions. If it's unlawful to follow Christ to obtain loaves, as shown in John six, how much more abominable is it to make of Him and religion a stalking-horse[7] to get and enjoy the world? Nor do we find anyone but heathen, hypocrites, devils, and sorcerers who hold this opinion."

Christian continued, "First—concerning the heathen, when Hamor and Shechem wanted the daughters and cattle of Jacob and saw there were no ways for them to get them except by becoming circumcised, they said to their companions, 'But the men will consent to live with us as one people only on the condition that our males be circumcised, as they themselves are. Won't their livestock, their property and all their other animals become ours?'[8] They sought to obtain their daughters and cattle, and their religion was the stalking-horse they used to obtain them. Read the whole story in Genesis thirty-four, twenty through twenty-three.

"Second—the hypocritical Pharisees were also of this religion. Long prayers were their pretense; but to gain the houses of widows was their intent, and greater damnation from God was their judgment. Read Luke twenty, forty-six and forty-seven.

"Third—that devil Judas was also of this religion. He was religious for the money bag so that he might possess that which was in it.[9] But he was lost, cast away, the very one doomed to destruction.[10]

"Fourth—Simon the sorcerer also was of this religion, for he wanted to have the Holy Spirit in order to use Him to get money. His sentence from Peter's mouth was according to his sin. See Acts eight, nineteen through twenty-two."

"Fifth," concluded Christian, "don't think this simply a fabrication of my own mind that a man who becomes religious for the purpose of gaining the world will be just as willing to throw away religion to obtain it. As surely as Judas had designs on the world in becoming religious, he just as surely sold religion and his Master for the same thing.[11] To answer the question in the affirmative, therefore, as I perceive you have done, and to accept such an answer as correct, is irreligious, hypocritical, and devilish. Your reward will be according to your works."[12]

They stood staring at each other but had nothing with which to answer Christian. Hopeful also approved of the soundness of Christian's answer, so there was a great silence among them. Mr. ByEnds and his group also staggered and kept behind so that Christian and Hopeful might outpace them.

Then Christian asked his friend, "If these men can't stand before the sentence of men, what will they do with the sentence of God? And if they're mute when dealt with by jars of clay,[13] what will they do when they're rebuked by the flames of a devouring fire?"[14]

Then Christian and Hopeful outpaced them again and went on until they came to a luxurious plain called Ease. They went through it with much contentment, but since the plain was only a narrow one, they were quickly through it.[15] Now on the other side of that plain was a little hill called Lucre, and in that hill a silver mine. Because of the rarity of it, some of those who had gone that way had turned aside to see it. However, when they went too near the brink of the pit, the ground (being deceitful under them) broke, and they were killed. Some also had been injured there and could not be their own selves again to their dying day.

Then I saw in my dream that a short distance off the road, over toward the silver mine, stood Demas[16] (in a gentlemanly manner) to call travelers to come and see. He said to Christian and his friend, "Hey! Turn aside here, and I'll show you something."

"What is a thing so deserving of our attention as to turn us out of the Way?" asked Christian.

Demas answered, "There is a silver mine here and some people digging in it for treasure. If you'll come, with a little effort you may provide richly for yourselves."

Then Hopeful said, "Let's go see."

"Not I," said Christian, "I've heard of this place before now and about how many have been slain here. Besides, that treasure is a snare to those who seek it, for it hinders them in their Pilgrimage."

Then Christian called to Demas, "Isn't that place dangerous? Hasn't it hindered many in their Pilgrimage?"[17]

"Not very dangerous," answered Demas, "except to those who are careless." But nevertheless he blushed as he spoke.

Then Christian said to Hopeful, "Let's not skip a step but continue on our way."

Hopeful responded, "I'll assure you, when ByEnds comes up, if he receives the same invitation as we, he'll turn in there to see."

"No doubt about it," said Christian, "for his principles lead him that way, and a hundred to one says he dies there."

Then Demas called again, saying, "But won't you come over and see?"

Then Christian firmly answered, "Demas, you're an enemy to the right ways of the Lord of this Way. You've already been condemned by one of His Majesty's judges for turning aside yourself. Why do you seek to bring us into the same condemnation? Besides, if we turn aside at all, our Lord the King will certainly hear about it and put us to shame at that time when we would otherwise stand with boldness before Him."

Demas cried out again and said he was also one of their comrades and that if they would tarry a little he himself would also walk with them.

Then Christian said, "What is your name? Isn't it the same as the one by which I've called you?"

"Yes, my name is Demas," he said. "I'm the son of Abraham."

"I know you," Christian stated. "Gehazi[18] was your great grandfather, and Judas was your father,[19] and you have walked in their steps. It's just a devilish prank that you're using. Your father was hanged for a traitor,[20] and you deserve no better reward. Assure yourself that when we come to the King, we'll bring Him word of your behavior." And with that, they went on their way.

By this time ByEnds and his companions had come again within sight, and at the first call they went over to Demas. Now, whether they fell into the pit by looking over the brink of it, or whether they went down to dig, or whether they were smothered in the bottom by the dampness that commonly arises, of these things I am not certain. But this I observed, that they were never again seen in the Way.

Then Christian sang:

By-ends and Silver Demas both agree;
One calls, the other runs, that he may be
A Sharer in his Lucre, so these two
Take up in this World, and no further go.

Now I saw, just on the other side of this plain, the Pilgrims came to a place where an old monument stood right next to the side of the Highway. At the sight of it they were both concerned because of the strangeness of its form, for it seemed to them as if it had been a woman transformed into the shape of a pillar. They stood, therefore, looking upon it, but for a time they didn't know what they should make of it. At last Hopeful looked up and saw written upon the head of it a writing in an unusual hand. He, being no scholar, called to Christian (for he was educated) to see if he could pick out the meaning. So he came, and after a little examination of the letters, he found the message to be this, "Remember Lot's Wife!"[21] So he read it to his friend, after which they both concluded it was the Pillar of Salt into which Lot's wife was turned for looking back with a covetous heart while she was fleeing for safety from Sodom.[22]

This sudden and amazing sight gave them the occasion for this discourse:

"Ah, my Brother!" said Christian, "this is a timely sight. It came to us opportunely after Demas' invitation to go over to view the Hill Lucre. Had we gone over as he desired us to do—and as you, my Brother, were inclined to do—for all I know we might have made ourselves like this woman, a spectacle to look upon for those who shall come after."

"I'm sorry I was so foolish," said Hopeful. "I'm made to wonder that I'm not now as Lot's wife, for what was the difference between her sin and mine? She only looked back, and I had a desire to go and see. Let grace be adored, and let me be ashamed that such a thing should ever be in my heart."

Then Christian said, "Let's take notice of what we see here to help us in times to come. This woman escaped one judgment, for she didn't fall from the destruction of Sodom.[23] Yet she was destroyed by another. As we see, she has been turned into a pillar of salt."

"True," said Hopeful, "and she may serve us as both caution and example: caution, in that we should shun her sin, or an example of what judgment will overtake those who will not be stopped by this caution. Korah, Dathan, and Abiram, with the two hundred and fifty men who perished in their sin, also became a sign or example to beware.[24] But, above all, I reflect on one thing: how Demas and his friends can walk so confidently over there to look for that treasure when this woman was turned into a pillar of salt for just looking behind her, for we don't read that she stepped one foot out of the Way. This is especially interesting since the judgment that overtook her set her up as an example within sight of where they are. They could have chosen to see her if they had only lifted up their eyes."

Then Christian spoke, "It's something to be wondered about, and it reveals that their heart has grown desperate in this case. I can't decide to whom they can accurately be compared— to those who pick pockets in the presence of the judge, or those who will steal purses under the gallows. It's said of the men of Sodom that they were sinners exceedingly because they were 'sinners before the Lord,'[25] that is, in His eyesight. This was in spite of the kindnesses He had shown them, for the land of Sodom was 'like the garden of the Lord'[26] prior to its destruction. This, therefore, provoked Him all the more to jealousy and made their plague as hot as the fire of the Lord out of Heaven could make it. It's most rationally to be concluded that those—even those like these who shall sin in His sight, yes, and even to do so despite such examples that are set continually before them to warn them to the contrary—must be partakers of the severest judgments."[27]

"You have no doubt spoken the truth," said Hopeful, "but what a mercy it is that neither you, nor especially I myself, have not become an example. This provides us an occasion to thank God, to fear before Him, and always to remember Lot's wife."

I saw then that they went on their way toward a pleasant river that David the king called "the river of God,"[28] but what John called "the river of the water of life."[29] Now their way lay right along the bank of this river. Here, therefore, Christian and his companion walked with great delight. They also drank of the water of the river, which was pleasant and rejuvenating to their weary spirits. Besides that, on the banks of both sides of this river there were green trees that bore all kinds of fruit,

Christian and Hopeful by "the river of God"

and the leaves of the trees were good for medicine.[30]
They were much delighted with the fruit of these trees;
for Pilgrims eat the leaves to prevent sicknesses of
overindulgence and other diseases that can afflict those
who heat their blood by traveling.

On either side of the river was also a meadow,
curiously beautified with lilies, and it was green all year
long. They lay down and slept in this meadow, for it was
here that they might lie down in safety.[31] When they
awoke, they again gathered of the fruit of the trees and
drank again of the water of the river and again lay down
to sleep. They did this several days and nights.

Then they sang:

Behold ye, how these Crystal Streams do glide
(To comfort Pilgrims) by the Highway side.
The Meadows green, besides their fragrant smell,
Yield dainties for them: And he that can tell
What pleasant Fruit, yea, Leaves, these Trees do yield,
Will soon sell all, that he may buy this Field.[32]

So when they were disposed to go on (for they were
not yet at their journey's end) they ate, drank, and departed.

NOTES ON CHAPTER 13

[1]   A by-end is an object lying aside from the main one; a
subordinate end or aim; especially a secret selfish purpose, a covert
purpose of private advantage.

[2]   **Proverbs 26:25.**

[3]   **He desires to keep company with Christian.**

[4]   Matthew 10:16.

[5]   Job 22:24 (KJV). Mr. Holdtheworld mishandles the
Scripture. Although these words are in the Book of Job, Eliphaz the
Temanite is quoted here. Holdtheworld uses Scripture to support
his beliefs.

⁶ 1 Corinthians 10:25-27—a godly passage used by Mr. Moneylove for ungodly gain.

⁷ A stalking-horse is a horse trained to allow a hunter to hide behind it while hunting. Bunyan presents the idea of an individual using religion and the person of Christ to hide behind while pursuing worldly gain.

⁸ Genesis 34:22-23.

⁹ John 12:4-6.

¹⁰ John 17:12.

¹¹ Luke 22:1-6, 22:47-48; John 18:1-3.

¹² Matthew 16:27.

¹³ 2 Corinthians 4:7; Romans 9:20-21.

¹⁴ Psalm 21:8-9, 50:3-4; Amos 5:6; 2 Peter 3:10-11; 1 Corinthians 3:10-15.

¹⁵ **The Ease that Pilgrims have, is but little in this life.**

¹⁶ **2 Timothy 4:10.**

¹⁷ Matthew 19:24; Mark 10:25; Luke 18:25.

¹⁸ **2 Kings 5:15-27.**

¹⁹ **Matthew 26:14-15, 27:1-6.**

²⁰ Matthew 27:3-5.

²¹ Luke 17:32.

²² **Genesis 19:26.**

²³ Genesis 18:1 to 19:29.

²⁴ **Numbers 26:9,10.**

²⁵ **Genesis 13:13** (KJV).

²⁶ **Genesis 13:10.**

²⁷ Luke 12:47-48.

²⁸ **Psalm 65:9** (KJV).

²⁹ **Revelation 22:1.**

³⁰ **Revelation 22:2; Ezekiel 47:1-12.**

³¹ **Isaiah 14:30; Psalm 23:2.**

³² Matthew 13:44.

14

THE PILGRIMS DEAL WITH GIANT DESPAIR

NOW I SAW IN my dream that they had not traveled far until the river and the Way parted for a time, at which they were very disappointed. The path away from the river was rough, and their feet were tender because of their travels, so they grew impatient on the way.[1] As they continued on, therefore, they wished for a better road. A short distance in front them was a meadow on the left hand side of the road. There was a set of steps constructed over the fence bordering the meadow, which is called By-path Meadow.

Then Christian said to his friend, "If this meadow lies alongside our pathway, let's go over into it."

Then he went to the steps to see. Sure enough, a path lay along the way they were going on the other side of the fence.

"It's just as I had hoped," said Christian; "here is the easiest going. Come, Hopeful, and let's go over."[2]

"But what if this path should lead us out of the Way?" asked Hopeful.

"That's not likely," said Christian. "Look, doesn't it go along by the wayside?"

So, being persuaded by his friend, Hopeful followed him over the steps. After they had gone over and had gotten into the path, they found it very easy for their feet; and with that, looking ahead of them, they saw a man walking as they did (and his name was Vain Confidence). So they called after him and asked him where that path led.

"To the Celestial gate," he said.

"Look," said Christian, "didn't I tell you so? By this you may see we are right."

So they followed, and he walked in front of them. But nighttime came, and it grew very dark, so that they who were behind lost sight of him who was in front. He who was in front (Vain Confidence by name), not seeing the way before him, fell into a deep pit that was put there on purpose by the owner of that property to catch conceited fools. With that he was dashed in pieces by his fall.[3]

Christian and his friend heard him fall, so they called out to know what the problem was; but there was no answer. They just heard groaning.

Then Hopeful asked, "Where are we now?"

His friend was silent, considering whether he had led him out of the Way. And it now began to rain and thunder in a dreadful manner. There was terrible lightning, and the water rose with force and suddenness.

Then Hopeful groaned in himself, saying, "Oh, if only I had kept on my Way!"

Christian said, "Who could have thought this path would have led us out of the Way?"

"I was afraid of it at the very beginning," responded Hopeful, "and therefore, I gave you that gentle warning. I would've spoken plainer, but you are older than I."

"Dear Brother," said Christian, "don't be angry. I'm sorry I've brought you out of the Way and that I've put you into such imminent danger. Please, my Brother, forgive me. I didn't do it with an evil intention."

Giant Despair

"Be comforted, my Brother," said Hopeful. "I forgive you and also believe this will turn out for our good."[4]

"I'm glad I have a merciful brother with me," responded Christian, "but we had better not stand here. Let's try to go back again."

"But, good Brother, let me go in front," suggested Hopeful.

"No." said Christian. "If you please, let me go first, so if there is any danger, I may be the first to encounter it. It's my fault we've both gone out of the path."

"No," replied Hopeful. "You won't go first. Since your mind is troubled, you may be led out of the Way again."

Then for their encouragement they heard the voice of one, saying, "Take note of the highway, the road that you take. Return."[5] But by this time the water had risen higher, and for that reason the way going back was very dangerous.

(Then the thought occurred to me that it is easier going out of the Way when we are in it than it is going in when we are out of it.) Yet they still attempted to go back, but it was so dark and the flood was so high that in going back they were almost drowned nine or ten times. Neither could they, with all the skill they had, get to the steps again that night. For that reason, they at last stopped under a little shelter and sat down there until daybreak. But being weary, they fell asleep.

Not far from the place where they lay was a castle called Doubting Castle. The owner of the castle was Giant Despair, and it was on his property they were now sleeping. When the Giant got up in the morning and walked up and down in his fields, he caught Christian and Hopeful asleep on his property. Then with a grim and surly voice, he commanded them to wake up and asked them where they came from and what they were doing on his land. They told him they were Pilgrims who had lost their way.

Then the Giant said, "You trespassed on me last night by trampling in and lying on my grounds. Therefore, you must go along with me."

They were forced to go because he was stronger than they. They also had very little to say, for they knew they were at fault. The Giant, therefore, drove them before him and put them into his castle in a very dark dungeon, which was nasty and stinking to the spirit of these two men. There they lay from Wednesday morning until Saturday night without one bit of bread or a drop to drink, and without light or anyone to ask how they were doing. They were, therefore, in a pitiful situation and were far from friends and acquaintances.[6] Now in this place Christian had double sorrow because it was through his ill-advised haste that they had been brought into this distress.

Giant Despair had a wife whose name was Diffidence. When the Giant went to bed, he told his wife what he had done, that he had taken a couple of prisoners and cast them into his dungeon for trespassing on his land. He then asked her what would be the best thing to do to them, and she asked him who they were, where they came from, and where they were going. When he had told her, she then advised him that when he arose in the morning he should beat them without any mercy.

So when he arose, he got himself a crab tree club and went down into the dungeon to them. There, he first started scolding them as if they were dogs, even though they never said a distasteful word to him. Then he attacked them and beat them fearfully in such a way that they were not able to help themselves or to turn themselves over on the floor. This done, he withdrew and left them there to sympathize with their misery and to mourn under their distress.

All that day, they spent the time doing nothing but sighing and bitterly wailing. The next night, while talking more with her husband about them, and realizing they were still alive, Diffidence advised him to tell them to do away with themselves. So when morning came, he went to them in a surly manner, as before, and seeing they were very sore with the stripes he had given them the day before, he told them that since they were likely never to come out of that place, their only way out would be to immediately put an end to themselves with either a knife, noose, or poison. "For why," he said, "should you choose life, seeing it is accompanied by so much bitterness?"

They asked him to let them go, and with that he made an ugly face and rushed upon them. He would have killed them himself if he had not fallen into one of his fits and lost for a time the use of his hand (for sometimes in sunny weather he falls into fits). For that reason, he withdrew as before and left them to consider what to do. Then the prisoners consulted one another about whether it would be best to take his advice. Thus they began to talk:

"Brother," said Christian, "what shall we do? The life we're now living is miserable! As for me, I don't know whether it's best to live like this or to die quickly. 'I prefer strangling and death, rather than this body of mine,'[7] and the grave seems more easy for me than this dungeon! Shall we be ruled by the Giant?"

Then Hopeful spoke. "Our present condition is indeed dreadful, and death would be far more welcome to me than to stay like this forever. But let's yet consider that the Lord of the country to which we are going has said, 'You shall not murder,'[8] no, not to murder another person. Much more, then, are we forbidden to take the Giant's advice to kill ourselves. Besides, he who kills someone else can only commit murder of that person's body, but for one to kill himself is to kill the body and soul at the same time."[9]

"And beyond that, my Brother," continued Hopeful, "you talk of ease in the grave, but have you forgotten Hell, where murderers most certainly go? For 'no murderer has eternal life in him.'[10] And let's consider again that all the law isn't in the hand of Giant Despair. As I understand it, others have been taken by him as well as we and have yet escaped out of his hands. Who knows but what God, who made the world, may cause that Giant Despair to die, or that at some time or other, he might forget to lock us in, or that he may soon have another one of his fits in front of us and lose the use of his limbs?"

"And if ever that should happen again," said Hopeful, "for my part, I'm resolved to muster up a manly heart and to try my best to get out from under his hand. I was a fool that I didn't try to do it before. But let's be patient, Brother, and endure a while longer. The time may come that provides us a happy release, but let's not be our own murderers."

With these words, Hopeful calmed the mind of his brother, so they continued together in the dark that day in their sad and dismal condition.

Well, toward evening the Giant went down into the dungeon again to see if his prisoners had taken his advice; but when he came there, he found them alive. And alive was truly all they were, for now, because of a lack of bread and water and by reason of the wounds they received when he beat them, they could do little more than breathe. But, I say, he found them alive, and at that, he went into a horrible rage and told them that seeing they had disobeyed his advice, it would be worse for them than if they had never been born.

At this, they trembled a great deal, and I think Christian fell into a swoon. But reviving a little, they renewed their discussion about the Giant's advice and whether they should yet take it. Again Christian seemed inclined toward doing it, but Hopeful made his second argument, as follows:

"My Brother," said Hopeful, "don't you remember how valiant you've been before now? Apollyon couldn't crush you, nor could all you heard, nor saw, nor felt in the Valley of the Shadow of Death. What hardship, terror, and amazement you've already gone through! And are you now nothing but fear? You see that I'm in the dungeon with you, and I'm a far weaker person by nature than you are. Also, this Giant has wounded me as well as you and has cut off the bread and water from my mouth, and I mourn with you here without light."

"But let's exercise a little more patience" continued Hopeful. "Remember how you displayed manliness at the Vanity Fair? And you weren't afraid of the chain, nor cage, nor even of a bloody death. So let's bear up with patience as well as we can, at least to avoid the shame that isn't suitable for a Christian to be found in."

Now night having arrived again, and the Giant and his wife being in bed, Diffidence asked him about the prisoners and whether they had taken his advice. Giant Despair replied, "They're sturdy rascals. They choose rather to bear all hardships than to do away with themselves."

Then Diffidence said, "Take them into the castle yard tomorrow and show them the bones and skulls of those you've already destroyed. And make them believe that within a week you'll also tear them in pieces as you've done to their friends before them."

So when morning came, the Giant went to them again, took them into the castle yard, and showed them what his wife had suggested to him. "These," said the Giant, "were once Pilgrims as you are, and they trespassed on my property as you have done. When I saw fit, I tore them in pieces, and within ten days I'll do the same to you. Go! Get yourselves down to your cell again!"

With that, he beat them all the way there. They lay, therefore, all day on Saturday in a pitiful condition as before. When night came, and when Diffidence and her husband the Giant had gone to bed, they began again their conversation about their prisoners. And then the old Giant wondered why he couldn't bring them to an end with either his beatings or his advice. Then his wife replied, "I fear that someone will come to rescue them, or that they may have some means to pick the locks, by the means of which they hope to escape."

"You think so, my Dear?" said the Giant. "Therefore, I'll search them in the morning."

Well, on Saturday about midnight the prisoners began to pray,[11] and they continued in prayer until almost daybreak. A little before dawn good Christian, as someone half amazed, broke out in this passionate declaration: "What a fool I am," he exclaimed, "to lay here in a stinking dungeon, when I could just as easily walk at liberty! In my coat, next to my heart, I have a Key called Promise.[12] I'm persuaded it will open any lock in Doubting Castle."[13]

"That's good news, Brother," said Hopeful. "Take it out and try."

Then Christian took it from his heart and began to try it on the dungeon door. As he turned the key, the bolt on the door gave way, and the door easily flew open. Christian and Hopeful both went out, and then Christian went to the iron gate, for it had to be opened, too. Well, that lock turned very hard, but the key opened it. Then they threw open the gate to quickly make their escape. However, that gate creaked so much as it opened that it woke Giant Despair. As he rose up to pursue his prisoners, he felt his limbs failing. He started to have one of his fits again, and so he could not by any means go after them. They went on and came back to the King's Highway, where they were safe and out of his jurisdiction.

After they had gone over the steps at the fence, they began to formulate between themselves what they should do at the steps to prevent those who would come after them from falling into the hands of Giant Despair. So they decided to erect a pillar there and to engrave upon the side of it this sentence: "Over these steps is the way to Doubting Castle, which is kept by Giant Despair, who despises the King of the Celestial Country and seeks to destroy His holy Pilgrims."

Many who followed after them, therefore, read what was written and escaped the danger. After this was done, they sang:

Out of the Way we went, and then we found
What 'twas to tread upon forbidden ground.
And let them that come after have a care,
Lest heedlessness makes them as we to fare,
Lest they for trespassing, his Pris'ners are,
Whose Castle's Doubting, and whose name's Despair.

NOTES ON CHAPTER 14

[1] **Numbers 21:4**.

[2] **Strong Christians may lead weak ones out of the way.** 1 Corinthians 8:9.

[3] **Isaiah 9:16. See what it is too suddenly to fall in with strangers.**

[4] Even in the dismal condition they have brought *themselves* into, Hopeful trusts God to use this experience to benefit the Pilgrims. Romans 8:28

[5] **Jeremiah 31:21**.

[6] **Psalm 88**.

[7] **Job 7:15**.

[8] Exodus 20:13.

[9] Matthew 10:28-31; 1 Corinthians 3:16-17.

[10] 1 John 3:15.

[11] Acts 16:25.

[12] Matthew 16:19; 2 Corinthians 1:20; Hebrews 8:6; 1 Peter 1:3; 1 John 2:25.

[13] **A Key in Christian's bosom called Promise, opens any lock in Doubting Castle.**

15

THE PILGRIMS REACH THE DELIGHTFUL MOUNTAINS

THEN CHRISTIAN AND HOPEFUL went on until they came to the Delightful Mountains, which belong to the Lord of the Hill, of whom we spoke earlier. So they went up to the mountains to see the gardens, vineyards, and fountains of water. There they drank and washed themselves and ate freely from the vineyards.

Now on top of those mountains there were Shepherds feeding their flocks, and they stood by the side of the Highway. The Pilgrims, therefore, went up to them, and leaning upon their walking sticks (as is common with weary Pilgrims when they stand to talk with anyone by the road), they asked, "Whose Delightful Mountains are these? And whose are the Sheep that feed upon them?"

"These mountains are Immanuel's Land,"[1] said one of the Shepherds, "and they're within sight of His city. The sheep are also His, and He laid down His life for them."[2]

"Is this the way to Celestial City?" asked Christian.

"You're in that Way," said the Shepherd.

"How far is it to there?" inquired Christian.

"Too far for anyone except those who indeed get there," answered the Shepherd.

"Is the way safe or dangerous?" asked Christian further.

"Safe for those for whom it is to be safe," said the Shepherd, "but the rebellious stumble in it."[3]

"Is there here a place of relief," asked Christian, "for Pilgrims who are weary and faint in the Way?"

"The Lord of these mountains has commanded us to 'not forget to entertain strangers,'"[4] answered the Shepherd. "Therefore, the goodness of the place lies before you."

I also saw in my dream that when the Shepherds realized they were wayfaring men, they asked them questions (which they had answered in other places). "Where did you come from?" they asked. "And how did you get in the Way? What have you done to persevere in the Way? For only a few of those who begin to come here actually show their faces on these mountains." But when the Shepherds heard their answers, and being pleased with them, they looked very lovingly upon them and said, "Welcome to the Delightful Mountains."

The Shepherds, whose names were Knowledge, Experience, Watchfulness, and Sincerity, led them by the hand, took them to their tents, and made them eat of that which was presently ready. Then the Shepherds said, "We want you to stay here awhile so you can get acquainted with us and, even more, to comfort yourselves with the good things of these Delightful Mountains."

The Pilgrims told them they were willing to stay, so they went and found their Rest that night, because it was very late.[5]

Then I saw in my dream that in the morning the Shepherds called on Christian and Hopeful to walk with them upon the mountains. So they went with them and walked for a while, having on all sides a pleasant view of the country.

The Shepherds said to one another, "Shall we show these Pilgrims some of the wonders?" And they decided to do it.

They first took them to the top of a hill called Error (which was very steep on the farthest side) and asked them to look down to the bottom. So Christian and Hopeful looked down and saw at the bottom several men dashed all to pieces by a fall they had taken from the top.

Christian asked, "What does this mean?"

The Shepherds answered, "Haven't you heard about those who were caused to err by listening to Hymenaeus and Philetus concerning the faith of the resurrection of the body?"[6]

"Yes," they answered.

The Shepherds said, "Those you see lying dashed in pieces at the bottom of this mountain are those individuals. As you see, they have continued to this day unburied for an example to others to take heed how they clamber too high or how they come too near to the edge of this mountain."

Then I saw that they took them to the top of another mountain called Caution and asked them to look far off in the distance. When they did, they thought they saw several men walking up and down among the tombs that were there, and they perceived that the men were blind because they sometimes stumbled over the tombs and could not get out from among them. Christian asked, "What does this mean?"

The Shepherds answered, "Didn't you see a short distance below these mountains a set of steps that led into a meadow on the left hand side of this way?"

"Yes," they answered.

Then the Shepherds said, "From those steps goes a path that leads directly to Doubting Castle, which is kept by Giant Despair; and these men (pointing to those among the tombs), once came on the Pilgrimage, as you are now, until they came to those same steps. Because the Right Way is rough in that place, they chose to leave it to go into that meadow and there were taken by Giant Despair and cast into Doubting Castle. There, after they'd been kept awhile in the dungeon, he finally put out their eyes and led them among those tombs. He has left them there to wander to this very day, so that the saying of the Wise Man might be fulfilled, 'A man who strays from the path of understanding comes to rest in the company of the dead.'"[7]

Christian and Hopeful looked at each other with tears pouring from their eyes, but yet they said nothing to the Shepherds.

Then I saw in my dream that the Shepherds led them to another place in a valley where a door existed in the side of a hill. The Shepherds opened the door and asked them to look in. They looked in, therefore, and saw it was very dark and smoky inside. They also thought they heard there a rumbling noise like fire and a cry of people tormented and smelled the scent of burning sulfur. Then Christian said, "What does this mean?"

The Shepherds told them, "This is an entrance to Hell, through which hypocrites go, such as those who sell their birthright with Esau,[8] such as those who sell their Master with Judas,[9] such as those who blaspheme the gospel with Alexander,[10] and who lie and pretend with Ananias and his wife Sapphira."[11]

Then Hopeful said to the Shepherds, "I suppose each and every one of these presented a show of going on the Pilgrimage just as we are now on, didn't they?"

"Yes," said a Shepherd, "and stayed on the Pilgrimage a long time, too."

"How far could they have gone on the Pilgrimage in their day if they had not been so miserably cast away?" asked Hopeful.

"Some farther," said the Shepherd, "and some not as far as these mountains."

Then the Pilgrims said to each other, "We have great need to cry out to The Strong for strength!"

"Yes," said another of the Shepherds, "and you'll have need to use it when you receive it, too."

By this time, the Pilgrims had a desire to continue on their journey, and the Shepherds agreed they should; so they walked together towards the end of the mountains.

Then the Shepherds said to one another, "If they have the skill to look through our perspective lens, let's now show the Pilgrims the gates of Celestial City."

The Pilgrims then lovingly accepted the idea. So the Shepherds took them to the top of a high hill called Clear, and gave them the lens to look through. They attempted to look, but the memory of that last thing the Shepherds had shown them made their hands shake, and because of that hindrance they could not look steadily through the lens. Yet, they thought they saw something like the gate and also some of the glory of the place.[12]

Then they went away and sang this song:

Thus by the Shepherds Secrets are reveal'd,
Which from all other men are kept conceal'd:
Come to the Shepherds then, if you would see
Things deep, Things hid, and that Mysterious be.

When they were about to depart, one of the Shepherds gave them a Map of the Way. Another of them warned them to beware of the Flatterer. The third told them to take heed not to sleep upon the Enchanted Ground, and the fourth bid them God Speed. And so, I awoke from my dream.

NOTES ON CHAPTER 15

[1] Immanuel is a Hebrew name meaning *God with us.* Isaiah 7:14, 8:7-10; Matthew 1:23.

[2] **John 10:11-15**.

[3] **Hosea 14:9**.

[4] **Hebrews 13:2**.

[5] Psalm 116:7-9; Hebrews 4:9-11.

[6] **2 Timothy 2:17-18**.

[7] **Proverbs 21:16**.

[8] Genesis 25:27-34.

[9] Luke 22:1-6, 22:47-48; John 18:1-3.

[10] 1 Timothy 1:18-20.

[11] Acts 4:32 through 5:10.

[12] Isaiah 33:15-17; Jeremiah 55:50.

16

THE PILGRIMS' DISCUSSION ABOUT LITTLE FAITH

I SLEPT AND DREAMED again, and I saw the same two Pilgrims going down the mountains along the Highway toward the City. Now a short distance below these mountains and on the left side there is the Country of Conceit. A little crooked lane comes from that country into the way in which the Pilgrims walked. Here, therefore, they met with a very spirited lad who came out of that country. His name was Ignorance. Christian asked him what parts he came from and where he was going.

"Sir," replied Ignorance, "I was born in the country that lies over there, a little to the left, and I'm going to Celestial City."

"But how do you think you'll get in at the gate?" inquired Christian. "For you may find some difficulty there."

"As other people do," said Ignorance.

"But what do you have to show at that gate in order for it to be opened to you?" asked Christian.

"I know my Lord's will," said Ignorance, "and I've lived a good life. I pay every man what I owe him; I pray, fast, pay tithes, and give offerings; and I've left my country to go where I'm now going."

Then Christian answered, "But you didn't come in at the Narrow Gate that is at the beginning of this path. You came in there, through that crooked lane. I fear, therefore, that whatever you may think of yourself, when the day of reckoning comes you will be charged with being a thief and a robber[1] instead of getting admittance into the City."

"Gentlemen," replied Ignorance, "you are absolute strangers to me. I don't know you. Be content to follow the religion of your country, and I will follow that of mine. I hope all will be well. And as for the Gate that you talk about, all the world knows that it's a great distance away from our country. I can't imagine that anyone in all our parts even so much as knows the way to it. Nor does it matter whether they do or not since, as you see, we have a fine pleasant green lane coming down from our country the next way into it."

When Christian saw that the man was wise in his own eyes, he said to Hopeful in a whisper, "'There is more hope for a fool than for him.'"[2] He continued and said, "'Even as he walks along the road, the fool lacks sense and shows everyone how stupid he is.'[3] Shall we talk further with him or outpace him and leave him to think about what he's already heard, and then stop again later for him and see if we can by degrees do him any good?"[4]

Then Hopeful said:

Let Ignorance a little while now muse
On what is said, and let him not refuse
Good Counsel to embrace, lest he remain
Still ignorant of what's the chiefest Gain.
God saith, Those that no Understanding have,
(Altho' he made them) them he will not save.[5]

Hopeful added further, "It isn't good, I think, to say everything to him at once. If you like, let's pass him by and talk to him again soon, even as he's able to stand it."[6]

So they both went on, and Ignorance followed after them. Now when they were a short distance past him, they entered into a very dark lane where they met a man whom seven evil spirits had bound with seven strong cords.[7] They were carrying him back to the door the Pilgrims had seen on the side of the hill.

Christian began to tremble, and so did Hopeful, his companion. Yet, as the devils led the man away, Christian looked to see if he knew him, and he thought it might be an individual named Turn Away who lived in the Town of Apostasy.

But after passing him, Hopeful looked after him and saw on his back a paper with this inscription: Wanton professor and damnable apostate. But he did not perfectly see his face, for he hung his head like a captured thief.

Then Christian said to his friend, "Now I remember what was told me about a thing that happened to a good man from around here. The name of the man was Little Faith, but he was a good man and lived in the Town of Sincere. The thing was this: at the entrance of this passage, a lane comes down from Broad Way Gate. The lane is called Deadman's Lane because of the killings that commonly take place there."

Christian went on with the story: "Little Faith—going on the Pilgrimage as we now do—chanced to sit down there and fell asleep. Now at that time, three stout hoodlums, named Faint Heart, Mistrust, and Guilt—three brothers—happened to come down that path on horseback from Broad Way Gate. They saw Little Faith lying there and quickly came galloping up to him. Now the good man was just waking up from his sleep and was getting up to go on his journey. So they all came up to him and with threatening language ordered him to stand. At this, Little Faith looked as white as a sheet and had no power to either fight or run away. Then Faint Heart said, 'Hand over your money.'"

"Little Faith was slow in doing it," continued Christian, "for he hated to lose his money. So Mistrust ran up to him, and thrusting his hand into the man's pocket pulled a bag of silver out of it. Little Faith then cried out, 'Thieves! Thieves!' Then Guilt, who had a large club in his hand, struck Little Faith on the head and with that blow knocked him flat on the ground. He lay there bleeding as one who would bleed to death. All this while, the thieves stood by; but finally hearing others on the road and fearing lest it should be a person named Great Grace, who lives in the City of Good Confidence, they took to their feet and left this good man to fend for himself. After a while, Little Faith came to himself and, getting up, made an effort to struggle on his way. This was the story."

"But did they take from him everything he ever had?" asked Hopeful.

"No," said Christian, "they never ransacked the place where his Jewels were, so he still retained those. But as I was told, the good man was much afflicted because of his loss, for the thieves got most of his spending money. That which they didn't get—as I said—were Jewels. He also had a bit of other money left, but hardly enough to sustain himself until the end of his journey. No, if I wasn't misinformed, he was forced to beg as he went to keep himself alive, for he dared not sell his Jewels. But begging and doing what he could, he went—as we say— with many a hungry belly for the most part of the rest of the way."[8]

"But isn't it a wonder they didn't get from him his Certificate by which he was to receive his admittance at the Celestial gate?" asked Hopeful.

"It's a wonder they didn't get it," remarked Christian, "though they didn't miss it due to his own cunning. Being frightened by their assault upon him, he had neither power nor skill to hide anything, so it was more by good providence than by his effort that they missed any of that good thing."[9]

Then Hopeful said, "But it has to be a comfort to him that they didn't get this Jewel from him."

"It might have been great comfort to him," responded Christian, "had he used it as he should. But they who told me the story said he made little use of it all the rest of the way, and that was because of the anxiety he had due to their taking away his money. Indeed, he forgot it a great part of the rest of his journey; and besides, when at any time it did come into his mind, and he began to be comforted by it, then fresh thoughts of his loss would come again upon him, and those thoughts would swallow up everything."

"Alas, poor man!" exclaimed Hopeful. "This couldn't be anything but a grief to him."

"Grief? Yes, a grief indeed!" said Christian. "Wouldn't it have been the same to any of us if we had been used as he was—to be robbed and wounded, too—and in a strange place as he was in? It's a wonder he didn't die with grief, poor thing. I was told that he went almost all the rest of the way scattering about nothing but dismal and bitter complaints. Also, as he went, he told everyone who passed him—or whom he passed in the Way—where and how he was robbed, who they were who did it, what he lost, how he was wounded, and that he barely escaped with his life."

Hopeful then said, "But it's a wonder his needs didn't cause him to start selling or pawning some of his Jewels so he could have something with which to relieve himself in his journey."

"You talk like one who still has the shell on his head to this very day,"[10] said Christian. "What would he pawn them for? Or to whom would he sell them? In all that country where he was robbed, his Jewels were of no importance, nor did he want the type of relief that could be given to him from there. Besides, if his Jewels had been missing at the gate of Celestial City, he would have been excluded from an inheritance there, and that he knew very well. That would have been worse to him than the appearance and evil deeds of ten thousand thieves."

"Why are you so sharp, my Brother?" asked Hopeful. "Esau sold his birthright, and that for a bowl of stew,[11] and that birthright was his greatest Jewel. If he did, then why might not Little Faith do so, too?"

Christian replied, "Indeed, Esau did sell his birthright, and so do many others besides. By doing so they exclude themselves from the chief blessing, as also that coward did. But you must place a difference between Esau and Little Faith, and also between their conditions. Esau's birthright was typical, but Little Faith's Jewels were not. Esau's desire lay in his fleshly appetite; Little Faith's didn't. Esau's belly was his god,[12] but

Little Faith's belly was not. Esau could see no farther than to the fulfilling of his desires. 'Look, I am about to die,' Esau said. 'What good is the birthright to me?'"[13]

Christian continued, "But Little Faith—though it was his lot to have only a little faith—was kept by his little faith from such wastefulness and made to see and prize his Jewels more than to sell them as Esau did his birthright. You haven't read anywhere that Esau had faith, not so much as a little. Therefore, where only the flesh bears influence—as it will in that man who has no faith to resist—it's not surprising if he sells his birthright and his soul and everything, even to the Devil of Hell. It is with such a person as it is with the wild donkey; 'in her heat who can restrain her?'[14] When their minds are set upon their cravings, they will have them, whatever the cost. But Little Faith was of another nature; his mind was on things divine. His livelihood depended upon things that were spiritual and from above. Therefore, why should he who is of such a nature sell his Jewels—had there been anyone who would have bought them—to fill his mind with empty things?[15] Will a man give a penny to fill his belly with hay? Or can you persuade the turtle dove to live upon decaying flesh like the crow? Though because of worldly desires, faithless ones can pawn, mortgage, or sell what they have—and themselves to boot—yet those who have faith, Saving Faith—though perhaps little of it—can't do it. Here, therefore, my Brother, is your mistake."

"I acknowledge it," confessed Hopeful, "but still, your severe rebuke almost made me angry."

"Why," said Christian in surprise, "I only compared you to some of the birds that are of the brisker sort, which run back and forth in well-worn paths with the shell still on their heads. But forget about that and consider the matter under debate, and all will be well between you and me"

"But Christian," responded Hopeful, "I'm persuaded in my heart that these three fellows are simply a company of cowards. Why else do you think they would have run as they did at the noise of someone who was coming on the road? Why didn't Little Faith respond with a greater heart? I think he could've withstood one battle with them and then yielded only when there was no way out."

"Many have said those thieves are cowards," answered Christian, "but few have found it that way during the time of trial. As for a great heart, Little Faith didn't have one,[16] and I perceive by you, my Brother, if you'd been the man concerned, you're simply for a battle and then to yield. Truly, since this is the extent of your courage, they are now at a distance from us, and should they appear to you as they did to him, they might cause you second thoughts."[17]

"But consider again," continued Christian, "that they're only hired thieves. They serve under the King of the Abyss,[18] who will, if need be, come to their aid himself; and his voice is as the roaring of a lion.[19] I myself have been engaged as Little Faith was, and I found it a terrible thing. These three villains assaulted me, and like a Christian I began to resist. But they simply called out, and in came their master. As the saying goes, I would've given my life for a penny, but as God would have it, I was clothed with proven armor. Yes, and yet even though I was so covered, I found it hard work to be a man. No man can comprehend what that combat is like unless he has been in the battle himself."

"Agreed," said Hopeful, "but they ran, you see, when they just supposed that Great Grace was on the road."

"True," responded Christian, "they have often fled, both they and their master, when Great Grace has simply appeared. And it's no wonder, for he is the King's Champion. But I trust you'll put some difference between Little Faith and the King's Champion. All the King's subjects are not His champions, nor when tried can they do such feats of war as he. Is it right to think that a little child should handle Goliath as David did,[20] or that there should be the strength of an ox in a bird? Some are strong; some are weak. Some have great faith; some have little. This man was one of the weak, and therefore, he was pressed to the walls."

"I wish it had been Great Grace for their sakes," said Hopeful.

"If it had been he," said Christian, "he might have had his hands full. For I must tell you that, though Great Grace is very good with his weapons—and as long as he keeps them at sword's point he has and can do well enough with them—yet if

Faint Heart, Mistrust, or the other get within him, it won't go well, and they'll cast him down. And you know that when a man is down, what can he do?"

Christian continued, "Whoever looks close upon Great Grace's face will see those scars and cuts there that will easily demonstrate what I say. Yes, once I heard he said—and that was when he was in combat—'we despaired even of life.'[21] How these stout hoodlums and their friends made David groan, mourn, and complain![22] Yes, Heman[23] and Hezekiah[24] too were forced to arouse themselves when they were assaulted by them, and though they were champions in their day, they had their coats soundly brushed by them. One time, Peter was determined to do what he thought he could do, but though some say of him that he is the prince of the Apostles, they handled him so well that they at last made him afraid of a weak girl."[25]

"Besides," continued Christian, "their king is at their whistle. He's never out of hearing, and he comes, if possible, to help them at any time they're being beaten. Of him it is said, 'The sword that reaches him has no effect, nor does the spear or the dart or the javelin. Iron he treats like straw and bronze like rotten wood. Arrows do not make him flee; slingstones are like chaff to him. A club seems to him but a piece of straw; he laughs at the rattling of the lance.'[26] What can a man do in this case? It's true; if a man could at all times have Job's horse, and have the skill and courage to ride him, he might do notable things. For his neck is clothed with 'a flowing mane;' he will not be afraid, 'like a locust, striking terror with his proud snorting. He paws fiercely, rejoicing in his strength, and charges into the fray. He laughs at fear, afraid of nothing; he does not shy away from the sword. The quiver rattles against his side, along with the flashing spear and lance. In frenzied excitement he eats up the ground; he cannot stand still when the trumpet sounds. At the blast of the trumpet he snorts, "Aha!" He catches the scent of battle from afar, the shout of commanders and the battle cry.'"[27]

"But for such foot soldiers as you and me," continued Christian, "let us never desire to meet with an enemy nor brag as if we could do better when we hear of others who have been foiled, nor be amused at the thoughts of our own manhood; for such individuals suffer the worst things when they are tried. For instance, Peter, of whom I made mention before, would strut arrogantly. Yes, he would. As his vain mind prompted him to say, he would stand up for his Master more than all men. But who was so foiled and run down by these villains as he?"

"Therefore," he continued, "when we hear that such robberies are committed on the King's Highway, it behooves us to do two things: First—to go out equipped, and to be sure to take a shield with us; for it was due to the lack of one that he who approached Leviathan so boldly could not make him yield.[28] For indeed, if that is lacking, he doesn't fear us at all. Therefore, he who had skill said, 'In addition to all this, take up the shield of faith, with which you can extinguish all the flaming arrows of the evil one.'"[29]

"Second," said Christian, "it's also good that we desire of The King that He give us an escort. Yes, that He go with us himself. This made David rejoice when he was in the Valley of the Shadow of Death.[30] And Moses would have rather died where he stood than to go one step without his God.[31] Oh, my Brother, if He will just go along with us, why should we be afraid of ten thousands that shall set themselves against us?[32] But without Him the proud helpers fall among the slain."[33]

"For my part," said Christian, "I've been in the fray before now. And yet, as you see, I'm alive through the goodness of Him who is best. Yet I can't boast of my manhood. I'll be glad if I don't meet with any more onslaughts, though I fear we haven't gotten beyond all danger. However, since the lion and the bear have not as yet devoured me, I hope God will also deliver us from the next uncircumcised Philistine."[34]

Then Christian sang:

Poor Little-Faith! Hast been among the Thieves?
Wast robb'd? Remember this; Whoso believes,
And gets more Faith, shall then a Victor be
Over ten thousand; else scarce over three.

So they went on, and Ignorance followed.

NOTE ON CHAPTER 16

[1] John 10:1.
[2] **Proverbs 26:12.**
[3] **Ecclesiastes 10:3.**
[4] **How to carry it to a fool.**
[5] Isaiah 27:10,11.
[6] 1 Corinthians 3:1,2.
[7] **Matthew 12:43-45; Proverbs 5:22-23.**
[8] **1 Peter 4:18.**
[9] **2 Timothy 1:14; 2 Peter 2:9.**
[10] This signifies silliness, immaturity, childishness, or lack of understanding. The poor bird may have thought differently, but it had not stopped long enough to consider it still had not gotten completely out of its shell.
[11] Genesis 25:27-34; **Hebrews 12:16.**
[12] Philippians 3:18,19.
[13] **Genesis 25:32.**
[14] **Jeremiah 2:24.**
[15] **Little-Faith could not live upon Esau's pottage.**
[16] **No great heart for God where there is but little faith.**
[17] **We have more courage when out, than when we are in.**
[18] Revelation 9:1-11.
[19] **1 Peter 5:8-9.**
[20] 1 Samuel 17.
[21] 2 Corinthians 1:8.
[22] Psalm 6:6, 32:3, Psalm 55.
[23] Probably referring to Heman, a minister of music mentioned in 1 Chronicles 6:31-33. Bunyan probably draws from Psalm 88, written by "Heman the Esrahite".
[24] 2 Kings 18, 19, 20.
[25] Matthew 26:31-35, 69-75.
[26] **Job 41:26-29.**
[27] **Job 39:19-20,** 39:21-25.
[28] Job 41:1; Isaiah 27:1
[29] **Ephesians 6:16.**
[30] Psalm 23.
[31] **Exodus 33:15-16.**
[32] **Psalm 3:5-8, 27:1-3.**
[33] **Isaiah 10:4.**
[34] Christian uses the reasoning of David, who after having God strengthen his hand against the lion and the bear, stood in faith before the uncircumcised Philistine, Goliath. 1 Samuel 17:33-36.

17

THE PILGRIMS MEET THE FLATTERERS

THEY WENT ON UNTIL they came to a place where they saw another way merge into their Way, and it seemed to lay as straight as the Way they should go. They did not know which of the two to take, for both seemed straight in front of them. Therefore, they stood still there to consider. And as they were thinking about the Way, a man with dark flesh and covered with a very light-colored robe came to them and asked why they stood there. They answered that they were going to Celestial City but did not know which of these ways to take.

"Follow me," said the man. "That is where I'm going."

So they followed him in the path that just there merged into the road. It turned slowly as it went, and in time it turned them so far away from the City where they wanted to go that soon their faces were turned away from it. Yet they followed him. But in time, before they were aware, he led them both within the confines of a net in which they were both so entangled that they did not know what to do. With that, the white robe fell off the Dark Man's back. Then they saw where they were. Therefore, they lay there for some time, crying, for they could not get themselves out.

Then Christian said to his friend, "Now I see myself to be in error. Didn't the Shepherds warn us to beware of the flatterers? As is the saying of the Wise Man, we have found it to be so this very day: 'Whoever flatters his neighbor is spreading a net for his feet.'"[1]

Hopeful responded, "They also gave us a map of directions about the Way to make it easier to find, but we've forgotten to read it and haven't kept ourselves from the paths of the violent. Here, David was wiser than we, for he said: 'As for the deeds of men—by the word of your lips I have kept myself from the ways of the violent.'"[2]

They lay like that, weeping for themselves in the net. Finally, they saw a Shining One coming toward them with a whip made of small cord in his hand. When he came to the place where they were, he asked them where they came from and what they were doing there. They told him they were poor Pilgrims going to Zion[3] but who were led out of their path by a Dark Man clothed in white, "who invited us," they said, "to follow him, for he was going there, too."

The one with the whip said, "It is Flatterer, a False Apostle who is masquerading as an angel of light."[4] He then ripped the net, letting the men out, and said to them, "Follow me, so I may set you in your way again."

So he led them back to the path they had left to follow the Flatterer. Then he asked them, saying, "Where did you stay last night?"

"With the Shepherds upon the Delightful Mountains," they answered.

He then asked them if they didn't get a Map of the Way from the Shepherds.

"Yes," they answered.

"But when you were at a stopping place, did you take out your Map and read it?" he asked.

"No," they answered.

"Why?" he asked them.

The Pilgrims meet Atheist

They told him they forgot.

He asked further if the Shepherds had warned them to beware of the Flatterer.

"Yes," they answered, "but we didn't imagine that this fine-spoken man had been he."[5]

Then I saw in my dream that he commanded them to lie down, and when they did, he chastised them severely to teach them the good way in which they should walk.[6] And as he chastised them he said, "'Those whom I love I rebuke and discipline. So be earnest, and repent.'"[7]

This done, he told them to go their way and take good heed to the other direction of the Shepherds. So they thanked him for all his kindness and went carefully along the Right Way, singing:

Come hither, you that walk along the Way,
See how the Pilgrims fare, that go astray:
They catched are in an intangling Net,
'Cause they good Counsel lightly did forget:
'Tis true, they rescu'd were, but yet you see
They're scourg'd to boot: Let this your Caution be.

After a while they saw at a distance a lone person coming quietly along the Highway to meet them.

Then Christian said to his friend, "Yonder is a man with his back toward Zion, and he's coming to meet us."

"I see him," said Hopeful. "Let's take heed to ourselves now, lest he should also prove to be a Flatterer."

So he drew nearer and nearer and at last came up to them. His name was Atheist, and he asked them where they were going.

"We're going to Mount Zion," answered Christian.

Then Atheist began laughing greatly.

"What's the meaning of your laughter?" inquired Christian.

"I laugh to see what ignorant persons you are to take upon yourselves such an exhausting journey," said Atheist. "And yet you're likely to have nothing but your travel for your pains."

"Why, Man?" asked Christian. "Do you think we won't be received?"

"Received!" exclaimed Atheist. "In all this world there is no such place as you dream of."

"But there is in the world to come," said Christian.

Atheist responded, "When I was at home in my own country, I heard the same thing you now say. And from that time I went out to see and have been seeking this City for twenty years, but I've found no more of it than I did the first day I set out."[8]

"We've both heard and believe there is such a place to be found," stated Christian.

Atheist then said, "Had I not believed when I was at home, I wouldn't have come this far seeking it. But not finding it—and I should have, had there been such a place to be found, for I've gone farther than you seeking it—I'm going back again and will seek to refresh myself with the things I had cast away for the sake of that which I now see doesn't exist."[9]

Then Christian said to his friend Hopeful, "Is it true what this man has said?"

"Take heed," answered Hopeful. "He is one of the Flatterers. Remember what it has already cost us once for listening to this kind of fellow. What? No Mount Zion? Didn't we see the gate of the City from the Delightful Mountains? Also, aren't we now to walk by faith?"[10]

"Let's go on," said Hopeful, "lest the man with the whip overtake us again.[11] You should have taught me the lesson that I will just now bring to your ears. That is, 'Cease, my son, to hear the instruction that causes you to err from the words of knowledge.'[12] I say, my Brother, stop listening to him, and let's believe and be saved."[13]

"My Brother," responded Christian, "I didn't ask you the question because I doubted the truth of our belief myself, but instead, to test you and to withdraw from you evidence of the nobleness of your heart.[14] As for this man, I know he is blinded by the god of this age.[15] Let's go on, knowing we believe the truth[16] and that 'no lie comes from the truth.'"[17]

"'Now I rejoice in the hope of the glory of God,'"[18] said Hopeful as they turned away from the man. And the man laughed at them and went his way.

NOTES ON CHAPTER 17

[1] **Proverbs 29:5.**

[2] **Psalm 17:4.**

[3] Jeremiah 50:5. Zion came to be used as a reference to the City of Jerusalem. Spiritually speaking, Zion is the City of God and is often used as a reference to the heavenly Jerusalem.

[4] **2 Corinthians 11:13-15.**

[5] **Daniel 11:32. Deceivers fine spoken.**

[6] **Deuteronomy 25:2**; Hebrews 12:11; **2 Chronicles 6:26-27.** Bunyan included **Romans 6:18** in his side notes to draw reference to the correction of a slave, which is something his contemporaries could identify with.

[7] **Revelation 3:19.**

[8] **Ecclesiastes 10:15**; Psalm 14:1.

[9] **Jeremiah 2:13.**

[10] **2 Corinthians 5:7.**

[11] **Remembrance of former chastisements is a help against present temptations.**

[12] **Proverbs 19:27** (KJV).

[13] **Hebrews 10:39.**

[14] Luke 8:15.

[15] 2 Corinthians 4:4.

[16] 2 Thessalonians 2:13.

[17] **1 John 2:21.**

[18] Romans 5:2.

18

HOPEFUL TELLS OF HIS CONVERSION

I SAW THEN IN my dream that they traveled until they
entered into a certain country whose air naturally tended to
make anyone drowsy who was a stranger to it. Here, Hopeful
began to be very listless and sleepy. He therefore said to
Christian, "I'm now beginning to grow so drowsy I can
scarcely hold my eyes open. Let's lie down here and take a nap."

"By no means," said Christian, "lest by sleeping we
never wake again."

"Why, my Brother?" asked Hopeful, "Sleep is sweet to
the laboring man.[1] We can be refreshed if we take a nap."

"Don't you remember," said Christian, "that one of the
Shepherds told us to beware of the Enchanted Ground? What
he meant was that we should beware of sleeping. 'So then, let
us not be like others, who are asleep, but let us be alert and
self-controlled.'"[2]

"I acknowledge my error," responded Hopeful, "and if
I'd been here alone, by sleeping I would've run the danger of

death. I see it's true that the Wise Man said, 'Two are better than one.'³ To this moment your company has been of great benefit to me, and you'll receive a good return for your work."

"Now then," said Christian, "to prevent drowsiness in this place, let's have a good discussion."⁴

"Gladly," said Hopeful.

Then Christian asked, "Where shall we begin?"

"Where God began with us," answered Hopeful. "But you begin if you would like."

"First I'll sing you this song," said Christian.

When Saints do sleepy grow, let them come hither,
And hear how these two Pilgrims talk together,
Yea, let them learn of them in any wise
Thus to keep ope' their drowzy slumb'ring eyes;
Saints Fellowship if it be manag'd well,
Keeps them awake, and that in spite of Hell.

Then Christian said, "I'll ask you a question. How did you at first come to think of doing as you now do?"

Hopeful responded, "Do you mean, how I at first came to look after the good of my soul?"

"Yes," answered Christian, "that's what I mean."

Hopeful explained, "I continued for a long time in the enjoyment of those things that were seen and sold at the Vanity Fair, things that I now believe would have plunged me into ruin and destruction had I continued in them."⁵

"What things were those?" questioned Christian.

"All the treasures and riches of the world," answered Hopeful. "Also, I enjoyed orgies, carousing, drinking, swearing, lying, impurity, Sabbath-breaking, and so on—those things that tended to destroy the soul.⁶ But I finally found by hearing and considering the things that are divine—which I heard from you and also from dear Faithful, who was put to death for his faith and good living in the Vanity Fair—that 'those things result in death!'⁷ 'For because of such things God's wrath comes on those who are disobedient.'"⁸

"And did you immediately fall under the power of this conviction?" asked Christian.

"No," said Hopeful. "I wasn't willing to recognize at once the evil of sin or the damnation that follows one's committing it. When my mind at first began to be shaken by the Word, I tried to shut my eyes against its light."[9]

"But what was the reason you responded like that until God's blessed Spirit began to move you?" inquired Christian.

Hopeful listed the causes: "First—I was ignorant that this was the work of God upon me. I never thought that God begins the conversion of sinners by awakening them to sin. Second—sin was still very sweet to my sinful nature, and I hated to leave it. Third—I didn't know how to part with my old companions, for their presence and actions were so desirable to me. Fourth—the times in which I felt the convictions were such troublesome and heart-frightening hours that I couldn't bear them, even the remembrance of them upon my heart."

"Then, as it seems, sometimes you got rid of your trouble," said Christian.

"Yes, of course," said Hopeful, "but it would come into my mind again, and then I would be as bad—no, even worse—than I was before."

"Why?" inquired Christian. "What was it that brought your sins to mind again?"

"Many things," answered Hopeful, "such as: One—if I just met a good man in the streets; or, two—if I heard anyone read from The Bible; or, three—if my head began to ache; or, four—if I'd been told some of my neighbors were sick; or, five—if I heard the bell toll for those who were dead; or, six— if I thought of dying myself; or, seven—if I heard that sudden death happened to others; but especially, eight—when I thought of myself, that I must soon arrive at judgment."

Christian then asked, "And could you ever easily get rid of the guilt of sin when it came upon you through any of these things?"

"No, not toward the end of that time," said Hopeful, "for then they got a firmer grip of my conscience. Then if I just thought of going back to sin—though my mind was turned against it—it would bring me twice the torment."

"And what did you do then?" asked Christian.

Hopeful then said, "I thought, 'I must try to mend my life or else I'm sure to be damned.'"

"And did you try to mend it?" asked Christian.

"Yes," answered Hopeful. "I fled from not only my sins but also sinful company. And I began performing religious duties, such as praying, reading, weeping for sin, speaking truth to my neighbors, and so forth. I did these things and also many others too many to relate now."

"And did you think well of yourself then?" asked Christian.

"Yes, for a while," said Hopeful, "but my trouble finally came tumbling down upon me again, despite all of my makeovers."

"How did that happen, since you were then reformed?" asked Christian.

"There were several things that caused them to fall upon me," responded Hopeful, "especially such sayings as these: all our righteous acts are like filthy rags;[10] by observing the law no one will be justified;[11] when you have done everything you were told to do, you should say 'We are unworthy servants;'[12] and with many more like those. From these I began to reason with myself, If all my righteous acts are filthy rags, if by observing the Law no man can be justified, and if when we've done everything we're still unworthy, then it's just foolishness to think of Heaven through the Law."

Hopeful continued, "I further thought that if a man runs a hundred dollars into a store owner's debt and then pays for everything he purchases thereafter, yet his old debt is still in the book, and the store owner may sue him and have him cast into prison until his debt is paid."

"Very well," said Christian. "And how did you apply this to yourself?"

"Why, I thought like this to myself," answered Hopeful. "Through my sins, I've run a great way into God's Book, and now, my reforming will not pay off that debt. Therefore, I should still consider—even after the recent mending of my ways—how I can be freed from the danger of that damnation that I've brought myself by my former transgressions."[13]

"A very good application," said Christian, "but please, go on."

Hopeful then said, "Another thing that has troubled me even since the recent changing of my ways, is that if I look narrowly into the best of what I now do, I still see sin, new sin, mixing itself with the best of what I do. Now I'm forced to conclude that in spite of my former fond conceited view of myself and my duties, I've committed enough sin in one act to send me to Hell, even if my former life had been faultless."

"And what did you do then?" asked Christian.

"Do!" exclaimed Hopeful, "I couldn't tell what to do until I shared my thoughts with Faithful. He and I were well acquainted, and he told me that unless I could obtain the righteousness of a Man who had never sinned, neither my own nor all the righteousness of the world could save me."

"And did you think he spoke the truth?" asked Christian.

Hopeful responded, "Had he told me that when I was pleased and satisfied with my own changes I'd made in my life, I would've called him a fool for his effort. But now, since I see my own weakness and the sin that cleaves to my best deed, I've been forced to be of his opinion."

Christian then said, "But when Faithful first suggested it to you, did you think there was such a Man to be found of whom it could be truly said that He never committed sin?"[14]

"I must confess," said Hopeful, "that at first the words sounded strange, but after a little more conversation and company with him, I was fully convinced."

"And did you ask him who this Man was," asked Christian, "and how you must be justified by Him?"

"Yes," answered Hopeful, "and he told me it was the Lord Jesus, who dwells on the right hand of the Most High.[15] And Faithful said this: 'You must be justified by Him, even by trusting in what He himself did during His life on earth as He suffered when He was hanging on the Tree.'[16] I asked him further how that Man's righteousness could be so powerful as to be able to justify another person before God. And he told me

He was the Mighty God,[17] and did what He did, and also died
the death not for himself, but for me to whom His works—and
the worthiness of them—would be ascribed if I believed on
Him."[18]

"And what did you do then?" inquired Christian.

"I stated my objections against believing," said Hopeful,
"because I thought He would not be willing to save me."

"And what did Faithful say to you then?" returned
Christian.

"He said I should go to Him and see," answered Hopeful.
"I said it would be presumptuous on my part, but he said no,
for I was invited to come.[19] Then he gave me a Book of the
words of Jesus to encourage me to feel better about going.
Concerning that Book he said the smallest letter and the least
stroke of the pen in it stood firmer than Heaven and earth.[20] I
then asked him what I must do when I arrived, and he told me
I must ask the Father upon my knees,[21] with all my heart and
soul, to reveal Him to me.[22] Then I asked him further how I
must make my prayer to Him, and he said, 'Go, and you will
find Him upon a Mercy Seat,[23] where He sits all year long to
give pardon and forgiveness to those who come.' I told him I
didn't know what to say when I arrived, and he told me to
speak to this effect:

> "'God be merciful to me a sinner, and make
> me to know and believe in Jesus Christ; for I
> see that if His righteousness had not been, or
> I have not faith in that righteousness, I am
> utterly cast away. Lord, I have heard that
> You are a merciful God and have ordained
> that Your Son Jesus Christ should be the
> Savior of the world; and moreover, that you
> are willing to bestow on such a poor sinner
> as I am—and I am a sinner indeed—Lord.
> Take therefore this opportunity, and magnify
> Your grace in the salvation of my soul
> through Your Son, Jesus Christ. Amen.'"[24]

"And did you do as you were told?" asked Christian.

"Yes, over and over and over," answered Hopeful.

"And did the Father reveal His Son to you?" asked Christian.

"Not the first time," said Hopeful, "or the second, or third, or fourth, or fifth, or at the sixth time either."

"What did you do then?" asked Christian.

"What!" exclaimed Hopeful. "Why, I couldn't tell what to do."

"Didn't you have thoughts of quitting your praying?" inquired Christian.

"Yes," said Hopeful, "a hundred times over."

"And why didn't you?" asked Christian.

Hopeful answered, "I believed it was true what had been told me, that without the righteousness of this Christ all the world could not save me. Therefore, I thought to myself, 'If I quit, I'll die, and I can't die except at the Throne of Grace.' With that, this came into my mind: 'Though it linger, wait for it; it will certainly come and will not delay.'[25] So, I continued praying until the Father showed me His Son."[26]

"And how was He revealed to you?" asked Christian.

"I didn't see Him with my bodily eyes," explained Hopeful, "but with the eyes of my heart.[27] This is the way it was: One day I was very sad—sadder, I think, than any one time in my life. And this sadness was due to a fresh sight of the greatness and vileness of my sins. As I was then looking forward to nothing but Hell and the everlasting damnation of my soul, suddenly I thought I saw the Lord Jesus looking down from Heaven on me and saying, 'Believe in the Lord Jesus, and you will be saved.'"[28]

Hopeful continued, "But I replied, 'Lord, I'm a great, very great sinner.' And He answered, 'My grace is sufficient for you.'[29] Then I said, 'But Lord, what is believing?' And then I saw from the saying, 'He who comes to me will never go hungry, and he who believes in me will never be thirsty,'[30] that believing and coming was all one thing, and that he who came—that is, ran out in his heart and affections after salvation by Christ—indeed believed in Christ. Then tears stood in my eyes, and I asked further, 'But, Lord, may such a great sinner as I am actually be accepted by You and be saved by You?' And I heard Him say, 'Whoever comes to me I will never drive away.'"[31]

Hopeful went on, "Then I said, 'But how, Lord, should I think of You in my coming to You, so that my faith may be correctly placed upon You?' Then He said, 'Christ Jesus came into the world to save sinners.'[32] 'He is the end of the law so that there may be righteousness for everyone who believes.'[33] 'He was delivered over to death for our sins and was raised to life for our justification.'[34] 'He loves us and has freed us from our sins by His blood.'[35] 'He is the mediator between God and men.'[36] 'He always lives to intercede for them.'[37] From all that, I gathered that I must look for righteousness in His person and for satisfaction for my sins to His blood. I also recognized that what He did in obedience to His Father's Law—and in submitting to the penalty of it—was not for himself but for him who will accept it for his salvation and be thankful. And then my heart was full of joy; my eyes were full of tears, and my affections were running over with love for the name, people, and ways of Jesus Christ."

"This was indeed a revelation of Christ to your soul," said Christian. "But tell me particularly what effect this had on your spirit."

Hopeful responded, "It made me see that, in spite of all the righteousness within it, all the world is in a state of condemnation. It made me see that God the Father, though He be just, can justly justify the coming sinner. It made me greatly ashamed of the vileness of my former life and confounded me with a sense of my own ignorance, for before then there never came a thought into my heart that so showed me the beauty of Jesus Christ. It made me love a holy life and long to do something for the honor and glory of the name of the Lord Jesus. Yes, I thought that if I'd had a thousand gallons of blood in my body, I could spill it all for the sake of the Lord Jesus."

NOTES ON CHAPTER 18

1 Ecclesiastes 5:12.
2 **1 Thessalonians 5:6.**
3 **Ecclesiastes 4:9.**
4 **Good discourse prevents drowsiness.**
5 1 Timothy 6:9.
6 Romans 13:12-14; Galatians 5:19-21; 1 Peter 4:3.
7 **Romans 6:21.** "For the wages of sin is death, but the gift of God is eternal life in Christ Jesus our Lord." **Romans 6:23.**
8 **Ephesians 5:6.**
9 John 3:19-21.
10 **Isaiah 64:6.**
11 **Galatians 2:16.**
12 **Luke 17:10.**
13 Revelation 20:11-12.
14 Hebrews 4:14-15.
15 **Hebrews 10:12.**
16 **Romans 4:25**; 1 Peter 2:24.
17 Isaiah 9:6-7; Colossians 2:8-9; John 1:1-3.
18 **Colossians 1:15-23; 1 Peter 1:3-12.**
19 **Matthew 11:28.**
20 Matthew 5:18, **24:35.**
21 **Psalm 95:6; Daniel 6:10.**
22 **Jeremiah 29:12-13.**
23 **Exodus 25:10-22,** especially 17-22 (KJV); **Leviticus 16:2; Numbers 7:89.**
24 **Hebrews 4:16.**
25 **Habakkuk 2:3.**
26 Galatians 1:15-16, 4:6; 1 John 5:20.
27 **Ephesians 1:18-21.**
28 **Acts 16:31.**
29 **2 Corinthians 12:9.**
30 **John 6:35.**
31 **John 6:37.**

[32] **1 Timothy 1:15**.
[33] **Romans 10:4**.
[34] Romans 4:25. **Romans 4**.
[35] Revelation 1:5.
[36] 1 Timothy 2:5.
[37] **Hebrews 7:25**.

CHAPTER 19

THE PILGRIMS DEAL WITH IGNORANCE

I THEN SAW IN my dream that Hopeful looked back and saw Ignorance, whom they had left behind, walking behind them. "Look how far that youngster lags behind," said Hopeful to Christian.

"Yes, yes, I see him," answered Christian. "He doesn't care for our company."

"But I don't think it would've hurt him to have kept up with us till now," said Hopeful.

"That's true," said Christian in return, "but I'll guarantee you he thinks otherwise."

"I'm sure he does," said Hopeful. "However, let's wait for him." And so they did.

Then Christian said to Ignorance, "Come on, Man! Why do you stay so far behind?"

Ignorance answered, "I enjoy walking alone, even a great deal more than in company, unless I like it better."

Then Christian spoke softly to Hopeful, "Didn't I tell you he didn't care for our company? However, let's go and talk away the time in this secluded place."

Then, directing his speech to Ignorance, he said, "Well now, how do you do? How are things between God and your soul now?"

"Good, I hope," answered Ignorance, "for I'm always full of good thoughts that come into my mind to comfort me as I walk."

"What good thoughts?" asked Christian. "Please, tell us."

"Why, I think of God and Heaven," answered Ignorance.

"So do the devils and damned souls,"[1] countered Christian.

"But I think of them and desire them," said Ignorance.

"So do many who are never likely to get there," said Christian. "'The sluggard craves and gets nothing.'"[2]

"But I think of them and leave everything for them," said Ignorance.

"I doubt that," responded Christian, "for leaving everything is a hard thing to do—yes, a harder thing than many realize. But why or by what are you persuaded that you have left everything for God and Heaven?"

"My heart tells me so," answered Ignorance.

"The Wise Man says, 'He who trusts in his own heart is a fool,'"[3] said Christian.

"This is spoken of an evil heart," protested Ignorance, "but mine is a good one."

"But how can you prove that?" inquired Christian.

"It comforts me with the hope of Heaven," answered Ignorance.

"That may be through its deceitfulness,"[4] said Christian, "for a man's heart may minister comfort to him with the hope of something that as yet he has no grounds to hope for."

"But my heart and life agree together," said Ignorance, "and therefore, my hope is well grounded."

"Who told you your heart and life agree together?" asked Christian.

"My heart tells me so," said Ignorance.

"Ask my friend if I'm a thief?" questioned Christian. "Your

heart tells you so! Unless the Word of God bears witness in this matter, other testimony is of no value."

"But isn't it a good heart that has good thoughts?" asked Ignorance. "And isn't that life good that is according to God's commandments?"

"Yes," agreed Christian, "that heart is good that has good thoughts, and that life is good that is according to God's commandments. But it's indeed one thing to have these and another thing to only think so."

"Please tell me," said Ignorance, "what do you consider good thoughts and a good life according to God's commandments?"

"There are good thoughts of many kinds," responded Christian, "some respecting ourselves, some of God, some of Christ, and some concerning other things."

"What are good thoughts respecting ourselves?" inquired Ignorance.

"Those that agree with the Word of God," answered Christian.

"When do our thoughts of ourselves agree with the Word of God?" asked Ignorance.

"When we pass the same judgment upon ourselves that the Word passes," said Christian. "To explain myself: The Word of God says of persons in their natural condition, 'There is no one righteous;'[5] 'there is no one who does good.'[6] It also says that every imagination of the heart of a man is only evil all the time,[7] and again, 'every inclination of his heart is evil from childhood.'[8] Now then, when we think of ourselves like that—having an understanding of it—then our thoughts are good ones because they are according to the Word of God."

"I'll never believe my heart is bad like that," stated Ignorance.

"Therefore," returned Christian, "you've never had one good thought concerning yourself in your life. But let me go on. As the Word passes a judgment upon our hearts, it also passes a judgment upon our ways; and when our thoughts of our hearts and ways agree with the judgment that the Word gives of both, then both are good because they are in agreement."

"Make your point," said Ignorance impatiently.

"Why," replied Christian, "the Word of God says that man's ways are crooked ways,[9] not good but perverse. It says they are naturally out of the Good Way, and they've not known it.[10] Now, when a man thinks of his ways like that—I say, when he thinks sensibly like that with humiliation of the heart—then he has good thoughts of his own ways because his thoughts now agree with the judgment of the Word of God."

"What are good thoughts concerning God?" asked Ignorance.

"As I've said concerning ourselves," said Christian, "good thoughts are when our thoughts of God agree with what the Word says of Him—that is, when we think of His person and attributes as the Word has taught, which is something I can't expound upon a great deal now. But, speaking of Him with reference to us, we have right thoughts of God when we think that He knows us better than we know ourselves and can see sin in us when and where we can see none, when we think He knows our innermost thoughts[11] and that our heart—with all its depths—is always open to His eyes.[12] In addition, good thoughts are when we think that all our righteousness stinks in his nostrils[13] and that therefore He can't bear to see us stand before Him in any self-confidence, even in all our best deeds."

Ignorance countered, "Do you think that I'm such a fool as to think God can see no farther than I or that I would come to God boasting of the best of my deeds?"

"How do you think regarding this matter?" asked Christian.

"To be brief," said Ignorance, "I think I must believe in Christ for Justification."

"Good!" exclaimed Christian. "You think you must believe in Christ when you don't see your need of Him! You see neither your original nor your present weaknesses, but you have such an opinion of yourself and of what you do that it plainly renders you to be one who has never seen the necessity of having Christ's personal righteousness to justify you before God. How then can you say, 'I believe in Christ?'"

"I believe well enough for that," said Ignorance.

"How do you believe?" asked Christian.

"I believe that Christ died for sinners," answered Ignorance, "and that I'll be justified before God from the Curse through His gracious acceptance of my obedience to his Law. Or this: I believe Christ makes my religious duties acceptable to His Father by virtue of His merits. In that way I will be justified."

"Let me give an answer to this confession of your faith," said Christian. "First—you believe with a bizarre faith, for this faith is not described anywhere in the Word. Second—you believe with a false faith because it takes justification away from the personal righteousness of Christ and applies it to your own. Third—this faith doesn't make Christ a justifier of your person but of your actions, and of your person for your actions' sake, which is false. Fourth—therefore, this faith is deceitful, even such as will leave you under wrath in the Day of God Almighty.[14] For true justifying faith causes the soul—understanding its lost condition by the Law—to flee for refuge unto Christ's righteousness.[15] His righteousness is not an act of Grace by which He for justification makes your obedience accepted with God, but it is His personal obedience to the Law in doing and suffering for us what punishment the Law prescribed for us. I say, true faith accepts this righteousness. Under the skirt of Christ's righteousness,[16] [having found refuge there], the soul, being covered, is presented by it as spotless before God. The soul is accepted and acquitted from condemnation."

"What!" exclaimed Ignorance. "Would you have us rely on what Christ has done personally without us? This conceit would loosen the reins of our evil desires and condone our living as we choose. If we believe that, what does it matter how we live if we may be justified for all things by Christ's personal righteousness?"

"Ignorance is your name," said Christian. "And as your name is, so you are. Even your answer here demonstrates what I say. You're ignorant of what justifying righteousness is, and just as ignorant of how to secure your soul through the faith of it from the heavy wrath of God. Yes, you're also ignorant of the true effects of saving faith in the righteousness of Christ, which is to bow and win over the heart to God in Christ, to cause it to love His name, His Word, ways, and people, and not as you ignorantly imagine."

Hopeful then spoke up and said, "Ask him if he ever had Christ revealed to him from Heaven."

"What!" exclaimed Ignorance once again. "You're a man for revelations! I believe that what both you and all the rest of you say about that matter is just the fruit of distracted brains."

"Why, man!" interjected Hopeful. "Christ is so hidden in God from the natural apprehensions of all flesh that He can't be known in salvation by anyone unless God the Father reveals Him."

"That's your faith, but not mine," stated Ignorance. "Yet I don't doubt that mine is as good as yours, even though I don't have as many fanciful thoughts in my head as you."

"Allow me to put in a word," said Christian. "You ought not to speak so carelessly of this matter, for this I'll boldly affirm—even as my good companion has done—that no man can know Jesus Christ except through the revelation of the Father.[17] Yes, and also faith—by which the soul lays hold upon Christ, if it be right—must be wrought by the exceeding greatness of His Mighty Power,[18] the working of which I see, poor Ignorance, you are ignorant of. Wake up then! See your own wretchedness and run to the Lord Jesus, and you'll be delivered from condemnation by His righteousness—which is the righteousness of God, for He himself is God."[19]

Ignorance then said, "You go so fast I can't keep up with you. Go on ahead of me. I must stay a distance behind."

Then Christian and Hopeful said:

Well, Ignorance, wilt thou yet foolish be
To slight good Counsel, ten times given thee?
And if thou yet refuse it, thou shalt know,
E're long, the Evil of thy doing so.
Remember, man, in time; stoop, do not fear;
Good Counsel taken well saves; therefore hear.
But if thou yet shalt slight it, thou wilt be
The Loser, Ignorance, I'll warrant thee.

Then Christian addressed himself like this to his friend: "Well, come, my good Hopeful. I see that you and I must walk by ourselves again."

So I saw in my dream that they went on at a fast pace in front, and as for Ignorance, he came hobbling after. Then Christian said to his companion, "I pity this poor man a great deal, for it will certainly go ill with him at the last."

"Alas!" sighed Hopeful. "There's an abundance of people in our town in his condition—whole families, even whole streets, and that of Pilgrims, too. And if there be so many in our parts, how many do you think there must be in the place where he was born?"

"Indeed," agreed Christian, "The Word says He has blinded their eyes lest they should see, and so forth.[20] But now that we are by ourselves, what do you think of such men? Do you think they have at any time felt convicted of sin and consequently felt that their manner of living is dangerous?"

"No," replied Hopeful. "You answer that question yourself, for you are the older and most experienced man."

Christian complied, "Then I say, sometimes—as I think—they may, but being naturally ignorant, they don't understand that such convictions work for their good. They desperately seek, therefore, to stifle them and presumptuously continue to flatter themselves in the way of their own hearts."

Hopeful then responded, "I believe, as you say, that fear works much for people's good and helps to prepare them to start their Pilgrimage."

"Without a doubt, it does if it be a proper fear," said Christian, "for the Word says, 'The fear of the Lord is the beginning of wisdom.'"[21]

"How would you describe proper fear?" asked Hopeful.

"True or proper fear is recognized by three things," answered Christian: "One—by its rise, for it's caused by saving convictions of sin. Two—it drives the soul to lay a firm hold of Christ for Salvation. Three—it produces and continues in the soul a great reverence for God, His Word, and His ways, keeping the soul tender and making it afraid to turn from them—to the right hand or to the left—toward anything that may dishonor God, break its peace, grieve the Spirit, or cause the enemy to speak reproachfully."

"Well said," commented Hopeful. "I believe you've said the truth. Have we now almost gotten past the Enchanted Ground?"

"Why? Are you weary of this discussion?" asked Christian.

"No, truthfully," answered Hopeful. "I just want to know where we are."

"We have no more than two miles farther to go through it," said Christian, "but let's return to our discussion. Now the ignorant don't know that such convictions—which tend to make them fear—are for their good. And, therefore, they seek to stifle them."[22]

"How do they seek to stifle them?" asked Hopeful.

Christian explained, "First—they think those fears are caused by the Devil—though they are actually caused by God—and thinking so, they resist them as things that directly work toward their overthrow. Second—they also think these fears work toward spoiling their faith when—alas for them, poor individuals that they are!—they have none at all! Therefore, they harden their hearts against them. Third—they presume they shouldn't fear, and, therefore, in contempt of them they become presumptuously confident. Fourth—they see those fears work to take away from them their pitiful old self-holiness. Therefore, they resist them with all their might."

"I know something of this myself," said Hopeful. "Before I knew myself, it was like that with me."

"Well," said Christian, "we'll leave our neighbor Ignorance by himself for now and deal with another profitable question."

"Gladly," said Hopeful, "but you shall still begin."

"Well then," said Christian, "didn't you know a temporary in your parts about ten years ago who was a bold man in religion then?"

"Know him!" exclaimed Hopeful. "Yes, he lived in Graceless, a town about two miles from Honesty. He lived next door to one named Turnback."

"Right," agreed Christian. "He lived under the same roof

with him. Well, that man was much awakened once. I believe that at that time he had some realization of his sins and of the wages that he owed for them."

"I think the same," said Hopeful, "for—my house not being more than three miles from him—he would often come to me with much weeping. I truly pitied the man and was not completely without hope for him. But, as one may see, it's not every one who cries, 'Lord, Lord . . .'"²³

Christian went on, "He told me once that he was resolved to go on Pilgrimage, as we do now; but all of a sudden he became acquainted with one named Saveself, and then he became a stranger to me."

"Now since we're talking about him," said Hopeful, "let's inquire a little into the reason of his sudden backsliding and that of others like him."

"It may be very profitable," remarked Christian, "but you begin."

"Well then," said Hopeful, "there are, in my judgment, four reasons for it: One—though the consciences of such people are awakened, their minds are still not changed. Therefore, when the power of guilt wears off, that which provoked them to be religious ceases; so they naturally turn to their own course again, just as we see the dog that is sick of what he has eaten— as long as its sickness prevails—vomits and casts it all up. It doesn't do this of a free mind—if we may say a dog has a mind—but because it troubles its stomach. But then, when its sickness is over and its stomach is eased, its desires being not at all alienated from its vomit, it turns itself about and licks it all up. And so it is that is written, 'A dog returns to its vomit.'²⁴ I say this about being hot for Heaven by virtue only of the sense and fear of the torments of Hell: as their sense of Hell and the fears of damnation chill and cool, so their desire for Heaven and salvation also cools. So then, it comes to pass that when their guilt and fear is gone, their desires for Heaven and happiness die, and they return to their course again."

"Two," continued Hopeful, "another reason is that they have slavish fears, which master over them. I speak now of the fears they have of people, for 'fear of man will prove to be a snare.'[25] So then, though they seem to be hot for Heaven as long as the flames of Hell are about their ears, yet when that terror has subsided a little they begin to foster second thoughts, such as, that it's good to be wise and not run—for all they know—the risk of losing everything or at least of bringing themselves into unavoidable and unnecessary troubles. Therefore, they fall in with the world again."

"Three," maintained Hopeful, "the shame that accompanies religion also lies as a roadblock in their way. They're proud and haughty, and religion is low and contemptible in their eye. When they've lost their sense of Hell and wrath to come, they return again to their former course."

"Four," stated Hopeful, "experiencing guilt and meditating upon terror is distressing to them. They don't like to see their misery before they come into it, though perhaps the sight of it at first—if they loved that sight—might make them run to where the righteous flee and are safe.[26] But, as I hinted before, because they shun the thoughts of guilt and terror, therefore when they once are rid of their awakenings about the terrors and wrath of God, they gladly harden their hearts and choose such ways as will harden them more and more."

"You're pretty near the crux of the matter," said Christian, "for the bottom of it all is their lack of a change in their mind and will. Therefore, they're simply like the felon who stands before the judge; he shakes and trembles and seems to repent most seriously, but the bottom of it all is the fear of the hangman's rope, not that he has any loathing for the crime. This is evident because, set this man free, and he'll be a thief and a rascal still. But, if his mind was changed, he would be otherwise."

"I've shown you the reasons of their going back," said Hopeful. "Now you show me the manner in which they do it."

"So I will, gladly," responded Christian. "First—they direct their thoughts—all that they can—away from the remembrance of God, death, and judgment to come.[27] Second—they gradually quit performing private duties, such as room-prayer,[28] curbing their desires,[29] watching,[30] sorrow for sin,[31] and the like.

Third—they shun the company of lively and warm Christians.[32] Fourth—then they grow cold to public duty such as hearing,[33] reading,[34] and godly consultation. Fifth—in a devilish manner they begin to pick holes, as we say, in the coats of some of the godly for some weakness they've seen in them, so they may have a seemingly good reason to throw religion behind their backs.[35] Sixth—they begin to adhere to and associate themselves with worldly, careless, and unrestrained people.[36] Seventh— they give way to doing worldly and unrestrained things in secret and are glad if they can see such things in anyone who is recognized as an honest person, so they may more boldly do it through their example.[37] Eighth—after this, they begin to play with little sins openly. Ninth—then being hardened, they show themselves as they are. Thus being launched again into the gulf of misery, they perish eternally in their own deceptions unless a miracle of grace prevents it."

NOTES ON CHAPTER 19

[1]   James 2:19.

[2]   **Proverbs 13:4**.

[3]   **Proverbs 28:26**.

[4]   Jeremiah 17:9.

[5]   **Romans 3:10**.

[6]   Ecclesiastes 7:20; Psalm 14:1, 53:1.

[7]   **Genesis 6:5**.

[8]   Genesis 8:21.

[9]   Deuteronomy 32:5; **Proverbs 2:15**; Philippians 2:15; **Psalm 125:5**.

[10] **Romans 3:17**; Isaiah 42:16.

[11] Psalm 94:11; Matthew 9:4, 12:25; Luke 5:22, 6:8, 11:17.

[12] Hebrews 4:12-13.

[13] Isaiah 64:6.

[14] Romans 2:5; Revelation 16:14.

[15] Cities of refuge were established under the Law for a place where an individual guilty of killing another could flee

in order to obtain fair treatment in a court of law. Numbers 35:6-34; also Joshua 20:1-6. The city of refuge was one's only hope to be delivered from "the avenger of blood." And so it is: Christ is our only hope to find refuge and to be delivered from the death sentence that sin prescribes. Psalm 57:1; Matthew 23:37.

16 Ezekiel 16:8.
17 **Matthew 11:27**; Galatians 1:15-16; **1 Corinthians 12:3**.
18 **Ephesians 1:17-19**.
19 Colossians 2:9.
20 John 12:40; Isaiah 6:9-10.
21 **Psalm 111:10; Proverbs 9:10, 1:7; Job 28:28**.
22 **Why ignorant persons stifle convictions.**
23 Matthew 7:21-23.
24 **2 Peter 2:22.**
25 **Proverbs 29:25**.
26 Proverbs 18:10.
27 Luke 22:19; 1 Corinthians 11:23-26; 2 Timothy 2:11-14; 2 Peter 1:12-15; Romans 1:28; Jude 17.
28 Matthew 6:6.
29 Galatians 5:16-24; 1 Peter 1:14, 2:11.
30 Matthew 24:42-44, 26:41; Mark 13:32-37, 14:38; Luke 12:35-40, 21:34-36; Acts 20:31; 1 Corinthians 16:13; Colossians 4:2; 1 Thessalonians 5:4-6; Revelation 3:2-3.
31 Psalm 51.
32 Hebrews 10:25.
33 Proverbs 28:9; Acts 28:27.
34 2 Kings 22:1-13 The public reading of God's Word ceased in Israel, which led to the Book being lost and contributed to their backsliding as a nation.
35 The religious leaders during Christ's time on earth were guilty of this act time and time again as they attempted to dismiss themselves from true religion taught by Christ. But even the Roman Procurator of Palestine could find no guilt in Him. Luke 23:1-25; John 18:28-40.
36 Proverbs 13:20; 1 Corinthians 5:9-11; 2 Thessalonians 3:14-15.
37 Psalm 90:8; Ecclesiastes 12:14; Luke 8:17; Romans 2:16.

20

THE PILGRIMS ENTER CELESTIAL CITY

NOW I SAW IN my dream that by this time the Pilgrims had gotten over the Enchanted Ground and entered into the country of Beulah,[1] whose air was very sweet and pleasant. With the Way lying directly through it, they comforted themselves there for a while. Yes, here they heard continually the singing of birds. Every day they saw the flowers appear on the earth and heard the voice of the turtledove in the land.[2]

In this country the sun shines night and day, and for that reason it was beyond the Valley of the Shadow of Death and also out of the reach of Giant Despair. Neither could they as much as see Doubting Castle from this place. Here they were within sight of the City where they were going. Also, some of the inhabitants of the country met them here, for in this land the Shining Ones commonly walked because it was next to the borders of Heaven. Also in this land, the contract between the Bride and the Bridegroom was renewed. Yes, here, "as a bridegroom rejoices over his bride, so will your God rejoice

Christian and Hopeful enter the Country of Beulah

over you."[3] They had no lack of corn and wine here, for in this place they met with an abundance of what they had sought in all their Pilgrimage.[4] Here, they heard voices from out of the City, loud voices, saying, "Say to the Daughter of Zion, 'See, your Savior comes! See, his reward is with him.'"[5] Here, all the inhabitants of the country called them "the Holy People, the Redeemed of the Lord, ...sought after,"[6] and so forth.

As they walked in this land, they rejoiced more than in parts more remote from the Kingdom to which they were headed; and, drawing near, they had an even more perfect view of the City. It was built of pearls and precious stones; and its streets were paved with gold.[7] Because of the natural glory of the City and the reflection of the sunbeams upon it, Christian fell sick with desire. Hopeful also had a fit or two of the same disease. Because of this, they lay there awhile, and because of their pangs cried out, "If you see my beloved, tell Him that I am lovesick."[8]

But being a little strengthened and better able to bear their sickness, they walked on their way and came yet nearer and nearer where there were orchards, vineyards, and gardens; and their gates opened onto the Highway. Now as they came up to these places, the Gardener stood in the path. To him the Pilgrims asked, "Whose pleasing vineyards and gardens are these?"

He answered, "They are the King's and are planted here for His own enjoyment and also for the comfort of Pilgrims." So the Gardener led them into the vineyards and invited them to refresh themselves with delicacies.[9] He also showed them there the King's walks and the arbors where He delighted to be, and they stayed here and slept.

Now I saw in my dream that they talked more in their sleep at this time than they ever did in all their journey. Reflecting upon it, the Gardener said to me, "Why do you ponder the matter? It's the nature of the fruit of the grapes of these vineyards to go down so sweetly as to cause 'the lips of those that are asleep to speak.'"[10]

I saw that when they awoke, they gave thought to going up to the City; but, as I said, the reflection of the sun upon the

City (for it was of pure gold)[11] was so extremely glorious that they could not as yet with an open face look at it except through an instrument made for that purpose. So, as they went on, I saw that two men met them. The men's clothing shined like gold, and their faces shone as the light.[12]

These men asked the Pilgrims where they came from, and they told them. They also asked them where they had stayed, and with what difficulties and dangers, what comforts and pleasures they had met in the Way; and they told them. Then the men who met them said, "You have only two more difficulties to experience, and then you are in the City."

Christian and his companion then asked the men to go along with them, so they told them they would. "But," they said, "you must obtain it by your own faith." So I saw in my dream that they went on together until they came within sight of the gate.

Now I saw further that between them and the gate was a River. But there was no bridge to go over, and the River was very deep. At the sight of this River, therefore, the Pilgrims were much astounded, but the men who went with them said, "You must go through, or you can't arrive at the gate."[13] The Pilgrims then began to inquire if there was another way to the gate, to which they replied, "Yes, but there have been none but two, Enoch[14] and Elijah,[15] who've been permitted to tread that path since the foundation of the world, nor shall there be until the Last Trumpet shall sound."[16]

Then the Pilgrims (especially Christian) began to despair in their minds. They looked this way and that but could find no way by which they might escape the River. Then they asked the men if the waters were all the same depth. They said, "No." Yet they could not help them in any case, "For," they said, "you shall find it deeper or shallower as you believe in the King of the place."

They then turned to the water, and, upon entering, Christian began to sink. He cried out to his good friend Hopeful, "I'm sinking in deep waters! The breakers go over my head! All the waves go over me. Selah"[17]

Hopeful responded, "Be of good cheer, my Brother! I feel the bottom, and it is good."

Then Christian said, "Ah, Friend! The cords of death have entangled me![18] I'll not see the land that flows with milk and honey!"[19]

With that, a great darkness and horror fell upon Christian, so that he could not see before him. Also, he lost his senses to a great degree, so that he could neither remember nor rationally talk of any of those sweet refreshments he had experienced in the course of his Pilgrimage. But all the words that he spoke tended to reveal that he had horror of mind and fear in his heart that he would die in that River and never obtain entrance in at the gate.

Here also, as those who stood by perceived, he had many troublesome thoughts of the sins he had committed both since and before he began to be a Pilgrim. It was also observed that he was troubled with apparitions of hobgoblins and evil spirits, and he would so refer to it by words ever and again.

Therefore, Hopeful had much commotion there keeping his brother's head above water. Yes, sometimes he would really be down, and then after a while he would rise up again half dead. Hopeful also would endeavor to comfort him, saying, "Brother, I see the gate and people standing by to receive us!"

But Christian would answer, "It's you! It's you they wait for! You have been Hopeful ever since I knew you!"

"And so have you!" said Hopeful to Christian.

"Ah, Brother," exclaimed Christian, "surely if I was right, He would rise now to help me! But because of my sins He has brought me into the snare and left me!"[20]

Then Hopeful said, "My Brother, you've quite forgotten the text where it is said of the wicked, 'They have no struggles; their bodies are healthy and strong. They are free from the burdens common to man.'[21] These troubles and distresses that you go through in these waters are no sign that God has forsaken you, but they're sent to try you, to see whether you will call to mind that which you've received before of His goodness and depend upon Him in your distresses."[22]

Then I saw in my dream that Christian was in contemplation for a while, to whom Hopeful also added these words, "Be of good cheer! Jesus Christ makes you whole!"

And with that, Christian broke out with a loud voice, "Oh, I see Him again! and He tells me, 'When you pass through the waters, I will be with you; and when you pass through the rivers, they will not sweep over you.'"[23]

Then they both took courage, and after that, the enemy was as still as a stone until they had gone over. Christian, therefore, presently found ground to stand upon, and so it followed that the rest of the River was just shallow. Thus, they got over.

Now upon the other bank of the River, they again saw the two Shining Men waiting for them. Therefore, as the two Pilgrims came up out of the River, the Men greeted them, saying, "We're ministering spirits sent to serve those who will inherit salvation."[24] Thus, they went along toward the gate.

Now, you must note that the City stood upon a mighty hill, but the Pilgrims went up that hill with ease because they had these two Men to lead them up by the arms. Also, they had left their mortal garments behind them in the River, for though they went in with them, they came out without them. They went up here with much agility and speed, though the foundation upon which the City was built was higher than the clouds. They went up, therefore, through the region of the air, sweetly talking as they safely got over the River and had such glorious companions to attend them.

The talk they had with the Shining Ones was about the glory of the place. They told them the beauty and glory of it was inexpressible. "There," they said, "is Mount Zion, the Heavenly Jerusalem, thousands upon thousands of angels, and the spirits of righteous men made perfect.[25] You are now going to the Paradise of God, in which you'll see the Tree of Life and eat of the never-fading fruits of it.[26] And when you arrive there, white robes shall be given you, and every day your walk and talk shall be with the King, even all the days of eternity.[27] You'll not see there again such things as you saw when you were in the lower region upon the earth[28]—that is, sorrow, sickness, affliction, and death, 'for the old order of things has passed away.'"[29]

The Shining Ones continued, "You are now going to Abraham, Isaac, and Jacob and to the prophets, men whom God has taken away from the evil to come and who are now resting upon their beds. Each one walks in His righteousness."[30]

The Pilgrims then asked, "What must we do in the holy place?"

To which was answered, "You must receive the comfort of all your toil and have joy for all your sorrow.[31] You must reap what you've sown, even the fruit of all your prayers, tears, and sufferings for the King while you were in the Way.[32] In this place you must wear crowns of gold[33] and enjoy the perpetual sight and vision of the Holy One, 'for we shall see Him as He is.'[34] There, you shall also serve Him continually with praise, shouting, and thanksgiving, even Him whom you desired to serve in the world, though with much difficulty because of the weakness of your flesh."[35]

"There," continued the Shining Ones, "your eyes shall be delighted with seeing Him,[36] and your ears with hearing the voice of the Mighty One. There you'll enjoy again your friends who have gone there before you.[37] And there you'll receive with joy everyone who follows after you into the holy place. Also, there you'll be clothed with glory and majesty, and put into a carriage that is fit to ride out in with the King of Glory.[38] When He comes with the sound of a trumpet in the clouds, as upon the wind, you'll come with Him.[39] Yes, and when He passes sentence upon all the workers of iniquity, be they angels or men, you'll also have a voice in that judgment because they were His and your enemies.[40] Also, when He shall again return to the City, you'll go too with the sound of a trumpet to be with Him forever."[41]

Now while they were thus drawing closer to the gate, a company of the Heavenly Host came out to meet them. The two Shining Ones said to the host, "These are the men who loved our Lord when they were in the world and who've left everything for His Holy Name. He has sent us to fetch them, and we've brought them this far on their desired journey, so they may go in and look their Redeemer in the face with joy."

Then the Heavenly Host gave a great shout, saying, "'Blessed are those who are invited to the wedding supper of the Lamb!'"[42]

At this time, there also came out to meet them several of the King's Trumpeters clothed in white and shining clothing; and with melodic and loud noises, they made even the heavens echo with their sound. These trumpeters saluted Christian and his friend with ten thousand welcomes from the world, and they did this with shouting and the sound of trumpets.

This done, they compassed them round about on every side. Some went ahead of them, some behind, some on the right hand, and some on the left (as it were, to guard them as they passed through the upper regions). As they went, they sounded continually with harmonious noise in notes on high, so that to them who could see it, the very sight of it was as if Heaven itself had come down to meet them.

Thus they walked on together, and as they walked on and on, these trumpeters (even with joyful sounds) would, by mixing their music with looks and gestures, continually signify to Christian and his brother how welcome they were into their company and with what gladness they came out to meet them.

And now, being swallowed up with the sight of angels, and with hearing their melodic notes, these two men seemed to be in Heaven before they got there. Here also, the City itself was in view, and they thought they heard all the bells in it ring to welcome them into it. But above all, they had such warm and joyful thoughts about having their own dwelling there with such a company forever and ever. Oh, what tongue or pen can express their glorious joy! Thus, they came up to the gate.

Now when they had come up to the gate, written over it were letters of gold: "Blessed are those who wash their robes, that they may have the right to the tree of life and may go through the gates into the city."[43]

Then I saw in my dream that the Shining Ones told them to call at the gate. And when they did, some from above looked over the gate. They were Enoch, Moses, Elijah, and others. It was said to them, "These Pilgrims have come from the City of Destruction because of the love they bring to the King of this

The King's Trumpeters salute the Pilgrims

place." And then, each of the Pilgrims gave to them the Certificate that he had received in the beginning. The Certificates then were carried in to the King, who, when He had read them, said, "Where are the men?"

It was answered Him, "They're standing outside the gate."

The King then commanded, "Open the gates that the righteous nation may enter, the nation that keeps faith."[44]

I saw in my dream that these two men went in at the gate, and as they entered, they were transfigured and had clothing put on them that shined like gold. There were also those who met them and gave to them harps and crowns: the harps with which to praise, and the crowns in token of honor. Then I heard in my dream all the bells of the City ringing again for joy, and it was said to them, "Come and share in your Master's happiness."[45]

I also heard the men themselves as they sang with a loud voice, saying, "To him who sits on the throne and to the Lamb be praise and honor and glory and power, for ever and ever!"[46]

Just as the gates were opened to let the men in, I looked in after them; and the City shined like the sun. The streets were paved with gold, and in them walked many people with crowns on their heads, palms in their hand, and golden harps with which to sing praises. There were also those who had wings, and they answered one another without ceasing, saying, "Holy, holy, holy is the Lord God Almighty."[47]

After that, they shut the gates; and, when I saw it, I wished myself to be among them.

Now, while I was gazing upon all these things, I turned my head to look back and saw Ignorance coming up to the riverside. He got over quickly and without half the difficulty that the other two men met with, for it happened that a man was there named Vainhope, a ferryman. And with his boat he helped him over. So, like the others, I saw him ascend the hill to go up to the gate, but he went alone, neither did anyone meet him with the least encouragement.

When he arrived at the gate, he looked up to the writing that was above it and then began to knock, supposing that entrance should have been quickly provided to him. The men who looked over the top of the gate asked him, "Where have you come from, and what do you want?"

Ignorance answered, "I've eaten and drunk in the presence of the King, and He has taught in our streets."[48]

Then they asked him for his Certificate, so they might go in and show it to the King.

He fumbled in his coat for one and found none.

Then they said, "Have you none?"

But the man didn't answer.

When they told the King, He would not come down to see him but instead commanded the two Shining Ones who had conducted Christian and Hopeful into the City to bind Ignorance hand and foot and take him away.[49] Then they picked Ignorance up and carried him through the air to the door that I had seen in the side of the hill and put him in there.

Then I saw that there was a way to Hell, even from the very gates of Heaven, as well as from the City of Destruction.

So, I awoke . . . and, yes, it was a dream.

NOTES ON CHAPTER 20

1 **Isaiah 62:4.**
2 **Song of Songs 2:11-12.**
3 **Isaiah 62:5.**
4 **Isaiah 62:8-9.**
5 **Isaiah 62:11.**
6 **Isaiah 62:12.**
7 Revelation 21:15-21.
8 Song of Solomon 5:8 (KJV).
9 **Deuteronomy 23:24.**
10 Song of Solomon 7:9 (KJV).
11 **Revelation 21:18.**
12 **2 Corinthians 3:18.**
13 **Death is not welcome to nature, though by it we pass out of this world into glory.**
14 Genesis 5:23-24; Hebrews 11:5.

15   2 Kings 2:11.
16   **1 Corinthians 15:51-52.**
17   Jonah 2:3; Psalm 69:1-2, 42:7; 2 Samuel 22:5.
18   Psalm 18:4, 116:3.
19   Exodus 3:7-8, 13:4-5; Numbers 13:26-27; Joshua 1:2, 11.
20   Ezekiel 17:20.
21   **Psalm 73:4-5.**
22   1 Peter 4:12-13.
23   **Isaiah 43:2.**
24   Hebrews 1:14.
25   **Hebrews 12:22-23.**
26   Genesis 2:9, 3:22; **Revelation 2:7**, 22:2,14-19.
27   **Revelation 3:4**, 19:8.
28   **Revelation 21:1**
29   Revelation 21:4; **Isaiah 65:16-17.**
30   **Isaiah 57:1-2.**
31   Revelation 7:17, 21:4.
32   **Galatians 6:7-9.**
33   Revelation 2:10, 4:4-10, 3:11.
34   **1 John 3:2.**
35   Revelation 19:5-7.
36   Isaiah 33:17.
37   2 Samuel 12:22.
38   Psalm 24:7-10.
39   **Jude 14.**
40   **Daniel 7:9-10; 1 Corinthians 6:2-3**; Revelation 20:11-15.
41   **1 Thessalonians 4:13-17.**
42   **Revelation 19:9.**
43   **Revelation 22:14.**
44   **Isaiah 26:2.**
45   Matthew 25:21-23.
46   **Revelation 5:13.**
47   Revelation 4:8.
48   Luke 13:26, Luke 13:22-28.
49   Matthew 22:13.

THE CONCLUSION

Now, READER, I HAVE told my Dream to thee,
See if thou canst Interpret it to me,
Or to Thyself, or Neighbour; but take heed
Of mis-interpreting; for that, instead
Of doing Good, will but thyself abuse:
By misinterpreting, Evil ensues.

Take heed also that thou be not extreme
In playing with the out-side of my dream:
Nor let my Figure or similitude
Put thee into a Laughter, or a Feud;
Leave this for Boys and Fools; but as for thee,
Do thou the Substance of my matter see.

Put by the curtains, look within my vail,
Turn up my metaphors, and do not fail;
There, if thou seekest them, such things thou'lt find
As will be helpful to an honest mind.
What of my dross thou findest here, be bold
To throw away, but yet preserve the Gold.
What if my Gold be wrapped up in ore?
None throws away the Apple for the Core.
But if thou shalt cast all away as vain,
I know not but 'twill make me dream again.

The End of the First Part

213

JOHN BUNYAN'S WAY OF SENDING FORTH HIS SECOND PART OF THE PILGRIM

GO NOW, MY LITTLE Book, to every place,
Where my first Pilgrim has but shewn his Face:
Call at their door: If any say, Who's there?
Then answer thou, Christiana is here.
If they bid thee Come in, then enter thou,
With all thy boys: And then as thou know'st how;
Tell who they are, also from whence they came;
Perhaps they'll know them by their looks or name:
But if they should not, ask them yet again,
If formerly they did not entertain
One Christian a Pilgrim? If they say,
They did, and were delighted in his Way,
Then let them know, that those related were
Unto him: Yea, his Wife and Children are.
Tell them that they have left their House and Home;
Are turned Pilgrims, seek a World to come:

That they have met with Hardships in the Way,
That they do meet with Troubles night and day:
That they have trod on Serpents, fought with Devils,
Have also overcome a many evils.
Yea, tell them also of the next, who have
Of Love to Pilgrimage, been stout and brave
Defenders of that Way, and how they still
Refuse this World, to do their Father's will.

  Go tell them also of those dainty things,
That Pilgrimage unto the Pilgrim brings:
Let them acquainted be too, how they are
Beloved of their King, under his Care;
What goodly Mansions for them he provides,
Tho' they meet with rough Winds and swelling Tides,
How brave a Calm they will enjoy at last,
Who to their Lord, and by his Ways hold fast.

  Perhaps with heart and hand they will embrace
Thee, as they did my firstling, and will grace
Thee, and thy fellows, with such cheer and fare,
As shew will, they of Pilgrims Lovers are.

1. OBJECTION

But how, if they will not believe of me
That I am truly thine; 'cause some there be
That conterfeit the Pilgrim and his Name,
Seek, by Disguise, to seem the very same,
And by that means have brought themselves into
The hands and houses of I know not who.

ANSWER

'Tis true, some have of late to counterfeit
My Pilgrim, to their own, my Title set;
Yea, others half my Name and Title too
Have stitched to their Book, to make them do;
But yet they by their Features do declare
Themselves not mine to be, whose e'er they are.

  If such thou meet'st with, then thine only way
Before them all, is, to Say out thy Say,
In thine own native Language, which no man

Now useth, nor with ease dissemble can.
If, after all, they still of you shall doubt,
Thinking that you, like Gipsies, go about
In naughty wise, the Country to defile,
Or that you seek good people to beguile
With things unwarrantable, send for me,
And I will testify you Pilgrims be;
Yea, I will testify that only you
My Pilgrims are; and that alone will do.

2. OBJECTION

But yet, perhaps, I may inquire for him,
Of those that wish him damned life and limb.
What shall I do, when I at such a door
For Pilgrims ask, and they shall rage the more?

ANSWER

Fright not thyself, my Book, for such bugbears
Are nothing else but Ground for groundless fears,
My Pilgrim's Book has travell'd Sea and Land,
Yet could I never come to understand
That it was slighted or turn'd out of door
By any Kingdom, were they Rich or Poor.
　　In France and Flanders, where men kill each other,
My Pilgrim is esteem'd a Friend, a Brother.
　　In Holland too, 'tis said, as I am told,
My Pilgrim is with some worth more than Gold.
　　Highlanders and Wild Irish can agree,
My Pilgrim should familiar with them be.
'Tis in New England under such advance,
Receives there so much loving contenance,
As to be trim'd, new-cloath'd, and deck'd with gems
That it may shew its features and its limbs,
Yet more, so comely doth my Pilgrim walk,
That of him Thousands daily sing and talk.
　　If you draw nearer Home, it will appear,
My Pilgrim knows no ground of shame or fear;
City and Country will him entertain
With, Welcome, Pilgrim, yea, they can't refrain,
From smiling, if my Pilgrim be but by,
Or shews his head in any Company.
　　Brave Gallants do my Pilgrim hug and love,
Esteem it much, yea, value it above

217

Things of a greater bulk; yea, with delight,
Say, my Lark's leg is better than a Kite.
    Young Ladies, and young Gentlewomen too,
Do no small kindness to my Pilgrim shew;
Their cabinets, their bosoms, and their hearts,
My Pilgrim has, 'cause he to them imparts
His pretty riddles, in such wholsome strains,
As yields them Profit double to their Pains
Of reading; yea, I think I may be bold
To say, some prize him far above their Gold.
    The very Children that do walk the street,
If they do but my Holy Pilgrim meet,
Salute him will, will wish him well, and say,
He is the only stripling of the day.
    They that have never seen him, yet admire
What they have heard of him, and much desire
To have his Company, and hear him tell
Those Pilgrim stories, which he knows so well.
    Yea, some who did not love him at the first,
Gut call'd him Fool and Noddy, say they must,
Now they have seen and heard him, him commend;
And to those whom they love, they do him send.
    Wherefore, my Second Part, thou need'st not be
Afraid to shew thy head; none can hurt thee,
That wish but well to him that went before,
'Cause thou com'st after with a second store,
Of things as good, as rich, as profitable,
For Young, for Old, for Stagg'ring, and for Stable.

3. OBJECTION

But some there be that say, He laughs too loud;
And some do say, His Head is in a Cloud.
Some say, His Words and Stories are so dark,
They know not how by them to find his mark.

ANSWER

One may (I think) say, Both his laughs and cries
May well be guess'd at by his wat'ry eyes.
Some things are of that nature, as to make
One's Fancy checkle, while his Heart doth ake;
When Jacob saw his Rachel with the sheep,
He did at the same time both kiss and weep.
    Whereas some say, A Cloud is in his Head,

218

That doth but shew how Wisdom's covered
With its own mantles, and to stir the mind
To a search after what it fain would find.
Things that seem to be hid in words obscure,
Do but the Godly mind the more allure,
To study what those sayings should contain,
That speak to us in such a cloudy strain.

I also know a dark Similitude
Will on the Fancy more itself intrude,
And will stick faster in the Heart and Head,
Than things from Similies not borrowed.

Wherefore, my Book, let no discouragement
Hinder thy travels: Behold, thou art sent
To Friends, not foes, to Friends that will give place
To thee, thy Pilgrims, and thy Words embrace.

Beside, what my first Pilgrim left conceal'd,
Thou, my brave Second Pilgrim hast reveal'd;
What Christian left lock'd up, and went his Way,
Sweet Christiana opens with her Key.

4. OBJECTION

But some love not the method of your first;
Romance they count it, throw't away as dust.
If I should meet with such, What should I say?
Must I slight them as they slight me, or nay?

ANSWER

My Christiana, if with such thou meet,
By all means in all Loving wise them greet;
Render them not reviling for revile;
But if they frown, I prithee on them smile:
Perhaps 'tis Nature, or some ill report,
Has made them thus despise, or thus retort.

Some love no cheese, some love no fish, and some
Love not their Friends, nor their own house or Home.
Some [flinch] at pig, slight chicken, love not fowl,
More than they love a cuckow, or an owl.
Leave such, my Christiana, to their Choice,
And seek those, who to find thee will rejoice;
By no means strive, but in all humble wise,
Present thee to them in thy Pilgrim's guise.

Go then, my little Book, and shew to all
That entertain, and bid thee Welcome shall,

219

What thou shalt keep close, shut up from the rest,
And wish what thou shalt shew them, may be blest
To them for good, may make them chuse to be
Pilgrims better by far, than thee or me.

Go then, I say, tell all men who thou art,
Say, I am Christiana, and my part
Is now with my four Sons to tell you what
It is for men to take a Pilgrim's lot.

Go also, tell them who and what they be,
That now do go on Pilgrimage with thee:
Say, Here's my neighbour Mercy, she is one,
That has long time with me a Pilgrim gone:
Come, see her in her Virgin face, and learn
'Twixt idle ones, and Pilgrims, to discern.
Yea, let young Damsels learn of her to prize
The World which is come, in any wise:
When little tripping maidens follow God,
And leave all doting Sinners to his Rod;
'Tis like those days wherein the young ones cry'd
Hosanna, to whom old ones did deride.

Next tell them of old Honest, who you found
With his white hairs treading the Pilgrim's ground
Yea, tell them how plain-hearted this man was,
How after his good Lord he bare his Cross:
Perhaps with some gray head this may prevail
With Christ to fall in Love, and Sin bewail.

Tell them also, how Master Fearing went
On Pilgrimage, and how the time he spent
In solitariness, with fears and cries;
And how, at last, he won the Joyful Prize.
He was a good man, tho' much down in spirit;
He is a good man, and doth Life inherit.

Tell them of Master Feeble-mind also,
Who, not before, but still behind would go;
Shew them also how he had like been slain,
And how one Great-Heart did his life regain:
This man was true of Heart, tho' weak in Grace,
One might true Godliness read in his face.

Then tell them of Master Ready-to-halt,
A man with Crutches, but much without fault,
Tell them how Master Feeble-mind and he
Did love, and in Opinions much agree.

And let all know, tho' Weakness was their chance,
Yet sometimes one would Sing, the other Dance.
    Forget not Master Valiant-for-the-Truth,
That man of courage, tho' a very Youth:
Tell every one his spirit was so stout,
No man could ever make him face about;
And how Great-Heart and he could not forbear,
But put down Doubting-Castle, slay Despair.
    Overlook not Master Despondency,
Nor Much-afraid his daughter, tho' they lie
Under such mantles, as may make them look
(With some) as if their God had them forsook.
They softly went, but sure, and at the End
Found that the Lord of Pilgrims was their Friend.
When thou hast told the World of all these things;
Then turn about, my Book, and touch these strings;
Which, if but touched, will such musick make,
They'll make a Cripple dance, a Giant quake.
    Those Riddles that lie couch'd within thy breast,
Freely propound, expound: And for the rest
Of thy mysterious lines, let them remain
For those whose nimble Fancies shall them gain.
    Now may this little Book a blessing be
To those that love this little Book, and me:
And may its Buyer have no cause to say,
His money is but lost, or thrown away;
Yea, may this Second Pilgrim yield that Fruit
As may with each good Pilgrim's fancy suit;
And may it persuade some that go astray,
To turn their Foot and Heart to the right Way,
Is the Hearty Prayer of

The AUTHOR,
JOHN BUNYAN.

PART 2

THE PILGRIMAGE OF CHRISTIANA, HER CHILDREN, AND HER FRIENDS

Christiana in the City of Destruction

21

CHRISTIANA BEGINS HER PILGRIMAGE

COURTEOUS COMPANIONS, SOME TIME ago it was profitable for you and pleasant to me to tell you the dream I had of Christian the Pilgrim and of his dangerous journey toward the Celestial Country. I also told you what I saw concerning his wife and children and how unwilling they were to go with him on the Pilgrimage, so much so that he was forced to go on his journey without them. He dared not run the danger of that judgment that he feared would come by staying with them in the City of Destruction. Therefore, as I showed you then, he left them and departed.[1]

Now, through the multiplicity of business, it just so has happened that I have been much hindered and kept back from my customary travels into those parts where he went. Until now I could not find an opportunity to make further inquiry into the lives of those he left behind, so I might give you an account of them. But lately, having had some concerns that way, I went down in that direction again; and having taken up my lodging in the woods about a mile away from the place, as I slept, I dreamed again.

As I was in my dream, I saw an aged gentleman come by where I lay; and, because he was to go part of the way I was traveling, I thought I got up and went with him. So, as we walked, it was as if we began discussing things (as travelers usually do), and our talk happened to be about Christian and his travels. Thus I began talking with the old man:

"Sir," I asked, "what town is that there below on the left side of our path?"

Then Mr. Sagacity (for that was his name) said, "It's the City of Destruction, a populous place but filled with a very ill-conditioned and idle sort of people."

"I thought it was that city," I said. "I went through that town once myself. Therefore, I know this report you give of it is true."

"Too true," said Mr. Sagacity. "I wish I could tell the truth by speaking better of those who dwell there."

"Well, Sir," I said, "then I perceive you to be a well-meaning man and therefore one who takes pleasure in the hearing and telling of that which is good. Please, did you ever hear what happened to a man some time ago in this town who went on a Pilgrimage up toward the higher regions? His name was Christian."

"Hear of him!" exclaimed Sagacity. "Yes, and I also heard of the molestations, troubles, wars, captivities, cries, groans, frights, and fears that he encountered and had in his journey. Besides, I must tell you, all our country rings of him. There are few houses that have heard of him and his doings which haven't sought after and gotten the records of his Pilgrimage. Yes, I think I may say that his hazardous journey has won many well-wishers over to his ways, for although he was a fool in every man's mouth when he was here, yet now that he is gone he is highly commended of all. For it's said that he lives bravely where he is. Yes, many of those who are resolved never to run his hazards yet have their mouths watering at his gains."

I said, "If they think anything that is true, they may very well think he lives well where he is, for he now lives at and in the Fountain of Life.[2] And he possesses what he has without labor and sorrow, for there is no grief mixed with it. But, please, what do people say about him?"

"Say!" exclaimed Mr. Sagacity again. "The people talk strangely about him. Some say he now walks in white,[3] that he has a chain of gold about his neck, or that he has on his head a crown of gold set with pearls. Others say the Shining Ones who sometimes showed themselves to him during his journey have become his companions, and that he is just as familiar with them in the place where he is as one neighbor is with another here. Besides, it's confidently affirmed concerning him, that the King of the place where he is already has bestowed upon him a very rich and pleasant dwelling at court[4] and that every day he eats and drinks and walks and talks with Him[5] and receives smiles and favors there from Him who is Judge of All."[6]

"Moreover," continued Sagacity, "it is expected by some that his Prince, the Lord of that country, will soon come into these parts and will desire to know the reason—if they can give any—why his neighbors treated him so lightly and made fun of him so much when they saw that he would be a Pilgrim. For they say that he is now held in so much affection by his Prince, and that his King is so much concerned with the indignities that were cast upon Christian when he became a Pilgrim, that He will look upon everyone as if those things were done to himself.[7] And it's not surprising, for it was because of the love Christian had for his Prince that he did what he did."

"I dare say I'm glad of that," said I. "I'm happy for the poor man's sake because now he has rest from his labor,[8] he now reaps with joy the benefit of his tears,[9] and he has now gotten out of range from his enemies and out of the reach of those who hate him. I'm also glad a rumor of these things has spread around the country; for who can tell but what it might have some good effect on some who are left behind. But tell me, Sir, while it's still fresh in my mind, do you hear anything of his wife and children? Poor things, I wonder in my mind what they're doing."

"Who?" questioned Mr. Sagacity. "Christiana and her sons? They're likely to do as well as Christian himself, for though they all played the fool at first and would by no means be persuaded by either Christian's tears or pleading, yet second thoughts worked wonders on them. They've packed up and have gone after him."

"Better and better," I said. "But what? Wife and children and all?"

"It's true," affirmed Mr. Sagacity. "I can give you an accounting of the matter, for I was at the spot at the time and was thoroughly acquainted with the whole affair."

"Then it seems a man may report it as a fact?" I asked in return.

"You need not fear to tell it," said Sagacity. "I mean, they're all gone on Pilgrimage, the good woman and her four boys. And since, as I perceive, we're going a considerable distance together, I'll give you an accounting of the whole matter."

(This is Mr. Sagacity's account.)

Concerning Christiana—for that became her name from the day she and her children took up a Pilgrim's life—after her husband had gone over the River and she could hear from him no more, her thoughts began to work upon her mind. The first reason for it was that she had lost her husband, and the loving bond of that relationship had been utterly broken between them. Nature can do no less than entertain the living with many heavy reflections in the remembrance of the loss of loving relatives. These reflections on her husband, therefore, cost her many tears. But that was not all, for Christiana herself began to consider whether her unbecoming behavior toward her husband was one reason why she saw him no more and for which he was taken away from her.[10]

After this, all her unkind, unnatural, and ungodly manner toward her dear friend came swarming into her mind, and these clogged her conscience and loaded her with guilt. Moreover, she was much broken by calling to remembrance the restless groans, the salty tears, and self-lamenting of her husband, and how she had hardened her heart against all his appeals and

Christiana

loving persuasions—to her and her sons—to go with him. Yes, there was not anything Christian either said to her or did in front of her all the while his burden hung on his back that did not return upon her like a flash of lightning and tear in two the enclosure of her heart, especially that bitter outcry of his, "What must I do to be saved?"[11] which rang most ominously in her ears.

Then Christiana said to her children, "Sons, we're all undone. I've sinned away your father, and he is gone. He wanted to have us with him, but I wouldn't go myself, and I hindered you from receiving life."

With that, the boys all began weeping and cried out to go after their father.

"Oh, that it had been our privilege to go with him!" exclaimed Christiana. "Then it would've fared well with us more than it's likely to now. For although I once imagined foolish things about your father's troubles—that they proceeded out of a silly idea that he had, or that he had been overrun with despondent moods—yet now I can't help but think that they sprang up from another cause, because the Light of Life[12] was given to him. By the help of that, as I see, he has escaped the snares of death."[13]

Then they all wept again and cried out "Oh, grief worth the day!"

The next night, Christiana had a dream, and in the dream she saw as if before her there was opened a broad parchment roll on which was recorded the sum of her ways. And, as she thought, the crimes looked very bad for her. Then she cried out aloud in her sleep, "God, have mercy on me, a sinner."[14] And the little children heard her.

After this, she thought she saw two very ugly beings standing by her bedside and saying, "What shall we do with this woman? She cries out for mercy when awake and asleep. If she's allowed to go on like this, we'll lose her as we lost her husband. Therefore, we must by one way or another seek to take her thoughts off of what shall be hereafter, or else all the world won't be able to stop it, and she'll become a Pilgrim."[15]

Now she awoke in a great sweat, and a trembling was upon her, but after a while she fell back to sleep. Then she thought she saw Christian, her husband, in a place of bliss among many Immortals with a harp in his hand, standing and playing upon it before One who sat on a throne with a rainbow about his head.[16] She also saw as if he bowed his head with his face to the floor under the Prince's feet, saying, "I sincerely thank my Lord and King for bringing me into this place." Then a group of them who stood round about and harped with their harps shouted, but no man living could tell what they said except Christian and his companions.[17]

The next morning, when she was up, had prayed to God, and had talked with her children awhile, someone knocked hard at the door. She called out, saying, "If you come in God's name, come in!"

The Visitor responded, "Amen!" Then he opened the door and greeted her with: "Peace to this house!" When he had done this, he said, "Christiana, do you know why I've come?"

Then she blushed and trembled, and her heart began to feel warm with desire to know where he came from and what his errand was to her.

So he said to her, "My name is Secret. I live with those who are high. It is talked of where I live that you have a desire to go there. Also, there is a report that you're aware of the evil you've formerly done to your husband in hardening your heart against his way and in keeping your babes in their ignorance."

"Christiana," said the Visitor, "the Merciful One has sent me to tell you that He is a God ready to forgive[18] and that He takes delight in multiplying the pardon of offenses.[19] He also wants you to know that He invites you to come into His presence, to His table, and that He will feed you with the fat of His house and with the heritage of Jacob your father."

He continued, "Christian, who was your husband, is there, with thousands more, his companions, ever beholding that Face who ministers life to beholders. And they'll all be glad when they hear the sound of your feet step over your Father's threshold."

At this, Christiana was greatly confounded in herself and bowed her head to the ground.

The Visitor proceeded and said, "Christiana, here also is a letter for you that I've brought from your husband's King."

So she took and opened it, and it smelled of the best perfume[20] and was written in letters of gold. The general content of the letter was that the King wanted her to do as Christian her husband had done, for that was the way to come to His City and to dwell in His presence with joy forever. At this, the good woman was quite overcome, so she cried out to her visitor, "Sir, will you take me and my children with you, so we also may go and worship this King?"

Then the Visitor said, "Christiana! The bitter comes before the sweet. You must enter Celestial City through troubles as did he who went before you. For that reason, I advise you to do as did Christian, your husband. Go across the plain to the Narrow Gate over there, for it stands at the head of the Way up which you must go, and I wish you good speed. Also, I advise you to put this letter next to your heart in your coat so you can read out of it to yourself and to your children until you have it memorized, for it's one of the songs you must sing while you're in the House of your Pilgrimage.[21] Also, you must deliver it at the gate at the end of your journey."

Now I saw in my dream that as Mr. Sagacity told me this story, the old gentleman seemed to be greatly affected with it himself. Moreover, he proceeded, and said:

So Christiana called her sons together and thus began to address herself to them: "My Sons, as you may perceive, of late I've been under much exercise in my soul about the death of your father—not that I doubt at all his happiness, for I'm satisfied now that he is well. I've also been much affected with the thoughts of my own condition and yours, which I really believe is miserable by nature.[22] My treatment of your father in his distress is also a great load on my conscience, for I hardened my own heart and yours against him and refused to go with him on Pilgrimage."

"The thoughts of these things," continued Christiana, "would now kill me outright if it weren't for a dream I had last night and for the encouragement that this stranger gave me this morning. Come, my Children, let's pack up and go to the Gate that leads to the Celestial Country, so we may see your father and be with him and his companions in peace according to the laws of that land."

Then her children burst into tears for joy that the heart of their mother was inclined to do so. Their visitor bid them farewell, and they began to prepare to set out on their journey.

But when they were about to leave, two of the women who were Christiana's neighbors came to the house and knocked at the door. To these she said as before, "If you come in God's name, come in."

At this, the women were stunned, for they were not used to hearing or perceiving this kind of language coming from the lips of Christiana. They came in, but they found the good woman preparing to leave her house.

So they said, "Neighbor, tell us what's the meaning of this?"

Christiana answered and said to the eldest of them, whose name was Mrs. Fearful, "I'm, preparing for a journey." (This Fearful was the daughter of him who met Christian on the Hill of Difficulty and would have had him go back for fear of the lions.)

Mrs. Fearful then asked, "For what journey, pray tell?"

"To go after my good husband," answered Christiana. And with that she began weeping.

"I hope you don't go," said Mrs. Fearful. "Please, for your children's sake, don't cast yourself away in such an unwomanly manner."

"No," said Christiana, "my children will go with me. Not one of them wants to stay behind."

"I wonder in my heart what or who has brought you into this state of mind," said Mrs. Fearful.

"Oh, Neighbor," said Christiana, "if you knew as much as I do, I don't doubt that you would go with me."

"I beg you," said Mrs. Fearful. "What new knowledge do you have that so takes your mind off your friends and tempts you to go no-one-knows-where?"

Then Christiana replied, "I've been sorely afflicted since my husband's departure from me, but especially since he went over the River. But what troubles me most is my rude treatment of him when he was under his distress. Besides, I'm now as he was then, for nothing will save me except going on Pilgrimage. I was dreaming last night that I saw him. Oh, that my soul were with him! He's living in the presence of the King of the Country. He sits and eats with Him at His table. He's become a companion of Immortals and has had a house given him to live in, to which if compared, the best palaces on earth seem to me to be only a dunghill.[23] The Prince of the place has also sent for me with the promise of receiving me if I'll come to Him.[24] His messenger was here just now and brought me a letter inviting me to come." And with that she plucked out her letter and read it, and said to them, "What do you say now to this?"

Mrs. Fearful exclaimed, "Oh, the madness that has possessed you and your husband to cause yourselves such difficulties! I'm sure you've heard what your husband met with, even—in a manner—at the first step he took on his way. Our neighbor Obstinate can yet testify to it, for he went along with him. Yes, and Pliable, too, until they—like wise men—were afraid to go any farther. Over and above that, we heard how he met with the lions, Apollyon, the Shadow of Death, and many other things. Nor should you forget the danger he met with at the Vanity Fair, for if he being a man was so challenged by it, what can you being a poor woman do? Consider also that these four sweet babes are your children, your flesh and your bones. Therefore, although you could be so rash as to cast yourself away, yet for the sake of the fruit of your body, keep yourself at home."

But Christiana said to her, "Don't tempt me, my Neighbor. I've now had placed in my hand the wherewithal to get gain, and I'd be a fool of the greatest size if I should have no heart to take advantage of the opportunity. And as for all these troubles you tell me about—which I'm likely to meet with in the Way— they're so far off from being a discouragement to me that they show me I'm in the right. The bitter must come before the sweet, and that will also make the sweet all the sweeter.[25]

The neighbors

Therefore, since you didn't come to my house in God's name, as I said, I ask you to please leave and not disturb me further."

Then Mrs. Fearful criticized her and said to her friend, "Come, neighbor Mercy, let's leave her in her own hands, since she scorns our counsel and company."

But Mercy was at a quandary and could not so readily comply with her neighbor, and that was for two reasons: First—she was deeply concerned for Christiana, so she said to herself, "I'll go a short way with her and help her." Second—she was deeply concerned over her own soul, for what Christiana had said had taken some hold upon her mind. She therefore said to herself again, "I'll yet have more discussion with this Christiana, and if I find truth and life in what she'll say, I'll also go with her with all my heart."

For that reason, Mercy thus began to reply to her neighbor, Mrs. Fearful: "Neighbor," said Mercy, "I indeed came with you this morning to see Christiana, and since she is—as you see—taking her last farewell of her country, I think I'll walk a short distance with her this sunshiny morning to help her on her way." She didn't tell her of the second reason, but she kept that to herself.

"Well," huffed Mrs. Fearful, "I see you have a mind to go playing the fool, too, but take heed in time and be wise. While we're out of danger, we are out, but when we're in, we're in."

So Mrs. Fearful returned to her house, and Christiana applied herself to her journey. But when Mrs. Fearful had gotten home to her house, she sent for some of her neighbors, that is, Mrs. Flirt,[26] Mrs. Inconsiderate, Mrs. Lightmind, and Mrs. Knownothing. When they arrived at her house she began telling the story of Christiana and of her intended journey. And thus, she began her tale:

"Neighbors," began Mrs. Fearful, "having had little to do this morning, I went to pay Christiana a visit. When I came to the door, I knocked, for you know it's our custom, and she answered, 'If you come in God's name, come in.' But when I went in, I found her preparing herself to leave town, she and also her children. So, I asked her what her meaning was of doing so, and she told me in short that she was now of a mind to go on Pilgrimage as did her husband. She also told me a dream she had and how the King of the country where her husband was had sent her a letter inviting her to come there."

"And what do you think she'll do?" asked Mrs. Knownothing.

"Yes," said Mrs. Fearful, "she'll go, whatever comes of it. I think I know it because of this: My great argument to persuade her to stay home—that is, the troubles she was likely to meet with in the Way—is one great argument she uses to embolden herself on her journey. For she told me in so many words, 'The bitter goes before the sweet; yes, and in doing so it makes the sweet all the sweeter.'"

"Oh, this blind and foolish woman," said Mrs. Flirt. "Won't she take warning by her husband's afflictions? For my part, I believe that if he were here again, he would rest himself in a whole body and never run so many hazards for nothing."

Mrs. Inconsiderate also replied, saying, "Away with such fantastical fools from the town! For my part, I say good riddance of her. Who could live quietly by her if she were to stay where she lives and retain such a mind, for she would either be gloomy or unneighborly, or talk of such matters that no wise person could tolerate. Therefore, for my part, I'll never be sorry about her departure. Let her go, and let someone better come in her place. It's never been a good world since these whimsical fools lived in it."

Then Mrs. Lightmind added, "Come, put this kind of talk away. Yesterday I was at Madam Wanton's,[27] where we were as merry as the maids. Who do you think should be there but me and Mrs. Lovetheflesh and three or four more, with Mr. Lechery, Mrs. Filth, and some others. So, there we had music, dancing, and what else was fitting to complete the pleasure. And I dare say, the Lady herself is an admirable, well-bred gentlewoman, and Mr. Lechery is a handsome fellow."

By this time Christiana had gone on her way, and Mercy went along with her. And as they went, her children being there also, Christiana began to talk:

"And Mercy," said Christiana, "I take this as an unexpected

237

favor that you should set foot out of doors with me to accompany me a short distance on my way."

Then young Mercy said (for she was but a young woman), "If I thought there was a good enough reason to go with you, I would never go near the town any more."

"Well, Mercy," said Christiana, "join with me. I know very well what will be the end of our Pilgrimage. My husband is where he would not leave for all the gold in the Spanish mines. Nor will you be rejected even though you go only upon my invitation. The King who sent for me and my children is one who delights in mercy. Besides, if you want, I'll hire you, and you can go along with me as my servant. Yet, we'll have all things in common between you and me; only go along with me."[28]

"But how can I be sure I'll be accepted?" asked Mercy. "If only I had this hope from one who could confirm it, I'd not pause at all but would go, being helped by Him who can help, even though the way might be never more difficult."

Well, loving Mercy," said Christiana, "I'll tell you what you shall do. Go with me to the Narrow Gate, and there I'll inquire further on your behalf. And if you don't find encouragement there, I'll be content for you to return to your place. I'll also pay you for the kindness you've shown to me and my children by accompanying us in our way as you do."[29]

"Then I'll go there," responded Mercy, "and will take whatever follows. And may the Lord grant that my good fortune will be for the King of Heaven to have compassion for me."

Then Christiana was glad in her heart, not only because she had a companion but also because she had convinced this poor girl to fall in love with her own Salvation. So they went on together, and Mercy began to weep.

Then Christiana said, "Why are you weeping so, Sister?"

"Alas!" exclaimed Mercy. "How can I keep from sorrowing when I rightly consider what a state and condition my poor relatives are in—those who yet remain in our sinful town. And what makes my grief even more heavy is that they have no instructor or anyone to tell them what is to come."

"Feelings of compassion befit a Pilgrim," said Christiana.

"You do for your friends as my good Christian did for me when he left me. He mourned because I wouldn't listen or take him seriously, but his Lord—and ours—gathered up his tears and recorded them.[30] Now both you and I, and these my sweet babes, are reaping the fruit and benefit of them. I have hope, Mercy, that these tears of yours won't be lost, for the Truth has said, 'Those who sow in tears will reap with songs of joy. He who goes out weeping, carrying seed to sow, will return with songs of joy, carrying sheaves with him.'"[31]

Then Mercy said:

Let the most Blessed by my Guide,
If't be his blessed Will,
Unto his Gate, into his Fold,
Up to his Holy Hill:

And let him never suffer me
To swerve or turn aside
From his Free grace, and Holy Ways,
Whate'er shall me betide.

And let him gather them of mine,
That I have left behind;
Lord, make them pray they may be thine,
With all their Heart and Mind.

NOTES ON CHAPTER 21

[1] Matthew 10:34-37; Mark 10:29-30.
[2] Psalm 36:8-9; Revelation 21:6.
[3] **Revelation 3:4 and 6:11.**
[4] **Zechariah 3:7.**
[5] **Luke 14:15.**
[6] Genesis 18:25; Hebrews 12:23; **Jude 14-15.**
[7] **Luke 10:16.**
[8] **Revelation 14:13.**
[9] **Psalm 126:5-6.**

¹⁰ **Mark this, you that are surly persons to your godly relations.**

¹¹ Acts 16:30.

¹² John 8:12.

¹³ Psalm 18:4-6; Proverbs 13:14, 14:27; **James 1:23-25**

¹⁴ **Luke 18:13**.

¹⁵ **This is the purest example of Hell.**

¹⁶ Revelation 4:2-3.

¹⁷ Revelation 14:2-3.

¹⁸ Psalm 86:5; Jeremiah 3:12

¹⁹ **Isaiah 55:7.**

²⁰ **Song of Songs 1:11-12**

²¹ **Psalm 119:54**

²² Ephesians 2:3

²³ **2 Corinthians 5:1-4.**

²⁴ John 6:37.

²⁵ **A pertinent reply to fleshly reasonings.**

²⁶ In the original, Bunyan used the name, "Mrs. Bats-eyes."

²⁷ **Madam Wanton, who was nearly too hard for Faithful in time past.**

²⁸ Acts 4:32.

²⁹ **Christiana allures her to the Gate, which is Christ, and promises to inquire for her there.**

³⁰ Psalm 56:8.

³¹ **Psalm 126:5-6.**

22

CHRISTIANA AND MERCY ENTER THE GATE

NOW MY FRIEND MR. Sagacity proceeded with his narrative:

When Christiana came to the Swamp of Despondence, she began to be in a standstill, for she said, "This is the place where my dear husband was nearly smothered with mud." She also recognized that in spite of the command of the King to make this place good for Pilgrims, yet it was actually worse than before.

So I asked if that was true, and the old Gentleman answered me:

"Yes, too true, for there are many who pretend to be the King's laborers. They say they are in favor of mending the King's Highway, but they bring dirt and manure instead of stones, and so they mar instead of mend it."[1]

Therefore, Christiana and her boys stopped here, but Mercy said, "Come, let's go on. But let's be careful."

They then looked carefully for the steps across the swamp and staggeringly made an attempt to get over it. Yet, Christiana almost fell in, and not just once or twice.

Now they no sooner had gotten across when they heard words that said to them, "Blessed is she who has believed that what the Lord has said to her will be accomplished!"[2]

Then they went on again, and Mercy said to Christiana, "If I had as good grounds to hope for a loving reception at the Narrow Gate as you, I don't think any Swamp of Despondence would discourage me."

"Well," said Christiana, "you know your sorrow, and I know mine. And, good Friend, we'll all experience enough evil before we come to our journey's end. For it couldn't be imagined that the people who desire and plan on attaining such excellent glories as we do, and whose happiness is so envied, would not meet with such fears and concerns over troubles and afflictions with which those who hate us can possibly assault us."

And now Mr. Sagacity left me to dream out my dream by myself. Therefore, I thought I saw Christiana, Mercy, and the boys go each of them up to the Gate. When they arrived, they began a short discussion among themselves about how they should manage their calling at the Gate and what they should say to him who opened it to them. So, it was concluded that since Christiana was the eldest she should knock for entrance and speak for the rest of them to him who opened.

So Christiana began to knock and, as her poor husband did, she knocked and knocked again. But instead of any who answered, they all thought they heard as if a dog came up to them barking. This dog (and a large one, too) made the women and children afraid, nor dared they for a while knock any more for fear the watchdog should attack them. They were greatly confused in their minds, therefore, and did not know what to do. They dared not knock for fear of the dog, and they dared not go back for fear the Keeper of the Gate would see them as they went and be offended with them. At last, they thought of knocking again, and knocked more vehemently than they did at first.

That time, the Keeper of the Gate said, "Who is there?" Then the dog stopped barking, and the Keeper opened to them.

Christiana bowed lowly and said, "Let not our Lord be offended with his handmaidens for knocking at His Princely Gate."

"Where did you come from?" asked the Keeper. "And what is it you want?"

"We came from where Christian came from," said Christiana, "and we've come on the same errand as he—that is, to be, if it pleases you, graciously admitted by this Gate into the path that leads to Celestial City. And in addition, I'm Christiana, once the wife of Christian, who has now gotten above."

With that, the Keeper of the Gate marveled, saying, "What? Has she who a while ago hated that life now become a Pilgrim?"

Then Christiana bowed her head and said, "Yes, and so also have these, my sweet babes."

Then the Keeper took her by the hand and let her in and said, "Let the little children come to me."[3]

And with that, He shut the Gate. This done, He called to a trumpeter who was above, over the Gate, to entertain Christiana with shouting and the sound of the trumpet for joy.[4] So he obeyed and sounded and filled the air with his melodious notes.[5]

Now while all this took place, poor Mercy stood outside trembling and crying for fear that she had been rejected. But when Christiana had gotten admittance for herself and her boys, she then began to make intercession for Mercy.

"My Lord," said Christiana, "I have a companion who yet stands outside. She came here for the same reason as I, but she's one who is much dejected in her mind, for she has come—as she thinks—without being sent for, whereas I was invited by my husband's King to come."

Mercy began to be very impatient, for each minute was as long to her as an hour. Therefore, by knocking at the Gate herself, she prevented Christiana from making a fuller intercession for her. She knocked so loudly that she startled Christiana.[6]

Then the Keeper of the Gate asked, "Who's there?"

And Christiana said, "It's my friend."

So He opened the Gate and looked out, but Mercy had fallen down outside in a swoon. She had fainted and was afraid that no Gate would be opened to her.

Then the Keeper took Mercy by the hand and said, "Young lady, I say to you, get up!"[7]

"Oh, Sir," said Mercy, "I'm faint. There's hardly any life left in me."

But the Keeper answered that a person once said, "'When my life was ebbing away, I remembered you, Lord, and my prayer rose to you, to your holy temple.'[8] Fear not," He said, "but stand upon your feet and tell me where you've come from."

Mercy then answered, "I've come for that unto which I was never invited, as my friend Christiana was. Her Invitation was from the King, and mine was only from her. Therefore, I fear I'm being presumptuous."

"Did she ask you to come with her to this place?" asked the Keeper.

"Yes," answered Mercy, "and as my Lord sees, I've come. And if there is any grace and forgiveness of sins to spare, I beg you that I, your poor handmaid, may be a partaker of them."

Then the Keeper took her again by the hand and led her gently in, saying, "I pray for all them who believe on me regardless of what brings them to me."[9] Then He said to those who stood by, "Fetch something and give it to Mercy to smell to stop her fainting." So they fetched her a bundle of myrrh, and a while later she had revived.

So Christiana, with her boys and Mercy, were received of the Lord at the head of the Way, and were kindly spoken to by Him. Then they yet further said to Him, "We're sorry for our sins and beg of our Lord His pardon and further information about what we must do."

He then said, "I grant pardon by word and deed: by word, in the promise of forgiveness; by deed, in the way I obtained it. Take the first from my lips with a kiss and the other as it shall be revealed."[10]

The Keeper of the Gate takes Mercy by her hand

245

Now I saw in my dream that He spoke to them many good words through which they were greatly gladdened. He also took them up to the top of the Gate and showed them by what deed they were saved and told them then that they would have that sight again to comfort them as they went along in the Way.[11] So He left them awhile below in a summer parlor where they entered into conversation by themselves. And thus Christiana began:

"Oh," exclaimed Christiana, "how glad I am that we have gotten in here!"

"You very well may be," remarked Mercy, "but more than anyone, I have cause to leap for joy."

Christiana then said, "I thought one time as I stood at the Gate—because I had knocked and no one answered—that all our labor had been lost, especially when that ugly mongrel made such a heavy barking against us."

Mercy then responded, "But my worst fears came after I saw you had been taken into His Favor and that I was left behind. I thought it was fulfilled which is written, 'Two women will be grinding with a hand mill; one will be taken and the other left.'[12] I had trouble keeping from crying out, 'Ruined! Ruined!'"[13]

"And I was afraid to knock any more," continued Mercy, "but when I looked up to what was written over the Gate,[14] I took courage. I also thought that I must either knock again or die, so I knocked. But I couldn't say how because my spirit struggled between life and death."

"Can't you tell how you knocked?" questioned Christiana. "I'm sure your knocks were so earnest that the very sound of them startled me. I thought I never heard such knocking in all my life. I thought you would've come in forcefully or would've taken the Kingdom by storm."[15]

"Alas," exclaimed Mercy, "considering my situation, who in the same position could have done otherwise? You saw that the Door was shut to me and that there was a most cruel dog thereabouts. Who, I say, that was so faint-hearted as I, would not have not knocked with all the strength available? But tell me, what did my Lord say about my rudeness? Wasn't He angry with me?"

Christiana answered, "When He heard your lumbering noise, He gave a wonderfully innocent smile.[16] I believe what you did pleased him well enough, for He showed no sign to the contrary. But I marvel in my heart why He keeps such a dog. Had I known that before, I fear I wouldn't have placed myself in such peril in this manner.[17] But now we are in. We're in, and I'm glad with all my heart."

"Next time He comes down," said Mercy, "if you don't mind, I'll ask why He keeps such a filthy mongrel in his yard. I hope He won't take it wrong."

"Yes, do," said the Children, "and persuade Him to get rid of him, for we're afraid he'll bite us when we go there."

So at last the Keeper came down to them again, and Mercy fell to the ground on her face before Him and worshipped, and said, "Let my Lord, accept the sacrifice of praise which I now offer unto You with the fruit of my lips."[18]

And He said to her, "Peace be to you. Stand up."

But she stayed on her face and said, "'You are always righteous, O Lord, when I bring a case before you. Yet I would speak with you about your justice.'[19] Why do you keep such a cruel dog in your yard? At the sight of him, women and children like us are ready to flee from your Gate for fear."

He answered, and said, "That dog has another owner. He is also kept close by in another man's ground, so my Pilgrims hear his barking. He belongs to the castle, which you see there at a distance, but he can come up to the walls of this place. He has frightened many an honest Pilgrim from worse to better by the great voice of his roaring. Indeed, he who owns him doesn't keep him because of any goodwill he has for me or mine, but with the intention of keeping the Pilgrims from coming to me and so they may be afraid to knock at this Gate for entrance."[20]

"Sometimes," He continued, "he has also broken out and has worried some whom I love. But I take it all patiently for now. I also give my Pilgrims timely help, so they aren't delivered up to his power to do with them what his doggish nature would prompt him to. But what? I suppose, my purchased One, if you hadn't known so much beforehand, you would not have been afraid of a dog."

He went on, "The beggars who go from door to door will run the hazard of the bawling, barking, and biting of a dog rather than lose expected alms. And shall a dog—a dog in another man's yard, a dog whose barking I turn to the profit of Pilgrims—keep any from coming to me? I deliver them from the lions, and 'my darling from the power of the dog.'"[21]

Then Mercy said, "I confess my ignorance. I spoke of what I didn't understand.[22] I acknowledge that you do everything well."[23]

Christiana began to talk about their journey and to inquire after the Way. Then He fed them and washed their feet and set them in the way of His Steps, as He had done with her husband before.

So I saw in my dream that they walked on in their way and had weather which was very comfortable to them.

Then Christiana began to sing, saying:

Blest be the Day that I began
A Pilgrim for to be;
And blessed also be that man
That thereto mov-ed me.

'Tis true, 'twas long ere I began
To seek to live for ever:
But now I run fast as I can;
'Tis better late, than never.

Our Tears to Joy, our Fears to Faith,
Are turned as we see;
Thus our Beginning (as one says)
Shows what our End will be.

NOTES ON CHAPTER 22

[1]   Matthew 7:15, 24:11; 1 John 4:1; 2 Peter 2; Jude 4-16.
[2]   **Luke 1:45**.
[3]   Mark 10:14.

CHRISTIANA AND MERCY ENTER THE GATE

4   2 Samuel 6:14-15.

5   **Luke 15:7.**

6   **The delays make the hungering soul more fervent.**

7   Mark 5:41.

8   **Jonah 2:7.**

9   **Mark this.**

10   **Song of Songs 1:2.**

11   **John 20:20.**

12   **Matthew 24:41.**

13   Isaiah 6:5.

14   "Knock and the door will be opened to you" (Luke 11:9). From the First Part.

15   **Matthew 11:12.**

16   **Christ pleased with loud and restless prayer.**

17   **If the soul at first knew all it should meet with in its journey to Heaven, it would hardly ever set out.**

18   Hebrews 13:15; Hosea 14:2.

19   **Jeremiah 12:1.**

20   **The dog, the Devil, an enemy to prayer.**

21   Psalm 22:20 (KJV).

22   Job 42:1-3.

23   Mark 7:37. **Christians when wise enough, acquiesce in the wisdom of their Lord.**

23

CHRISTIANA AND MERCY MEET THE INTERPRETER

A GARDEN WAS ON the other side of the Wall that fenced in the path up which Christiana and her companions were to go. The garden belonged to him who owned the barking dog, which was mentioned before. Some of the fruit trees that grew in the garden shot their branches over the Wall; and, the fruit being ripe, they who found them often gathered them and ate from the trees to their harm.

So Christiana's boys (as boys are apt to do), being pleased with the trees and the fruit that hung from them, jumped up and grabbed the branches. They bent them down and began to eat. Their mother rebuked them for doing so, but the boys still went on.

"Well," said Christiana, "you transgress, for none of that fruit is ours." But she did not know that they belonged to the enemy. If she had, I will assure you she would have been ready to die for fear. But that passed, and they went on their way.

When they had gone about two bowshots from the place that had let them into the Way, they saw two very rough-looking individuals coming down quickly toward them. With that, Christiana and Mercy, her friend, covered themselves with their veils and continued on their journey. The children also went on ahead of them, but at last they met together.

Then they who came down toward them came right up to the women as if they would embrace them, but Christiana said, "Stand back or go peaceably by as you should."

Yet these two, as men who are deaf, did not regard Christiana's words but began to lay hands on them. At that, becoming very angry, Christiana began kicking at them with her feet. Mercy also, as well as she was able, did what she could to budge them.

Christiana again said to them, "Stand back and be gone, for we have no money to lose. We're Pilgrims, as you see, and such also who live upon the charity of our friends."

Then one of the two men said, "We're not assaulting you for money but have come out to tell you that if you'll grant one small request, which we'll ask, we will make women of you forever."

Now, imagining what they meant, Christiana said again, "We'll neither hear nor regard nor yield to what you'll ask. We're in a hurry and can't stay. Our business is a business of life and death."

Again, she and her companions made a fresh attempt to go past them, but they hindered them in their way.[1]

And they said, "We intend no harm to your lives. It's another thing we want."

"Yes," said Christiana, "you want us body and soul, for I know it's for that purpose you've come. But we'd rather die on the spot than allow ourselves to be brought into such snares as shall endanger our well-being hereafter."

And with that, they both screamed and cried, "Murder! Murder!" and put themselves under those laws which are provided for the protection of women.[2] But the men still made their approach upon them, intending to prevail against them. Therefore, they cried out again.

Now being, as I said, not far from the Gate through which they had come, their voices were heard there from where they were. So, some individuals of the House came out and, knowing it was Christiana's voice, made haste to relieve her.[3] By the time they got within sight of them, the women were in a very great scuffle; the children also stood crying nearby.

Then he who came to help them called out to the ruffians, "What are you doing? Would you make my Lord's people to transgress?"[4] He also attempted to take them, but they made their escape over the Wall and into the garden of the man to whom the great dog belonged. So, the dog became their protector.[5]

This Reliever then came up to the women and asked them how they were.

So the women answered, "We thank your Prince quite sincerely, but we've been somewhat frightened. We also thank you for coming to our help, for otherwise we would've been overcome."

After a few more words, the Reliever said, "When you were entertained at the Gate above, I was amazed—seeing you knew you were weak—that you didn't ask the Lord there for a Guide. Then you might have avoided these troubles and dangers, for He would have granted you one."

"Alas," exclaimed Christiana, "we were so involved with our present blessing that we forgot the dangers to come.[6] Besides, who could've thought that such naughty individuals would be lurking so near the King's palace? Indeed, it would've been good for us if we had asked our Lord for a Guide; but since our Lord knew it would be for our profit, I wonder why He didn't send one along with us."

"It's not always necessary to grant things not asked for,"[7] explained the Reliever, "lest by doing so, they become of little value. But when the desire of a thing is felt, it then comes to be valued properly as it is worth in the eyes of the person who feels it, and who will consequently thereafter use it. Neither— had my Lord granted you a Guide—would you have so lamented your oversight in not asking for one, as you now have opportunity to do. So all things work for good and tend to make you more careful."[8]

"Should we go back again to my Lord, confess our folly, and ask for one?" questioned Christiana.

The Reliever answered, "I'll present Him with your confession of folly. You need not go back again, for in all the places where you go, you'll find no lack at all. For in every one of my Lord's lodgings, which He has prepared for the reception of His Pilgrims, there are sufficient things there to equip them with everything they need for avoiding any and all temptations to go back. But as I said, He will be asked of them to do it for them,[9] and it is a worthless thing that is not worth asking for."

After he had said these things, he went back to his place, and the Pilgrims went on their way.

Then Mercy said, "What a surprise this is. I'd reasoned that we had gotten past all danger and that we should never sorrow any more."

"Your innocence, my Sister, may well excuse you," said Christiana to Mercy, "but as for me, my fault is so much greater in that I saw this danger before I came out of the doors and yet didn't provide for it where provision might have been obtained. Therefore, I'm much to be blamed."

"How did you know this before you came from home?" asked Mercy. "Please, open to me this riddle?"

"Why, I'll tell you," answered Christiana. "Before I set foot out of doors, one night as I lay in my bed I had a dream about this. I thought I saw two men who as sure as the world looked like these. They stood at the foot of my bed, plotting how they might prevent my salvation. I'll tell you their very words: They said—it was when I was in my troubles—'What shall we do with this woman? For she cries out for forgiveness when awake and asleep. If she's allowed to go on like this, we'll lose her as we've lost her husband.' You know this might have made me take heed and have provided when provision might have been obtained."

"Well," said Mercy, "through this neglect we have an opportunity ministered unto us to see our own imperfections.

So our Lord has taken the opportunity to manifest the Riches of His Grace through it. As we see, He has accompanied us with kindness not asked for, and out of His mere good pleasure He has delivered us from the hands of those who were stronger than we."

When they had talked away a little more time, they came close to a house that stood in the Way. This house was built for the relief of Pilgrims (as you will find more fully related in the first part of these records of *The Pilgrim's Progress.*) They drew closer to the House (of the Interpreter), and when they came to the door, they heard a great discussion inside. Listening, they thought they heard Christiana mentioned by name, for you must know that word of her and her children's travel on Pilgrimage went before her. This thing was even more pleasing to those inside because they had heard she was Christian's wife, that woman who some time ago was so unwilling to hear of going on Pilgrimage.

They stood still, therefore, and heard the good people within the house commending her whom they didn't consider would be standing at the door. At last, Christiana knocked as she had done at the Gate before. Now when she had knocked, a young girl came to the door, opened it, and looked; and there, two women were standing.

The girl asked them, "With whom would you speak in this place?"

Christiana answered, "We understand this is a privileged place for those who've become Pilgrims. We who are at this door are such, so we ask that we may be sharers of that for which we at this time have come. As you see, it's very late in the day, and we hate to go any farther tonight."

Then the girl asked, "Please, what may I call your name so I can tell it to my master inside?"

"My name is Christiana," she said. "I was the wife of that Pilgrim who some years ago traveled this way, and these are his four children. This girl is also my companion and is going on Pilgrimage, too."

Then Innocent, for that was her name, ran in and said to those inside, "Can you imagine who is at the door? Christiana and her children and companion are there, all waiting for acceptance here."

They leaped for joy and went and told the head of the house. So he came to the door, and looking upon her asked, "Are you that Christiana whom the good man Christian left behind him when he applied himself to a Pilgrim's life?"

Christiana answered, "I'm the woman who was so hard-hearted as to slight my husband's troubles and who allowed him to go on his journey alone, and these are his four children. Now I've come also, for I'm convinced that no way is right but this one."

The Interpreter then said to her, "Then that is fulfilled which is written of the man who said to his son, 'Go and work today in the vineyard.'[10] And he said to his father, 'I will not, but later he changed his mind and went.'"[11]

Then Christiana said, "So be it, Amen. May God make it a true saying for me and grant that I may be found spotless, blameless and at peace with Him."[12]

"But why are you standing like this at the door?" asked the Interpreter. "Come in, you Daughter of Abraham. We were just now talking about you, for word had come to us how you had become a Pilgrim. Come, Children, come in! Come, Young Lady, come in!"

So he brought them all into the house, and when they were inside he invited them to sit down and rest themselves. When they had done that, those who waited upon the Pilgrims in the house came into the room to see them. One smiled, and another smiled, and they all smiled for joy that Christiana had become a Pilgrim.[13] They also looked upon the boys and stroked their faces with their hands in token of their kind reception of them. They also lovingly received Mercy and welcomed them all into their Master's house.

After a while, because supper was not ready, the Interpreter took them into his significant rooms and showed them what Christian, Christiana's husband, had seen some time before. Here, therefore, they saw the man in the cage, the man and his dream, the man who cut his way through his enemies, and the picture of the biggest of them all, together with the rest of those things that were then so profitable to Christian.

This done, and after these things had been somewhat digested by Christiana and her group, the Interpreter took them aside again and led them first into a room where there was a man who could look no way but downwards and who had a muckrake in his hand.[14] Another individual stood over his head with a celestial crown in his hand and offered to trade him the crown for his muckrake, but the man neither looked up nor regarded it, but raked to himself the straw, the small sticks, and dust of the floor.

Then Christiana said, "I'm persuaded that I know something of the meaning of this, for this is a figure of a man of this world, is it not, Good Sir?"

"You've said it rightly," said the Interpreter, "and his muckrake shows his sinful mind. And in that you see him rather paying attention to raking up straw, sticks, and the dust of the floor rather than to what He who calls to him from above says, it is to show that Heaven is only like a fable to some and that things here are accounted the only things substantial. Now, in that it was also showed you that the man could look no way but downwards, it is to let you know that when they are with power upon men's minds, earthly things quite carry their hearts away from God."

Then Christiana said, "Oh, deliver me from this muckrake!"

"The prayer, 'Give me neither poverty nor riches,'"[15] said the Interpreter, "has been laid aside until it's almost rusty. It's the prayer of scarcely one in ten thousand. Straw, sticks, and dust are considered by most to be the great things to be sought after."

With that, Mercy and Christiana wept and said, "It is, alas, too true!"

When the Interpreter had showed them this, he took them into the very best room in the house. A very fine room it was! So he asked them to look around and see if they could find anything profitable there. They looked around and around, for

The man with the muckrake

there was nothing to be seen except for a very large spider on the wall, which they overlooked.

Then Mercy said, "Sir, I see nothing." But Christiana remained silent.

"But," said the Interpreter, "look again."

Mercy looked again therefore and said, "There is nothing here except an ugly spider who hangs by its hands upon the wall."

"Is there only one spider in all this spacious room?" questioned the Interpreter.

Then tears formed in Christiana's eyes, for she was a woman quick of apprehension. She said, "Yes, Sir, there are more than one here. Yes, and spiders whose venom is far more destructive than that one."

The Interpreter then looked pleasantly upon her and said, "You've said the truth."

This made Mercy blush and the boys to cover their faces, for they all began now to understand the riddle.

Then the Interpreter said again, "As you see, 'the spider takes hold with her hands, and is in the king's palaces.'[16] And for what reason is this recorded but to show you that no matter how full you may be of the venom of sin, yet you may, by the hand of faith, lay hold of and dwell in the best room which belongs to the King's House above."

"I thought of something like this," said Christiana, "but I couldn't imagine it all. I thought that we were like spiders, and that we looked like ugly creatures in whatever fine room we were. But it didn't cross my mind that by this spider—this venomous and ugly-looking creature—we were to learn how to display faith. And yet, as I see, it has taken hold with its hands and dwells in the best room in the house. God has made nothing in vain."

Then they all seemed to be glad, but tears stood in their eyes. They looked upon one another and also bowed before the Interpreter. He then took them into another room where a hen and chicks were, and he asked them to observe for a while. So one of the chicks went to the trough to drink; and every time it drank, it lifted up its head and eyes towards Heaven.

"Watch what this little chick does," said the Interpreter, "and learn through it to acknowledge where your mercies come from by receiving them with looking up." And again he said, "Observe and look."

So they gave heed and perceived that the hen walked in a fourfold manner towards her chicks: First—she had a common call, and she had it all day long. Second—she had a special call, and she had it only occasionally. Third—she had a brooding sound. And Fourth—she had an outcry.

"Now," said the Interpreter, "compare this hen to your King, and these chicks to His obedient ones. In like manner as she, He himself has His methods through which He approaches His people: By His common call He gives nothing; by His special call He always has something to give; He also has a brooding voice for them who are under His wing; and He has an outcry to give the alarm when He sees the enemy come.[17] I choose, my Dear Ones, to lead you into the room where such things are because you are women, and they are easy for you."

"And sir," said Christiana, "please let us see some more."

So he led them into the Slaughter House where a butcher was killing a sheep, and the sheep was quiet, taking its death patiently.

The Interpreter said, "You must learn from this sheep to suffer and to put up with wrongs without murmurings and complaints. See how quietly it takes its death, and how without objection it allows its skin to be pulled over its ears? Your King calls you His Sheep."[18]

After this, he led them into his garden, where there was a great variety of flowers. And he asked, "Do you see all these?"

Christiana answered, "Yes."

Then the Interpreter said again, "See, the flowers are different in stature, quality, color, fragrance, and virtue; and some are better than others. Also, they stand where the gardener has set them, and they don't quarrel with one another."[19]

Again, he led them into his field, which he had sown with wheat and corn. But when they looked, the tops of all of it were cut off, and only the straw remained.

"This ground was fertilized, plowed, and sown," said the Interpreter, "but what shall we do with the crop?"

"Burn some of it," answered Christiana, "and make compost of the rest."

Then the Interpreter said, "You see, fruit is the thing you look for, and for lack of that you condemn it to the fire or to be trodden under foot by men. Beware that in this you don't condemn yourselves."[20]

Then as they were coming in from outside, they spied a little robin with a large spider in its mouth. So the Interpreter said, "Look here."

They looked, and Mercy wondered; but Christiana said, "What a disparagement it is to such a pretty little bird like the Robin-red-breast, being also a bird above many, who loves to maintain a kind of sociableness with man. I had thought they lived upon crumbs of bread or upon other such harmless matter. I don't like him as much as I did."

The Interpreter then replied, "This robin is an emblem very suited to be likened to some professors of faith. For, like this robin, they are by sight pretty of note, color, and carriage. They seem also to have a very great love for professors who are sincere, and above all others appear to desire to associate with them and to be in their company, as if they could live upon the good man's crumbs. Therefore, they're also pretenders in that they frequent the house of the godly and the appointments of the Lord, but when they're by themselves they can catch and gobble up spiders like the robin. They can change their diet, drink iniquity, and swallow down sin like water."

When they had entered again into the house, and because supper was not as yet ready, Christiana again desired that the Interpreter would either show or tell of some other profitable things.[21]

Then the Interpreter began to teach proverbs, and said:

"The fatter the sow is, the more she desires the mire; the fatter the ox is, the more playfully he goes to the slaughter; and the more healthy the lusty man is, the more prone he is to evil.

"There is a desire in women to dress neatly and finely,

and it is an attractive thing to be adorned with that which in God's sight is of great price.

"It's easier staying awake a night or two than to sit up a whole year at a time. So, it's easier for a person to begin to profess well than to hold out, as one should, to the end.

"When in a storm, every ship's captain will willingly cast overboard that which is of the least value in the vessel; but who will throw the best out first?—none but he who doesn't fear God.

"One leak will sink a ship, and one sin will destroy a sinner.

"He who forgets his friend is ungrateful to him, but he who forgets his Savior is unmerciful to himself.

"He who lives in sin and looks for happiness thereafter is like him who sows cockleburs and thinks to fill his barn with wheat or barley.[22]

"If a man intends to live well, let him fetch his last day to himself and make it always his companion.

"Whispering and change of mind prove that sin is in the world.

"If the world, which God accounts as less significant, is considered by people to be a thing of worth, how is Heaven considered, which is commended by God?

"If we so hate to let go of the life that is accompanied with so many troubles, what is our feeling for the life above?

"Everyone will cry out and commend the goodness of people, but who is there who will, as one should, be so affected with the goodness of God?

"We seldom sit down to eat food that we don't eat and leave some. So in Jesus Christ there is more merit and righteousness than the whole world has need of."

When the Interpreter was done, he took them out into his garden again and led them to a tree whose inside was all rotten and gone, and yet it grew and had leaves.

Then Mercy asked, "What does this mean?"

"This tree whose outside is fair and whose inside is rotten," said the Interpreter, "is that to which may be compared many who are in the Garden of God—those who with their mouths speak well in behalf of God but indeed who will do nothing for Him, and those whose leaves are fair but whose hearts are good for nothing but to be tinder for the devil's tinderbox."[23]

Then supper was ready, the table was spread, and all things were set on the dining table. So, after one had given thanks, they sat down and ate. The Interpreter usually entertained those who lodged with him with music at meals, so the musicians played. There was also one who sang with a very fine voice. His song was this:

The Lord is only my support,
And he that does me feed;
How can I then want any thing
Whereof I stand in Need?

When the song and music had ended, the Interpreter asked Christiana what it was that at first caused her to thus take upon herself a Pilgrim's life.

"First," answered Christiana, "the loss of my husband came into my mind, at which I was truly grieved. But all that was based on natural affection. Then after that, the troubles and Pilgrimage of my husband came into my mind, and also how, like a rascal, I had treated him about it. So guilt took hold of my mind and would have drawn me into the pond, but opportunely I had a dream of the well-being of my husband. Also, I received a letter sent to me from the King of that country where my husband lives, a letter inviting me to come to Him. The dream and the letter together so worked on my mind that they forced me to this way."

"Didn't you meet with any opposition before you set out of doors?" inquired the Interpreter.

"Yes," answered Christiana, "from a neighbor of mine, Mrs. Fearful. She was related to him who would have persuaded my husband to go back for fear of the lions. She ridiculed me for—as she called it—my intended desperate adventure. She also did what she could to discourage me from it by talking of the hardship and troubles my husband met with in the Way. I got over all this pretty well, but I had a dream of two bad

Supper at the house of the Interpreter

looking fellows who I thought plotted how to make me unsuccessful in my journey. That troubled me a great deal. It still runs in my mind and makes me afraid of everyone I meet, lest they should meet me to do me harm and turn me out of the Way. Yes, I may tell you, Sir—although I wouldn't want everybody to know it—that between here and the Gate through which we got into the Way, we were both so sorely assaulted that we were made to cry out 'Murder!' And the two who made this assault upon us were like the two whom I saw in my dream."

Then the Interpreter said, "Your beginning is good. Your latter end shall greatly increase."[24] He then addressed himself to Mercy and asked her, "And what moved you to come here, Sweetheart?"

Mercy blushed, trembled, and continued silent for a while.

Then the Interpreter said, "Don't be afraid, just believe[25] and speak your mind."

So Mercy began, saying, "Truly, Sir, my lack of experience is what makes me desire to remain silent and also fills me with fears of coming up short at last. I can't tell of visions and dreams, as my friend Christiana can; nor do I know what it is to mourn for my refusing the counsel of those who were good relations."

"What was it, then, Dear Heart, that convinced you to do as you've done?" asked the Interpreter.

"Why," said Mercy, "when our friend here was packing up to leave our town, I and another went to see her for a casual visit. We knocked at her door and went in. When we were inside and saw what she was doing, we asked what her meaning was. She said she was sent for, to go to her husband; and then she up and told us how in a dream she had seen him living in a curious place among Immortals, wearing a crown, playing upon a harp, eating and drinking at his Prince's table, and singing praises to Him for bringing him there. While she was telling these things to us, I thought my heart burned within me, and I said in my heart, 'If this is true, I'll leave my father and my mother, and the land of my birth, and will—if I may—go along with Christiana.'"

"So," continued Mercy, "I asked her further about the truth of these things and if she'd let me go with her, for I saw there was no longer in our town any dwelling that wasn't in danger of ruin. But I still came away with a heavy heart, not because I was unwilling to leave but because so many of my relatives were left behind. I've come with all the desire of my heart, and, if I may, I'll go with Christiana unto her husband and his King."

Then the Interpreter said, "Your leaving is good, for you've given credit to the truth. You're a Ruth, who for the love she had for Naomi and the Lord her God left father, mother, and the land of her birth to leave and go with a people whom she didn't know before.[26] 'May the Lord repay you for what you have done. May you be richly rewarded by the Lord, the God of Israel, under whose wings you have come to take refuge.' Ruth two, twelve."

Now supper was over, and preparations were made for bed. The women were lodged singly alone and the boys by themselves. When Mercy was in bed, she could not sleep because of her joy, for now her doubts of finally missing out were removed farther from her than ever before. So she lay blessing and praising God, who had such favor for her.

In the morning they arose with the sun and prepared themselves for their departure, but the Interpreter wanted them to tarry awhile, "For," he said, "you must go from here orderly." Then he said to the girl who first opened the door to them, "Take them into the garden to the Bath and wash them there. Make them clean from the soil which they've gathered by traveling."

Then Innocent, the girl, took them, led them into the garden, and brought them to the Bath.[27] So she told them they must wash there and be clean, for that is what her master would have the women who called at his house to do as they were going on Pilgrimage. Then they went in and washed—yes, they and the boys and all—and they came out of that bath not only sweet and clean but also much enlivened and strengthened in their joints. So when they came in the house, they looked a deal fairer than when they went out to the washing.

When they had returned out of the garden from the Bath, the Interpreter took them, looked at them, and said, "Fair as the moon."[28] Then he called for the Seal which was used for sealing those who were washed in his bath. So the Seal was brought, and he set His mark upon them that they might be known in the places where they were yet to go. Now the Seal was the content and sum of the Passover, which the Children of Israel ate when they came out from the land of Egypt. This mark was set between their eyes.[29] The Seal added greatly to their beauty, for it was an ornament to their faces. It also added to their seriousness and made their countenance more like that of angels.

Then the Interpreter said again to the girl who waited upon these women, "Go into the vestry[30] and fetch out garments for these people."

So she went and got out white clothing and laid it down before him, and he commanded them to put it on. It was 'fine linen, white and clean.'[31] When the women were thus adorned, they seemed to be a terror to one another, for they each could not see on themselves the glory which they could see on the other. They began, therefore, to esteem each other better than themselves.[32] "You are fairer than I am," said one; "And you are more lovely than I am," said the other. The children also stood amazed to see into what form they were brought.

The Interpreter then called for a manservant of his, one called Great Heart, and told him, "Take Sword, Helmet, and Shield; and take these, my daughters, and guide them to the house called Beautiful, where they will next rest."

So, Great Heart took his weapons and went before them, and the Interpreter said, "God speed!" Those also who belonged to the Family sent them away with many good wishes.

So they went on their way, singing:

This place has been our second stage,
Here we have heard, and seen
Those good things, that from Age to Age
To others hid have been.

267

The Dunghill-raker, Spider, Hen,
The Chicken too, to me,
Has taught a lesson, let me then
Conformed to it be.

The Butcher, Garden, and the Field,
The Robin, and his bait,
Also the rotten Tree does yield
Me argument of weight;

To move me for to Watch and Pray,
To strive to be sincere;
To take my Cross up day by day,
And serve the Lord with fear.

NOTES ON CHAPTER 23

1 Genesis 24:56

2 **Deuteronomy 22:23-27.**

3 **'Tis good to cry out when we are assaulted.**

4 1 Samuel 2:24 (KJV).

5 **The ill ones fly to the Devil for relief.** The dog barked at those with the best of intentions but became the protector of those with the worst.

6 **Mark this.**

7 Matthew 21:22; John 16:24; James 4:2-3; also 1 John 3:21-22.

8 Romans 8:28.

9 **Ezekiel 36:37.**

10 Matthew 21:28.

11 **Matthew 21:29.**

12 2 Peter 3:14.

13 **Old Saints glad to see the young ones walk in God's ways.**

14 A muckrake is a rake used for moving heavy, moist, earth, most usually mixed with manure.

15 **Proverbs 30:8.**

[16] **Proverbs 30:28** (KJV).

[17] **Matthew 23:37**.

[18] Romans 8:36; Psalm 79:13, 100:3; Jeremiah 23:1; Ezekiel 34:11-12; Matthew 10:16; John 10:1-29, 21:16; Isaiah 53:7; Acts 8:32.

[19] 1 Corinthians 3:1-3, 6:1-11.

[20] Matthew 21:18-19; Luke 13:6-9, also John 15:1-8.

[21] **Pray, and you will get at that which yet lies unrevealed.**

[22] Galatians 6:7-8.

[23] Tinder is a readily combustible material. A tinderbox is a box in which to store tinder and the flint and steel to use for producing a spark.

[24] Job 8:7

[25] Mark 5:36.

[26] **Ruth 2:11**.

[27] **The bath of sanctification.**

[28] Song of Songs 6:10.

[29] **Exodus 13:8-10**; Revelation 7:2-3.

[30] A vestry is a room in a church where robes are kept.

[31] Revelation 19:14. Revelation 19:8.

[32] Philippians 2:3.

24

GREAT HEART AND THE HILL OF DIFFICULTY

NOW I SAW IN my dream that they went on, and Great Heart went before them. So they went on and came to the place where Christian's burden fell off his back and tumbled into a tomb. Here, then, they paused and blessed God.

"What was said to us at the Gate now comes to mind," said Christiana, "that we should receive pardon by word and deed. By word, that is, by the promise; and by deed, that is, in the way it was obtained. I know something about what the promise is, but what does it mean to have pardon by deed or in the way it was obtained? Mr. Great Heart, I suppose you know. If you please, therefore, let us hear your explanation of it."

Great Heart then answered, "Pardon by the deed done is pardon obtained by someone for another who has need of it. This is not speaking of a deed done by the person pardoned, but it refers to the way—as says another—in which I've obtained it.[1] So then, to speak to the question more in general, the pardon that you, Mercy, and these boys have attained was

271

obtained by Another—that is, by Him who let you in at the Gate. And He has obtained it in this double way: He has performed righteousness to cover you and has spilled blood in which to wash you."[2]

"But if He imparts His righteousness to us, what will He have for himself?" inquired Christiana

"He has more righteousness than you have need of, or than He himself needs," answered Great Heart.

"Please clarify that," said Christiana.

"Gladly," said Great Heart, "but first I must premise my remarks by saying that He of whom we are now about to speak is an Individual who has no equal. He has two natures in one person, and they are plain to be distinguished but impossible to be divided. A righteousness belongs to each of these natures, and each righteousness is essential to that nature; so that one may just as easily cause the nature to be extinct as to separate it from its justice or righteousness. We're not, therefore, made partakers of these righteousnesses, in that they or any of them would be put upon us to make us just and lively by them. Besides these, there is a righteousness which this Person has as these two natures are joined in one. And this is not the righteousness of the Godhead as distinguished from the manhood; nor is it the righteousness of the manhood as distinguished from the Godhead; but it is a righteousness which appears in the union of both natures. This righteousness may properly be called the righteousness that was essential to His preparation by God for the responsibility of the position of Mediator, with which He was to be entrusted."[3]

"If He parts with his first righteousness," continued Great Heart, "He parts with His Godhead. If He parts with his second righteousness, He parts with the purity of His manhood. If He parts with His third, He parts with the perfection which qualifies Him for performing mediation. He has another righteousness, therefore, which is demonstrated through performance or obedience to a revealed will, and that is the righteousness that He puts upon sinners and which covers their sins. He said, therefore, 'For just as through the disobedience of the one man the many were made sinners, so also through the obedience of the one man the many will be made righteous.'"[4]

Then Christiana asked, "But aren't the other righteousnesses of use to us?"

"Yes," answered Great Heart, "for although they are essential to His natures and position—and so can't be given away to another—yet, it's by the virtue of them that the righteousness that justifies is empowered for that purpose. The righteousness of His Godhead gives virtue to His obedience; the righteousness of His manhood gives capability to His obedience to justify; and the righteousness that stands in the union of these two natures to His position gives authority to that righteousness to do the work for which it was ordained."

"So," continued Great Heart, "here then is a righteousness that Christ, as God, has no need of; for He is God without it. Here is a righteousness that Christ, as Man, has no need of to make Him so; for He is perfect Man without it. Again, here is a righteousness that Christ, as God-man, has no need of; for He is perfectly so without it. Here then is a righteousness that Christ, as God, Man, and God-man, has no need of with reference to himself. So He can set aside a justifying righteousness that He doesn't need for himself, and therefore, He gives it away. That's why it's called the Gift of Righteousness."[5]

Great Heart continued, "Since Christ Jesus the Lord has made himself righteous under the Law, this righteousness must be given away; for the Law not only binds the one who is under it to do justly but to also use love. Since He must do these, according to the Law he who has two coats ought to give one to him who has none.[6] Now our Lord, indeed, has two coats, one for himself and one to spare. He, therefore, freely places one upon those who have none; and so, Christiana and Mercy, and the rest of you who are here, your pardon comes by deed, or by the work of another Person. Your Lord Christ is He who has worked, and what He labored for He has given away to the next poor beggar He meets."

"But again," Great Heart went on, "in order to pardon by deed, something must be paid to God as a price as well as for something prepared with which to cover us.[7] Sin has delivered us up to the just curse of a righteous Law. Now from this curse we must be justified by way of redemption, a price being paid for the harms we have done; and this is by The Blood of your Lord who came and stood in your place and stead, and who died your death for your transgressions.[8] Thus, He has ransomed you from your transgressions by blood and covered your polluted and deformed souls with righteousness. For the sake of this, God passes by you and will not hurt you when He comes to judge the world."[9]

"This is wonderful," said Christiana. "Now I see there was something to be learned by our being pardoned by word and deed. Good Mercy, let's labor to keep this in mind. And, my Children, you remember it, too. But, Sir, wasn't this what made my good Christian's burden fall from off his shoulder? And what made him give three leaps for joy?"

"Yes," responded Great Heart, "it was the belief of this that cut out those strings that couldn't be cut by other means, and he was permitted to carry his burden to the Cross to give him proof of the virtue of this."

"I thought so," said Christiana, "for although my heart was light and joyous before, yet it's ten times more lightsome and joyous now. And I'm persuaded by what I've felt—even though I've felt only a little as yet—that if the most burdened man in the world was here, and he saw and believed as I now do, it would make his heart more merry and glad."

Then Great Heart said, "Not only is comfort and ease from a burden brought to us by the sight and consideration of these, but also an endearing affection is conceived in us by it. For if a person just once considers that pardon comes not only by promise but from this, who could keep from being affected with the way and means of redemption, and also with the Man who worked to prepare it for him?"

"True," agreed Christiana, "I think it makes my heart bleed to think He should bleed for me. Oh, You loving One! Oh, You blessed One! You deserve to have me, for You have bought me. You deserve to have me all, for You paid for me ten thousand times more than I'm worth. It's no marvel this made the tears stand in my husband's eyes and made him step so nimbly on. I'm persuaded he wished me to be with him, but vile wretch that I was, I let him come all alone. Oh, Mercy, if only your father and mother were here! Yes, and Mrs. Fearful also! No, with all my heart I now wish that Madam Wanton were here, too. Surely, surely, their hearts would be affected; nor could the fear of one nor the powerful lusts of the other convince them to go home again and cause them to refuse to become good Pilgrims."

Great Heart then said, "You now speak in the warmth of your affections. Do you think it will always be like this with you? Besides, this is not communicated to everyone nor to everyone who saw your Jesus bleed.[10] There were those who stood by and saw the Blood run from His heart to the ground, and yet they were so far off this that instead of lamenting, they laughed at Him; and instead of becoming His disciples, they hardened their hearts against Him. So, all you have, my Daughters, you have by a peculiar impression made by a divine contemplating upon what I've spoken to you. Remember, it was told you that the hen, by her common call, gives no meat to her chickens. This, therefore, you have by a special grace."

Now I saw still in my dream that they went on until they had come to the place where Simple, Sloth, and Presumption lay and slept when Christian went by on Pilgrimage. And there, they were hanged up in irons a short distance off on the other side.

Then Mercy asked him who was their Guide and Leader, "Who are those three men? And why were they hanged there?"

Great Heart answered, "These three were men of very bad qualities. They had no mind to be Pilgrims themselves, and they hindered whomever they could. They were in favor of slothfulness and folly themselves, and they made whomever they could persuade with these things the same way, too, and thereupon taught them to presume they should do well at last. They were asleep when Christian went by, and now as you go by they are hanged."

"But could they persuade anyone to be of their opinion?" asked Mercy.

"Yes," answered Great Heart, "they turned several out of the Way. There was Slow Pace, whom they persuaded to do as they do. They also convinced one named Shortwind, one named Noheart, one named Linger Afterlust, one named Sleepy Head, and a young woman named Dull, to turn out of the Way and become like them. Besides that, they brought up a bad report of your Lord, persuading others that He was a taskmaster. They also brought up an evil report of the Good Land, saying it wasn't half as good as some pretended it to be. They also began to denounce His servants and to count the very best of them as meddlesome, troublesome busybodies. Furthermore, they would call the Bread of God, husks; the comforts of His children, fancies; and the travel and labor of Pilgrims, things to no purpose."

"No," said Christiana, "if they were such, they'll never be wept for by me. They have just what they deserve. And I think it's good they hang so near the Highway, so that others may see and take warning. But wouldn't it have been good if their crimes had been engraved in some plate of iron or brass and left here—even where they made their mischief—for a caution to other bad men?"

"So it is," answered Great Heart, "as you may very well see if you'll go a little toward the Wall."

"No, no," said Mercy, "let them hang, their names rot, and their crimes live forever against them. I believe it to be a high favor that they were hanged before we came here. Who knows what else they might have done to such poor women as we?"

Then she turned it into a song, saying:

Now then you three hang there, and be a Sign
To all that shall against the Truth combine.
And let him that comes after, fear this End,
If unto Pilgrims he is not a Friend.
And thou, my Soul, of all such men beware,
That unto Holiness opposers are.

Thus, they went on until they came to the foot of the Hill Difficulty, where their good friend Mr. Great Heart took an occasion to tell them about what happened there when Christian himself went by. He took them first to the Spring and said, "Look, this is the Spring from which Christian drank before he went up this hill. It was clear and good then, but now it's dirty from the feet of some who aren't desirous that Pilgrims should quench their thirst here."[11]

At that, Mercy asked, "Why do you suppose they're so envious?"

"But it'll do if it's taken up and put into a sweet and good vessel," said the Guide, "for then the dirt will sink to the bottom, and the water will come out by itself more clear."

Therefore, that is what Christiana and her companions had to do. They took it up and put it into an earthen pot and let it stand until the dirt had gone to the bottom, and then they drank of it.

Great Heart next showed them the two byways at the foot of the hill where Formality and Hypocrisy lost themselves. "These," he said, "are dangerous paths. Two were cast away when Christian came by, and although, as you see, these ways have been barricaded with chains, posts, and a ditch, there are yet those who will choose to venture here rather than take the pains to go up this hill."[12]

"The way of transgressors is hard,"[13] said Christiana. "It's a wonder they can get into those ways without the danger of breaking their necks."

"They'll attempt it," responded Great Heart. "Yes, if at any time any of the King's servants happen to see them, call to them, tell them they're in the wrong ways, and advise them to beware of the danger, then in return they'll scornfully answer them and say, 'We will not listen to the message you have spoken to us in the name of the King! We will certainly do everything we said we would.'"[14]

"No," he continued, "if you look a little farther, you'll see that these ways are made ominous enough, not only by these posts, ditch, and chain, but also by being bordered by thorn hedges. Yet, they'll choose to go there."

"They're idle," said Christiana. "They love not to take pains. The Up-hill Way is unpleasant to them, so it is fulfilled to them as it is written, 'The way of the sluggard is blocked with thorns.'[15] Yes, they'll rather choose to walk upon a snare than to go up this hill and the rest of this way to the City."

Then they set forward and began to climb the hill, and up the hill they went. But before they got to the top, Christiana began to pant and said, "I dare say, this is a breathing hill. It's no marvel that they who love their ease more than their souls choose a smoother way for themselves."

Then Mercy said, "I must sit down."

Also, the youngest of the children began to cry.

"Come, come!" said Great Heart. "Don't sit down here, for a short distance above is the Prince's Arbor." Then he took the little boy by the hand and led him up to it.

When they had come to the Arbor, they were very willing to sit down, for they were all beaten down from the heat. Then Mercy said, "How sweet rest is to them who labor.[16] And how good the Prince of Pilgrims is to provide such resting places for them. I've heard much about this Arbor, but I never saw it before. Let's beware of sleeping here, though, for I heard it cost poor Christian dearly."

Then Mr. Great Heart said to the little ones, "Come, my fine Boys, how are you doing? What do you think now about going on Pilgrimage?"

"Sir, I had almost lost heart," said the youngest, "but I thank you for lending me a hand in my need. I remember now what my mother has told me, namely that the way to Heaven is like a ladder and the Way to Hell is like down a hill. But I'd rather go up the ladder to life than down the hill to death."

Then Mercy said, "But the proverb is: 'To go down the hill is easy.'"

But James (for that was his name) said, "In my opinion, the day is coming when going down the hill will be the hardest of all."[17]

"That's a good boy," said Great Heart. "You've given her a right answer."

Then Mercy smiled, but the little boy blushed.

"Come," said Christiana, "will you eat a bit, a little to sweeten your mouths while you sit here to rest your legs? For I have here a piece of pomegranate that Mr. Interpreter put into my hand just as I went out of his doors.[18] He also gave me a piece of honeycomb and a little bottle of spirits."[19]

"I thought he gave you something," said Mercy, "for he called you aside."

"Yes, so he did," said Christiana. "But, Mercy, it will still be as I said it would when we first left home. You'll be a sharer of all the good I have because you so willingly became my companion."

Then she gave to them, and they ate, both Mercy and the boys. Christiana said to Mr. Great Heart, "Sir, will you do as we?"

But he answered, "You're going on Pilgrimage, and I'll soon return. May what you have to eat do much good for you. Every day at home I eat the same as you do now."

Now when they had eaten and drunk, and had chatted a little longer, their Guide said to them, "The day wears away. If you think it good, let's prepare to be going."

So they got up to go, and the little boys went in front. However, Christiana forgot to take her bottle of spirits with her, so she sent her little boy back to fetch it.

Then Mercy said, "I think this is a Place of Losing. Here Christian lost his Book, and here Christiana left her bottle behind her. Sir, what is the cause of this?"

So their Guide answered and said, "The cause is sleep or forgetfulness. Some sleep when they should stay awake, and some forget when they should remember. This is the exact cause why often at the resting places some Pilgrims, in some things, come away losers.[20] During their times of greatest enjoyment, Pilgrims should watch and remember what they've already received.[21] But for failing to do so, oftentimes their rejoicing ends in tears, and their sunshine in a cloud. Witness the story of Christian in this place."

When they had come to the place where Mistrust and Fearful met Christian to persuade him to go back for fear of the lions, they saw as it were a platform and in front of it, towards the road, a wide plate with a copy of verses written upon it. Underneath was written the reason of the construction of the platform in that place. The verses were these:

Let him that sees this Stage, take heed
Unto his Heart and Tongue:
Lest if he do not, here he speed
As some have long agone.

The words underneath the verses were: "This platform was built to punish upon those who through fearfulness or mistrust shall be afraid to go further on Pilgrimage. Also, on this platform, both Mistrust and Fearful were burnt through the tongue with a hot iron for endeavoring to hinder Christian on his journey."

Then Mercy said, "This is similar to the saying of the Beloved, 'What will he do to you, and what more besides, O deceitful tongue? He will punish you with a warrior's sharp arrows, with burning coals of the broom tree.'"[22]

So they went on until they came within sight of the lions. Now Mr. Great Heart was a strong man, so he was not afraid of a lion; but, when they had come up to the place where the lions were, the boys who walked in front were glad to cringe behind, for they were afraid of the lions. So they stepped aside and went to the back.

At this, their Guide smiled, and said, "How's this, my Boys? Do you love to take the lead when no danger approaches but love to take the rear as soon as the lions appear?"[23]

Now, as they went up, Mr. Great Heart drew his Sword with the intention of making a way for the Pilgrims in spite of the lions. Then there appeared one who, it seemed, had taken upon himself to support the lions and said to the Pilgrims' Guide, "What's the reason you've come here?" The name of that man was Grim (or Bloody Man) because of his slaying of Pilgrims, and he was of the race of the Giants.

The Pilgrim's Guide then said, "These women and children are going on Pilgrimage, and this is the way they must go. And go it they shall, in spite of you and the lions."

"This isn't their road," answered Grim, "neither shall they travel in it. I've come here to withstand them, and to that end I'll back the lions."

Giant Grim

Now to tell the truth, by reason of the fierceness of the lions and of the grim behavior of him who backed them, this way had lately been much unoccupied and was almost grown over with grass.

Then Christiana said, "Though the roads were abandoned, and though the travelers have been made at times to walk on winding paths, it must not be so now that I've risen to be 'a mother in Israel.'"[24]

Then Grim swore by the lions that it should be so. Therefore, he commanded the Pilgrims to turn aside, for they should not have passage there. But their Guide approached Grim the first time and attacked him so heavily with his Sword that he forced him to retreat.

Then Grim asked, "Will you kill me upon my own ground?"

"It's the King's Highway we're in," said Great Heart, "and it's in this path that you've placed your lions. But these women and children, though weak, shall continue on their way in spite of your lions."

And with that, he again gave him a tremendous blow and brought him to his knees. With the next blow he broke his helmet, and with the next he cut off an arm. Then the Giant roared so hideously that his voice frightened the women, but they were glad to see him lie, sprawled out on the ground.

Now the lions were chained, and so of themselves could do nothing. Therefore, when old Grim, who intended to back them, was dead, Great Heart said to the Pilgrims, "Come now and follow me. You'll not be hurt by the lions."

They therefore went on, but the women trembled as they passed by them. The boys also looked as if they would die, but they all got by with no further harm.

NOTES ON CHAPTER 24

[1]   Titus 3:5. **A comment upon what was said at the Gate, or a discourse of our being justified by Christ.**

[2]   Revelation 1:5 (KJV); Revelation 7:14.

³   1 Timothy 2:5; Hebrews 8:6-9:15, 12:24.

⁴   **Romans 5:19.**

⁵   **Romans 5:17.**

⁶   Luke 3:11.

⁷   1 Corinthians 6:20, 7:23.

⁸   **Romans 4:23-25; Galatians 3:13.**

⁹   Psalm 98:8-9; Exodus 12:12-13, 21-23.

¹⁰   **To be affected with Christ, and with what he has done, is a thing special.**

¹¹   **'Tis difficult getting of good doctrine in erroneous times. Ezekiel 34:17-19.**

¹²   **By-paths, though barred up, will not keep all from going in them.**

¹³   **Proverbs 13:15 (KJV).**

¹⁴   **Jeremiah 44:16-17.**

¹⁵   **Proverbs 15:19.**

¹⁶   **Matthew 11:28.**

¹⁷   **Which is hardest, up hill or down hill?**

¹⁸   Deuteronomy 8:6-10.

¹⁹   The Honeycomb mentioned in the Bible is a symbol for the good provision of the land. The word "spirits" is often used to speak of good moods, positive feelings, and courage. The pomegranate figured prominently in the Old Testament text. Its fruit provided food and drink, and images and carvings of pomegranates were used to adorn buildings and clothing, including the clothing of the Hebrew priests.

²⁰   **Mark this.**

²¹   Revelation 2:25; Philippians 3:16.

²²   **Psalm 120:3-4.**

²³   **An emblem of those who go on bravely when there is no danger, but shrink when troubles come.**

²⁴   Judges 5:7; **Judges 5:6-7.**

The Porter

25

CHRISTIANA AND MERCY MEET THE FAMILY

THEY WERE NOW WITHIN sight of the Porter's lodge, and they soon came up to it. But after this they went on more hastily because it was dangerous traveling at night. When they arrived at the gate, the Guide knocked, and the Porter cried out, "Who is there?"

The Guide said, "It is I."

And as soon as he had said that, the Porter recognized his voice and came down, for the Guide had come there often before as a Leader of Pilgrims. When he came down, he opened the gate and, seeing the Guide standing in front of it but not yet seeing the others because they were behind him, the Porter said, "Say now, Mr. Great Heart, what is your business here so late tonight?"

"I've brought some Pilgrims here, where by the Lord's commandment they must stay," answered Great Heart. "I would've been here some time ago had I not been opposed by the Giant who used to back the lions. After a long and tedious combat with him, I've cut him off and have brought the Pilgrims here in safety."

"Won't you go in and stay until morning?" asked the Porter.

"No," replied Great Heart, "I'll return to my Lord tonight."

"Oh, Sir," interjected Christiana, "I don't know how to let you leave us in our Pilgrimage. You've been so faithful and so loving to us. You've fought so courageously for us. And you've been so kind in counseling us. I'll never forget your favor towards us."

Then Mercy said, "Oh, that we might have your company to our journey's end! How can such poor women as we hold out in a way so full of troubles as this way without a friend and defender?"

Then James, the youngest of the boys, said, "Please, Sir, be persuaded to go with us and help us. We're so weak, and the Way is so dangerous."

"I'm at my Lord's command," said Great Heart. "If he'll appoint me to be your Guide the entire way, I'll willingly wait upon you. But here you failed in the beginning, for when he told me to come this far with you, you should've asked him to have me go completely through with you, and he would have granted your request. For now, however, I must withdraw. And so, good Christiana, Mercy, and my brave Children, farewell."

Then the Porter, Mr. Watchful, asked Christiana about her country and her relatives, and she said, "I came from the City of Destruction. I'm a widow woman, and my husband is dead. His name was Christian, the Pilgrim."

"Well," said the Porter, "was he your husband?"

"Yes," answered Christiana, "and these are his children. And this," she said, pointing to Mercy, "is one of my town's women."

Then the Porter rang his bell, as was his habit at such times, and to the door came one of the girls whose name was Humblemind. The Porter said to her, "Go tell it inside that Christiana, the wife of Christian, and her children have come here on Pilgrimage."

Oh, what a noise of gladness there was when the girl just dropped that message out of her mouth! So they came with haste to the Porter, for Christiana still stood at the door.

Then some of the most serious said to her, "Come in, Christiana! Come in, wife of that good man! Come in, you blessed woman! Come in with all those who are with you!"

So she went in, and her children and companion followed her. Now when they had gone in, they were taken into a very large room, where they were invited to sit down; and the Leaders of the House were called to see and welcome the guests. When they came in, and understanding who they were, they saluted them with a kiss and said, "Welcome, you vessels of the Grace of God! Welcome to us, your faithful friends!"

Now because it was somewhat late, and because the Pilgrims were weary with their journey and made faint with the sight of the fight and the terrible lions, they therefore desired to prepare to retire to rest as soon as they could.

"No," said those of the Family, "refresh yourselves with a morsel of meat." They had prepared for them a lamb with the customary sauce belonging to it,[1] for the Porter had heard of their coming earlier and had told it to them within. So when they had eaten and ended their prayer with a Psalm, they desired that they might retire.

"But if we may be so bold as to choose," said Christiana, "let us be in that room that was my husband's when he was here."

So they took them up there, and they all lay in one room. When they were at rest, Christiana and Mercy entered into discussions about things that came to mind.

Christiana said, "Little did I once think when my husband went on Pilgrimage that I would follow him."

"And you thought as little about lying in his bed and in his room to rest as you do now," responded Mercy.

"And much less," said Christiana, "did I ever think of seeing his face with comfort and of worshipping the Lord, the King, with him. Yet now I believe I shall."

"Listen!" exclaimed Mercy. "Don't you hear a noise?"

The Family welcomes the Pilgrims

"Yes," answered Christiana. "I believe it's a sound of music for joy that we're here."

"Wonderful!" said Mercy excitedly. "There's music in the house, music in the heart, and music also in Heaven, for joy that we're here."[2]

They talked like this for a while and at last fell asleep.

In the morning when they were awake, Christiana said to Mercy, "What was the matter that you laughed in your sleep last night? I suppose you were dreaming."

"So I was," answered Mercy, "and a sweet dream it was, but are you sure I laughed?"

"Yes, you laughed heartily," said Christiana. "Please tell me your dream, Mercy."

"I was dreaming that I sat all alone in a solitary place and was lamenting over the hardness of my heart," explained Mercy. "I hadn't sat there long before I thought that many were gathered around me to see me and hear what I was saying. So they listened, and I went on lamenting the hardness of my heart. At this, some of them began to laugh at me. Some called me a fool, and some started to push me around. With that, I thought I looked up and saw one with wings coming towards me. So he came directly to me, and said, 'Mercy, what ails you?'"

"Now when he'd heard my complaint," Mercy went on, "he said, 'Peace be to you.' He also wiped my eyes with his handkerchief and dressed me in silver and gold. He put a chain about my neck, earrings in my ears, and a beautiful crown on my head.[3] Then he took me by the hand and said, 'Mercy, come after me.' So he went up, and I followed until we came to a Golden Gate. Then he knocked, and when those inside had opened it, the man went in, and I followed him up to a throne upon which One sat. And to me He said, 'Welcome, Daughter.' The place looked bright and twinkling like the stars, or rather like the sun; and I thought I saw your husband there. Then I awoke from my dream. But did I laugh?"

"Laugh!" exclaimed Christiana. "Yes, and well you might to see yourself doing so well. For you must allow me to tell you it was a good dream and that as you've begun to find the first part true, so you'll also find the second part at last. 'For

289

Mercy has a sweet dream

God does speak—now one way, now another—though man may not perceive it. In a dream, in a vision of the night, when deep sleep falls on men as they slumber in their beds . . .'⁴ When in bed, we need not lie awake to talk with God. He can visit us while we sleep and cause us then to hear His voice. Our heart often wakes when we sleep, and God can speak to it either by words and proverbs or by signs and similitudes, as well as if one were awake."

"Well, I'm glad of my dream," said Mercy, "for I hope before long to see it fulfilled to make me laugh again."

"I think it's now high time to rise and know what we must do," said Christiana.

"Please," petitioned Mercy, "if they invite us to stay for a while, let's willingly accept the offer. I'm most willing to stay here awhile to grow better acquainted with these girls. I think Prudence, Piety, and Charity have very attractive and serious appearances."

"We'll see what they want to do," answered Christiana.

When they were up and ready, they came down and asked one another about their rest and whether or not it was comfortable.

"Very good," said Mercy. "It was one of the best night's lodgings that I've ever had in my life."

Then Prudence and Piety said, "If you'll be persuaded to stay here awhile, you'll have what the House can supply."

"Yes, and gladly," said Charity.

So they consented and stayed there about a month or more being profitable to one another. And, because Prudence wanted to see how Christiana had brought up her children, she asked her permission to question them in order to teach them doctrine.⁵ Christiana gave her free consent, so she began with the youngest, whose name was James.

"Come, James," said Prudence; "can you tell me who made you?"

"God the Father, God the Son, and God the Holy Spirit," answered James.

"Very good, Young Man," said Prudence. "And can you tell me who saves you?"

"God the Father, God the Son, and God the Holy Spirit," answered James once more.

"Good again," said Prudence, "but how does God the Father save you?"

"By His grace,"[6] answered James.

"How does God the Son save you?" asked Prudence.

"By His righteousness,[7] death,[8] blood,[9] and life,"[10] replied James.

"And how does God the Holy Spirit save you?" asked Prudence.

"By His illumination,[11] by His renovation,[12] and by His preservation,"[13] answered James.

Then Prudence said to Christiana, "You're to be commended for bringing up your children like this. I suppose I don't need to ask the rest these questions since the youngest of them can answer them so well. Therefore, I'll apply myself to Joseph, the next to the youngest."

Then she said, "Come, Joseph, will you let me test and teach you?"

"Gladly," said Joseph.

"What is Man?" asked Prudence.

"A reasonable creature, made that way by God, as my brother said," answered Joseph.

"What is assumed by this word 'saved'?" she inquired.

"That by sin Man has brought himself into a state of captivity and misery," said Joseph.

"What is assumed by his being saved by the Trinity?" inquired Prudence further.

Joseph answered, "That sin is so great and mighty a tyrant, that no one but God can pull us out of its clutches, and that God is so good and loving to people as to indeed pull them out of this miserable state."

Prudence continued, "What is God's design in saving poor people?"

"The glorifying of His name, grace, and justice, and the everlasting happiness of His creature," said Joseph.

"Who are those who must be saved?" asked Prudence.

"Those who accept His salvation," he answered.

"Very good, Joseph," said Prudence. "Your mother has taught you well, and you've listened to what she has said to you."

Then Prudence said to Samuel, the next to the oldest, "Come, Samuel, are you willing for me to test and teach you, too?"

"Yes, indeed, if you please," answered Samuel.

"What is Heaven?" asked Prudence.

"A place and state most blessed because God lives there," said Samuel.

"What is Hell?" she asked.

"A place and state most wretched because it is the dwelling place of sin, the Devil, and death," answered Samuel.

"Why do you want to go to Heaven?" questioned Prudence.

Samuel answered, "So I may see God and serve Him without weariness, so I may see Christ and love Him forever, and so I may have a fullness of the Holy Spirit in me such as I can't enjoy here."

"You are a good young man, also," responded Prudence, "and one who has learned well."

Then she addressed herself to the oldest, whose name was Matthew. And she said to him, "Come, Matthew, shall I also test and teach you?"

"I'm most willing for you to do so," said Matthew.

"Then I ask," began Prudence, "if there was ever anything that lived antecedent to or before God."

"No," said Matthew, "for God is eternal, nor is there anything, excepting himself, that had an existence until the beginning of the first day.[14] 'For in six days the Lord made the heavens and the earth, the sea, and all that is in them.'"[15]

"What do you think of the Bible?" asked Prudence.

"It is the Holy Word of God," answered Matthew.

"Is there anything written in it that you understand?" inquired Prudence.

"Yes, a great deal," said Matthew.

"What do you do when you come across in it places that you don't understand?" she asked.

"I think that God is wiser than I," said Matthew. "I also

pray that He will please let me know everything in it that He knows will be for my good."

"What do you believe regarding the resurrection of the dead?" asked Prudence.

"I believe the same people who were buried shall rise the same in nature but not in corruption,"[16] answered Matthew. "And I believe this for two reasons: First—because God has promised it.[17] Second—because He is able to perform it."[18]

Then Prudence said to the boys, "You must still listen to your mother, for she can teach you more. You must also diligently give ear to what good talk you'll hear from others, for they speak good things for your sakes. Also, carefully observe what the heavens and the earth teach you. But especially be much in meditation of that Book that was the cause of your father becoming a Pilgrim. For my part, my Children, I'll teach you what I can while you're here, and I'll be glad if you'll ask me questions that tend toward godly edifying."

Now seeing these Pilgrims had been at this place a week, Mercy had a visitor who pretended good intentions toward her. His name was Mr. Brisk, a man of some breeding who pretended to be religious but who stuck very close to the world. So he came once or twice or more to Mercy and offered love to her.

Now Mercy was of a fair appearance, and therefore, all the more alluring. It was also her mind to be ever busying herself with doing things, for when she had nothing to do for herself she would make stockings and garments for others and would give them to those who had need. And Mr. Brisk, not knowing where or how she disposed of what she made, seemed to be greatly impressed, for he never found her idle.

"I'm sure she would be a good housewife," he said to himself.

Mercy then revealed the business to the girls who were of the House and inquired of them concerning him, for they knew him better than she. So they told her that he was a very busy young man and one who pretended to be religious but was, as they feared, a stranger to the power of that which is good.

"No then," said Mercy, "I'll not see him anymore, for I aim to never have an obstruction to my soul."

Prudence then told her there need not be any great matter of discouragement given to him, for her continuing the things she had begun to do for the poor would quickly cool his courage.

So the next time he came he found her at her old work of making things for the poor. Then he said, "What, always at it?"

"Yes," said Mercy, "either for myself or for others."

"And what can you earn in a day?" asked Mr. Brisk.

Then Mercy answered, "I do these things to be rich in good deeds and to lay up treasure for myself as a firm foundation for the coming age, so that I may take hold of the life that is truly life."[19]

"Why, pray tell?" questioned Mr. Brisk. "What do you do with them?"

"Clothe the naked," she answered.

With that, his expression fell. So he stopped coming to see her, and when he was asked the reason why, he said that Mercy was a pretty girl but troubled with ill conditions.

When he had left her, Prudence said, "Didn't I tell you that Mr. Brisk would soon forsake you? Yes, he'll raise up an ill report of you, for in spite of his pretense toward religion and his seeming love for mercy, yet Mercy and he are of such different dispositions that I believe they'll never come together."[20]

"I could've had husbands before now, although I didn't speak of it to anyone," said Mercy. "But they were such as didn't like my conditions, even though none of them found fault with my person. So they and I couldn't agree."

"Mercy in our days is valued little beyond its name," said Prudence. "There are only a few who can endure the practice set forth by the conditions."

"Well," said Mercy, "if nobody will have me, I'll die unmarried or my conditions will be to me like a husband. For I can't change my nature, and I purpose to never, as long as I live, allow myself to have one who lies crosswise to me in this. I had a sister named Bountiful, and she was married to one of these rascals. He and she could never agree, but because my sister was resolved to do as she had begun—that is, to show

295

kindness to the poor—her husband, therefore, first verbally abused her and then threw her out of his house."

"Yes," said Prudence, "and yet I'll assure you he professed religion and compassion."

"Yes," agreed Mercy, "he did. The world is now filled with such as he. But I want none of them."

Now Matthew, the oldest son of Christiana fell sick, and he suffered greatly from his sickness. He had much pain in his bowels, so that at times he was doubled up with pain. Not far from there lived Mr. Skill, an ancient and well approved physician. So at Christiana's request, they sent for him, and he came. When he entered the room and had observed the boy a little, he concluded he was sick with the Gripes.[21]

Then Mr. Skill asked the young man's mother, "What diet has Matthew fed upon lately."

"Diet?" questioned Christiana. "Nothing but what is wholesome."

The Physician then said, "This boy has been tampering with something that lies inside undigested and which will not go away without help. And I tell you he must be purged or he'll die."

Then Samuel said, "Mother, mother, what was it that my brother picked up and ate as soon as we came from the Gate at the head of this Path? You know, there was an orchard on the left on the other side of the Wall, and some of the trees hung over the Wall. My brother knocked the fruit down and ate them."

"True, my Child," said Christiana, "he did take from it and eat. Naughty boy as he was! I scolded him, and yet he would eat it."

Mr. Skill then said, "I knew he'd eaten something that wasn't wholesome food. That fruit is the most harmful of all, for it's the fruit of Beelzebub's Orchard. I'm amazed that nobody warned you about it. Many have died from it."

Then Christiana began to cry and she said, "Oh, naughty Boy! And, oh, careless Mother! What shall I do for my son?"

"Come," said the Physician, "don't be too much dejected. The boy may do well again, but he must purge and vomit."

"Please, Sir," pleaded Christiana. "Try the utmost of your skill with him, whatever it costs."

"No," replied Mr. Skill. "I hope I'll be reasonable." So he made him a laxative, but it was too weak. It is said it was made of the blood of a goat, the ashes of a heifer,[22] and with some of the juice of hyssop,[23] and other ingredients. When Mr. Skill saw that the laxative was too weak, he made him one for the purpose. It was made *Ex Carne et Sanguine Christi*,[24] (you know, physicians give strange medicines to their patients) and it was made up into pills with a promise or two and a proportional quantity of Salt.[25]

Matthew was to take the pills three at a time while fasting, and with fifty-nine milliliters of the Tears of Repentance.[26] When this medicine was prepared and brought to the boy, he was hesitant to take it, even though he was so torn with the Gripes it was as if he'd be pulled in pieces.

"Come, come," said the Physician, "you must take it."

"It goes against my stomach," said the boy.

"I must have you take it," said his mother.

"I'll vomit it up again," said the boy.

"Please, sir," said Christiana to Mr. Skill, "how does it taste?"

"It has no bad taste," said the doctor, and with that, she touched one of the pills with the tip of her tongue.

"Oh, Matthew," she said, "this medicine is sweeter than honey.[27] If you love your mother, if you love your brothers, if you love Mercy, and if you love your life, take it."

So, with much commotion, after a short prayer for the blessing of God upon it, he took it, and it worked kindly with him. It caused him to purge and to sleep and rest quietly. It put him into a fine fever and breathing sweat, and it completely cured him of his gripes. So in a short time he got up and walked about with a cane and talked with Prudence, Piety, and Charity about his distemper and how he was healed.

When the boy was healed, Christiana asked Mr. Skill, "Sir, what will satisfy you for your efforts and care for my child?"

And he said, "You must pay the Head of the College of Physicians according to rules made and provided for such a

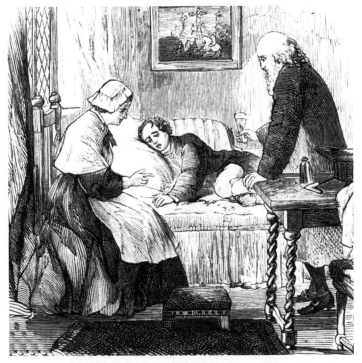

Christiana gives Matthew the medicine

case."[28]

"But, Sir," said Christiana, "is this pill good for anything else?"

"It's a universal pill," said Mr. Skill. "It's good against all the diseases to which Pilgrims are susceptible. When it's prepared well, it will be potent for longer than you can imagine."

"Please, Sir," said Christiana, "make me up twelve boxes of them, for if I can get these, I'll never take any other laxative."

"These pills are good to prevent diseases as well as to cure when one is sick," said the Physician. "Yes, I dare say and stand behind it that if a person will use this laxative as he should, it'll make him live forever.[29] But, good Christiana, you must give these pills no other way but as I've prescribed, for if you do they will do no good." So he gave the laxative to Christiana for herself, her boys, and Mercy and told Matthew to take heed how he ate any more green plums. He then kissed them and went his way.

You were told before how Prudence told the boys that if at any time they wanted to ask her some questions that might be profitable, she would say something to them. Then Matthew, who had been sick, asked her why laxative, for the most part, should be bitter to the taste.

Prudence therefore answered, "To show how unwelcome the Word of God and the effects of it are to a worldly heart."[30]

"Why does laxative, if it is good, purge and cause us to vomit?" asked Matthew.

"To show that when it works effectually, the Word cleanses the heart and mind," said Prudence. "For you see, what one does to the body the other does to the soul."

Matthew asked, "What should we learn by seeing the flame of our fire go upwards and the beams and sweet influences of the sun strike downwards?"

Prudence answered, "By the going up of the fire, we are taught to ascend to Heaven by fervent and hot desires. By the sun sending its heat, beams, and sweet influences downwards, we're taught that, though high, the Savior of the world reaches down to us below with His grace and love."

"Where do the clouds get their water?" asked Matthew.

"Out of the sea," answered Prudence.

"What may we learn from that?" he questioned.

"That ministers should get their doctrine from God," she replied.

"Why do they empty themselves upon the earth?" he asked.

"To show that ministers should give out to the world what they know of God," she said.

"Why is the rainbow caused by the sun?" asked Matthew.

"To show that the covenant of God's grace is confirmed to us in Christ," answered Prudence.[31]

"Why do some of the springs rise out of the top of high hills?" he asked.

"To show that the Spirit of Grace shall spring up in some who are great and mighty as well as in many who are poor and low," she answered.

"Why does fire fasten upon the candle wick?" he inquired.

"To show that unless grace kindles upon the heart, there will be no true Light of Life in us," answered Prudence.[32]

"Why are the wick and tallow and everything spent to maintain the light of the candle?" he asked.

"To show that body and soul and everything should be at the service of and spend themselves to maintain in good condition that grace of God that is in us," she answered.[33]

"Why does the pelican pierce her own breast with her bill?" asked Matthew.

"To nourish her young ones with her blood, and thereby to show that Christ the blessed so loves His young, His people, as to save them from death by His Blood," answered Prudence.[34]

"What may one learn by hearing the rooster crow?" he asked.

"Learn to remember Peter's sin and repentance,"[35] answered Prudence. "The rooster's crowing also shows that day is coming on. Let then the crowing of the rooster put you in mind of that last and terrible day of judgment."[36]

Now about this time, their month was over, so they indicated to those of the House that it was convenient for them to rise and be going.

Then Joseph said to his mother, "We mustn't forget to

send to the house of Mr. Interpreter to ask him to allow Mr. Great Heart to be sent to us so he may be our Guide the rest of our way."[37]

"Good idea!" said Christiana. "I'd almost forgotten."

So she drew up a petition and asked Mr. Watchful, the Porter, to send it by some fit man to her good friend, Mr. Interpreter. When it arrived, and he had seen the contents of the petition, the Interpreter said to the messenger, "Go tell them that I will send him."

When the Family with whom Christiana was staying saw that they were planning to go, they called the whole house together to give thanks to their King for sending them such profitable guests as these. When that was done, they said to Christiana, "And shall we not, as is according to our custom, show you something upon which you can meditate when you're on the Way?"

So they took Christiana, her children, and Mercy into the closet and showed them one of the apples that Eve ate and that she also gave to her husband.[38] It was the fruit that for the eating of which they were both turned out of Paradise, and they asked her what she thought it was.

Then Christiana said, "It's food or poison, I don't know which." So they explained the matter to her, and she held up her hands and wondered.

Then they led her to a place and showed her Jacob's Stairway.[39] At that time, there were some angels ascending upon it. So Christiana looked and looked to see the angels go up, and so did the rest of the company. Then they were going into another place to show them something else, but James said to his mother, "Please ask them to stay here a little longer, for this is a curious sight." So they turned back again and stood, feeding their eyes with this pleasant prospect.[40]

After this, they led them into a place where a golden anchor was hanging up. So they invited Christiana to take it down, saying, "You shall take it with you, for it's an absolute necessity that you have it so you may lay hold of that which is behind the curtain[41] and stand steadfast in case you should meet with turbulent weather."

Then they led them to the mountain upon which Abraham our father had offered up Isaac his son.[42] And they showed them the Altar, the Wood, the Fire, and the Knife, for they remain to be seen to this very day.

When they had seen it, they held up their hands and consecrated themselves as they exclaimed, "Oh, what a man for love to his master and for self-denial was Abraham!"[43]

After they had shown them all these things, Prudence took them into the dining room where a pair of excellent harpsichords stood. So she played upon them and turned what she had shown them into this wonderful song, saying:

> Eve's Apple we have showed you;
> Of that be you aware:
> You have seen Jacob's Ladder too,
> Upon which Angels are.
>
> An Anchor you received have,
> But let not these suffice,
> Until with Abra'm you have gave
> Your Best, a Sacrifice.

About this time, someone knocked at the door. So the Porter opened, and there was Mr. Great Heart. What joy there was after he came in, for now again it came freshly into their minds how just a while ago he had slain old Grim (Bloody Man) the Giant and had delivered them from the lions.

Then Mr. Great Heart said to Christiana and Mercy, "My Lord has sent each of you a bottle of wine and also some parched corn, together with a couple of pomegranates. He's also sent the boys some figs and raisins to refresh you in your way."[44]

Then they addressed themselves to their journey, and Prudence and Piety went along with them. When they came to the gate, Christiana asked the Porter if anyone had gone by lately. He said, "No, only one some time ago who told me there had recently been a great robbery committed on the King's Highway in the direction you're going. But, he said the thieves were apprehended and will shortly be tried for their lives."

Then Christiana and Mercy were afraid, but Matthew said, "Mother, fear nothing as long as Mr. Great Heart is to go with us and be our Guide."

Then Christiana said to the Porter, "Sir, I'm much obliged to you for all the kindnesses you've shown me since I came here and also for being so loving and kind to my children. I don't know how to repay your kindness. Therefore, please accept this small mite as a token of my respect for you." So she put a gold coin in his hand.[45]

He bowed lowly before her and said, "'Always be clothed in white, and always anoint your head with oil.'[46] Let Mercy live and not die, nor let her deeds be few."[47] And to the boys he said, "Do flee the evil desires of youth and follow after godliness with those who are serious and wise,[48] and in so doing you shall put gladness into your mother's heart[49] and obtain praise of all who are sober minded."

Then they thanked the Porter and departed.

Then I saw in my dream that they went forward until they had come to the brow of the hill. There, thinking to herself, Piety cried out, "Alas, I've forgotten what I intended to give to Christiana and her companions! I'll go back and get it." So she ran to get it.

While she was gone, Christiana thought she heard in a grove a little way off to the right hand a most curious melodious note with words much like these:

Through all my Life Your Favor is
So frankly showed to me,
That in Your House for evermore
My dwelling-place shall be.

And still listening, she thought she heard another answer it, saying:

For why? The Lord our God is good;
His Mercy is forever sure:
His Truth at all times firmly stood,
And shall from Age to Age endure.

Christiana asked Prudence what it was that made those curious notes.

Prudence answered, "They're our country birds. They sing these notes only seldom, except when it's spring. When the flowers appear and the sun shines warm, then you may hear them all day long.[50] I often go out to hear them. Often we keep them tame in our house. They're very fine company for us when we're unhappy. Also, they make solitary places, the woods, and groves desirous places in which to be."

By this time, Piety had gotten back, and she said to Christiana, "Look here, I've brought you a diagram of all those things you've seen at our house. You can look at it when you find yourself forgetful, and you can call those things to remembrance again for your edification and comfort."

NOTES ON CHAPTER 25

[1] **Exodus 12:3-8; John 1:29.**

[2] Luke 15:3-10.

[3] **Ezekiel 16:10-12.**

[4] **Job 33:14-15.**

[5] In the original, Bunyan used the religious term "catechize them," which is not a common term in many Christian circles today. In its place, phrased meanings of "catechize" are used here and elsewhere.

[6] Ephesians 2:4-10.

[7] Romans 5:17.

[8] Romans 5:6; Hebrews 2:14-15; 1 Peter 3:18.

[9] Romans 5:9; Ephesians 1:7-8, 2:13; Colossians 1:19-20; Hebrews 9:11-14, 13:12; 1 Peter 1:18-19.

[10] John 1:4; Romans 5:10, 6:4, 23, 8:11, 34.

[11] John 14:16-17, 15:26, 16:13; 1 Corinthians 2:13; 1 John 5:6.

[12] Acts 1:8; Romans 8:1-27; 2 Corinthians 3:18; Titus 3:5.

[13] Luke 12:11-12; Acts 9:31; Romans 15:13.

[14] Genesis 1:1-3; John 1:1-3.

[15] Exodus 20:11.

[16] 1 Corinthians 15:12-58.

[17] 1 Thessalonians 4:13-18; John 5:25, 28-29.

[18] His ability to perform rests with the firstfruits of the resurrection, the resurrection of Jesus Christ. 1 Corinthians 6:14, 15:20-24.

[19] **1 Timothy 6:17-19.**

[20] **Mercy in the practice of mercy rejected, while Mercy in the name of mercy is liked.**

[21] **Gripes of conscience.**

[22] Hebrews 9:11-14, **10:1-4.**

[23] Exodus 12:21-23; Psalm 51:7; Hebrews 9:19.

[24] **The Latin I borrow.** This Latin phrase means "of the flesh and blood of Christ." **John 6:53-58; Hebrews 9:14.** The medicine of the Law was not enough to cure the sickness. The blood and flesh of Christ is the only medicine strong enough to overcome the effects of sin. Romans 8:3.

[25] **Mark 9:49** (KJV).

[26] **Zechariah 12:10.**

[27] Psalm 119:103; Ezekiel 3:3.

[28] **Hebrews 13:11-15**; Romans 12:1.

[29] **John 6:48-51.**

[30] John 3:19-21.

[31] Genesis 9:12-16; Hebrews 9:15; 2 Corinthians 3:13-16.

[32] John 8:12.

[33] Matthew 22:37-38.

[34] John 3:16.

[35] John 13:31-38, 18:15-18, 25-27, 20:3-9, 21:14-19.

[36] Mark 13:35-37; Luke 21:34-36.

[37] **The weak may sometimes call the strong to prayers.**

[38] **Genesis 3:6.**

[39] **Genesis 28:10-17.**

[40] **John 1:51.**

[41] **Hebrews 6:19-20.**

[42] **Genesis 22:1-19.**

[43] Matthew 16:24; Mark 8:34; Luke 9:23.

[44] Philippians 4:19.

[45] In the original, the coin was a "gold angel," an old English coin having as its device the archangel Michael standing upon and piercing the dragon.

[46] Ecclesiastes 9:8; Psalm 133:1-2.

[47] Compare this statement to Deuteronomy 33:6.

[48] 2 Timothy 2:22.

[49] Proverbs 1:8-9, 6:20-22, 10:1, 23:24-25, 29:15, and 30:17.

[50] **Song of Songs 2:11-12.**

26

CHRISTIANA AND MERCY IN THE VALLEYS

NOW THEY BEGAN TO go down the hill into the Valley of Humiliation. It was a steep hill, and the Path was slippery; but they were very careful and got down quite well. When they were down in the valley, Piety said to Christiana, "This is the place where Christian, your husband, met with the foul fiend Apollyon and where they had that great fight. I know you couldn't have helped hearing of it. But be of good courage, for as long as you have Mr. Great Heart here to be your Guide and Leader, we hope you'll fare better."

So when Prudence and Piety had committed the Pilgrims to the conduct of their Guide, he went forward, and they followed.

Mr. Great Heart then said, "We don't need to be so afraid of this valley, for there is nothing here to hurt us, unless we bring it upon ourselves. It's true, Christian did meet here with Apollyon, with whom also he had a horrible fight, but that fray was the fruit of those slips that he made going down the hill.

They who slip there must look for battles here, and this is how this valley got so hard a name. For when the common people hear that some frightful thing has befallen such an individual in such a place, they form an opinion that the place is haunted with some foul fiend or evil spirit; but, alas, it's because of the fruit of their actions that such things befall them here."

"Of itself," he continued, "this Valley of Humiliation is as fruitful a place as any the crow flies over. If we could be so fortunate, I'm persuaded we might find somewhere around here something that could give us reasons why Christian was so grievously beset in this place."

Then James said to his mother, "Look, yonder stands a pillar, and it looks as if something is written on it. Let's go and see what it is."

So they went and found written there: "Let Christian's slips before he came here and the battles that he met with in this place be a warning to those who come after."

"Oh," said their Guide, "didn't I tell you there was something around here that would allude to the reason why Christian was so grievously beset in this place?" Then turning to Christiana, he said, "It's no more disparagement to Christian than to many others whose chance and lot it was for these things to happen, for it's easier going up than down this hill; and that can be said of all but a few hills in these parts of the world. But we'll leave the good man; for he's at rest and also had a brave victory over his enemy. Let Him who Lives Above grant that we fare no worse than he when we come to be tried."

"But," continued Mr. Great Heart. "we'll return to talking about this Valley of Humiliation. It's the best and most fruitful piece of ground in all these parts. It's a fertile ground, and as you see, it consists of much meadow land. And if a man were to come here in the summertime, as we do now, if he didn't know anything about it before and if he delighted himself in the sight of his eyes, he might see these things and find them delightful to him. See how green this valley is and how beautified it is with lilies?[1] I've also known many laboring men who've gotten good estates in this Valley of Humiliation—For God opposes the proud but gives more, more grace to the humble[2] —

for it's indeed a very fruitful soil, and it yields fruit by the handfuls. Some have also wished that the next way to their Father's house were here, so they might not be troubled any more with either hills or mountains to go over. Yet, the Way is the Way, and there is an end."

As they were going along and talking, they saw a boy feeding his father's sheep. The boy was in very poor clothing, but he had a very fresh and good-looking face. And he sang as he sat by himself.

"Listen to what the Shepherd Boy sings," said Mr. Great Heart.

So they listened, and he sang:

He that is down, needs fear no Fall;
He that is low, no Pride:
He that is humble, ever shall
Have God to be his Guide.

I am content with what I have,
Little be it or much:[3]
And, Lord, Contentment still I crave,
Because thou savest such.

Fulness to such, a Burden is,
That go on Pilgrimage:
Here little, and hereafter Bliss,
Is best from Age to Age.[4]

Then their Guide said, "Do you hear him? I'll dare say, this boy lives a merrier life and wears more of that herb called Heart's Ease in his inner man than he who is clothed in silk and velvet. But we'll proceed in our discussion."

"Our Lord formerly had His country house in this valley,"[5] continued Mr. Great Heart. "He loved being here a great deal. He also loved to walk in these meadows, for He found the air was pleasant. Besides, here an individual shall be free from the noise and hurryings of this life. All states are full of noise and confusion, but only the Valley of Humiliation is that empty and

The Shepherd Boy

solitary place. Here, a person won't be so prevented and hindered in his contemplation as in other places he's likely to find. This is a valley in which nobody walks except those who love a Pilgrim's life, and although Christian had the sad misfortune to meet with Apollyon here and to enter into a brisk encounter with him, yet I must tell you that in former times people have met with angels here,[6] have found pearls here,[7] and have found in this place the Words of Life."[8] ✔

"Did I say our Lord had His country house here in former days, and that He loved to walk here?" asked Mr. Great Heart. "I'll add that in this place He has left a yearly revenue to the people who live and traverse these grounds. It's to be faithfully paid to them at certain times for their expenses in the Way and to further encourage them to go on their Pilgrimage."[9]

As they went on, Samuel said to Mr. Great Heart, "Sir, I understand my father and Apollyon had their battle in this valley, but where was the fight? For I recognize this valley is large."

Mr. Great Heart answered, "Your father had that battle with Apollyon at a place before us, yonder in a narrow passage just beyond Forgetful Green. And that place is indeed the most dangerous place in all these parts. For if at any time the Pilgrims meet with any battle shock, it's when they forget what favors they've received and how unworthy they are of them. This is also the place where others have been severely challenged, but we can speak more about that place when we come to it. I'm persuaded that to this day some sign of the battle or some monument remains there to testify that such a battle was fought."

Then Mercy said, "I think I'm as well in this valley as I've been anywhere else in all our journey. I think the place suits my spirit. I love to be in such places where there's no rattling of coaches or rumbling of wheels. I think a person may, without much annoyance, consider who he is, where he came from, what he has done, and what the King has called him to. Here, one may think, and tear one's heart, and melt in one's spirit until one's eyes become like the Pools of Heshbon.[10] Those who go the right way through this Valley of Baca make it a well. The rain that God sends down from Heaven upon those who are here also fills the pools.[11] This valley is that from where also the King will give them vineyards, and they who go through it shall sing[12]—as Christian did even after meeting Apollyon."

"It's true," said their Guide; "I've gone through this valley many times, and I was never better than when here. I've also been a Leader of several Pilgrims, and they've confessed the same. 'This is the one I esteem' says the King, 'he who is humble and contrite in spirit, and trembles at my word.'"[13]

Now they came to the place where the battle mentioned earlier was fought. Then the Guide said to Christiana, her children, and Mercy, "This is the place. Christian stood on this ground, and up came Apollyon against him. And look, didn't I tell you? Here is some of your husband's blood upon these stones to this day. Also, see how there are yet to be seen here and there upon the place some of the splintered pieces of Apollyon's broken arrows. See also how they beat the ground with their feet as they fought in order to make firm their positions against each other and also how with their missed blows they actually split the stones in pieces. To be sure, Christian played the man here and showed himself as stout as even Hercules himself could have, had he been here."

"When Apollyon was beaten," continued Mr. Great Heart, "he made his retreat to the next valley, which is called the Valley of the Shadow of Death,[14] unto which we shall soon come. Look! Yonder also stands a monument to his fame throughout all ages. On it is engraved this battle and Christian's victory."

So, because it stood on the wayside before them, they stepped up to it and read the writing, which word for word was this:

Hard-by here was a Battle fought,
Most strange, and yet most true;
Christian and Apollyon fought
Each other to subdue.
The Man so bravely play'd the Man,

312

He made the Fiend to fly:
Of which a Monument I stand,
The same to testify.

When they had passed by this place, they came upon the borders of the Shadow of Death, and this valley was longer than the other one, a place also most strangely haunted with evil things, as many are able to testify. But these women and children went through it better because they had daylight and because Mr. Great Heart was their Guide.

When they had entered this valley, they thought they heard groaning, as of dead men—a very great groaning. They also thought they heard words of weeping, spoken as of people in extreme torment. These things made the boys shudder. The women also looked pale and faint, but their Guide told them to be of good comfort.

Going on a little farther, they felt the ground begin to shake under them as if some hollow place were there. They also heard a kind of hissing as of serpents, but nothing yet appeared. Then the boys said, "Aren't we almost at the end of this dismal place?"

But the Guide also told them to be of good courage and to pay close attention to their feet, "lest by chance," he said, "you're caught in some snare."

James began to be sick, but I think the cause of it was fear, so his mother gave him some of that glass of spirits that was given to her at the Interpreter's house and three of the pills that Mr. Skill had prepared; and the boy began to revive. Thus, they went on until they came to about the middle of the valley, and then Christiana said, "I think I see something yonder upon the road in front of us, a thing of such a shape as I've not seen."

Then Joseph said, "Mother, what is it?"

"An ugly thing, Child," said Christiana. "An ugly thing."

"But mother," he said, "what's it like?"

"I can't tell what it's like," she answered.

And now it was just a little way off, and she said, "It's near."

"Well," said Mr. Great Heart, "let them who are most afraid keep close to me."

So the Fiend came on, and the Guide met it; but when it just got up to him it vanished to all their sights. Then they remembered what had been said some time ago: "Resist the devil, and he will flee from you."[15]

Being a little refreshed, therefore, they went on.

But they hadn't gone far before, looking behind her, Mercy saw, as she thought, something like a lion coming at a great padding pace toward them. It had a hollow voice of roaring, and at every roar it made all the valley echo and their hearts to ache, except the heart of him who was their Guide. So it came up, and Mr. Great heart stepped to the rear and put all the Pilgrims behind him. The Lion also came on quickly, and Mr. Great Heart prepared himself to battle him. But when the Lion saw it was determined that resistance should be made, he also drew back and came no farther.[16]

They went on again, and their Leader went before them until they came to a place where a pit had been dug across the whole width of the Path. And before they could prepare themselves to go over it, a great mist and a darkness fell upon them so that they could not see.

Then the Pilgrims said, "Alas! Now what shall we do?"

But their Guide answered them, "Don't fear. Stand still and see what kind of end this also will come to."

So they stayed there because their path was damaged. Then, they thought they heard more clearly the noise and rushing of the enemies. The fire and the smoke of the pit also was much easier to be discerned.

Then Christiana said to Mercy, "Now I see what my poor husband went through. I've heard much about this place, but I never was here before now. Poor man, he went here all alone in the night. He had night almost through the entire way, and these fiends were busy around him as if they would've torn him in pieces. Many have spoken of it, but no one can tell what the Valley of the Shadow of Death should mean until they come into it themselves. 'Each heart knows its own bitterness, and no one else can share its joy.'[17] To be here is a fearful thing."

Great Heart then said, "This is like doing business in great waters,[18] or like going down into the deep. This is like being in the heart of the sea, and like going down to the roots of the mountains. Now it seems as if the earth, with its bars, were about us forever.[19] But let them who walk in the dark, who have no light, trust in the name of the Lord and rely on their God.[20] For my part, As I've already told you, I've often gone through this valley, and I've been much more challenged than I am now; and yet you see I'm alive. I wouldn't boast because I'm not my own savior. But in order to obtain light, let's pray to Him who can lighten our darkness,[21] and who can rebuke not only these, but all the devils in Hell."

So they cried and prayed, and God sent light and deliverance, for there was now no hindrance in their way—no, not there where they had been stopped by a pit. Yet, they had not gotten through the valley, so they still traveled on and experienced great stinks and loathsome smells to their great annoyance.

Then Mercy said to Christiana, "There isn't such pleasantness here as there is at the Gate, or at the Interpreter's house, or at the house where we last lay."

"Oh," said one of the boys, "but it's not as bad going through here as it is to live here always. And for all I know, one reason why we must go this way to the house prepared for us is so that our home might be made all the sweeter to us."

"Well said, Samuel," stated the Guide. "You've now spoken like a man."

"Why, if I ever get out of here again," said the boy, "I think I'll prize light and a good path better than I ever did in all my life."

Then the Guide said, "We'll be out soon."

So on they went, and Joseph said, "Can't we see to the end of this valley yet?"

The Guide replied, "Watch your feet, for you'll soon be among snares."

So they watched their feet and went on but were much troubled with the snares. When they came among the snares, they saw a man who had been cast into the Ditch on the left hand side of the path. His flesh was all lacerated and torn.

The Guide said, "That is one named Heedless who was traveling this way. He has lain there a great while. There was one named Takeheed with him when he was taken and killed, but he escaped their hands. You can't imagine how many are killed hereabouts, and yet men are so foolishly venturous as to set out lightly on Pilgrimage and to come without a guide. Poor Christian! It was a wonder that he escaped here, but he was beloved of his God. He also had a good heart of his own, or else he never could've done it."

Now they approached the end of the Way. It was there that Christian had seen the Cave when he went by, and out of the Cave came a Giant named Maul, who used to spoil young Pilgrims with Sophistry.[22] He called Great Heart by name and said to him, "How many times have you been forbidden to do these things?"

"What things?" asked Mr. Great Heart.

"What things!" exclaimed the Giant. "You know what things! But I'll put an end to your trade."

"But please," said Mr. Great Heart, "before we begin it, let us understand the reason why we must fight."

Now the women and children stood trembling and did not know what to do.

Then the Giant answered, "You rob the country, and you rob it with the worst kind of thefts."

"These are just generalities," said Mr. Great Heart. "Come to the particulars, Man."

The Giant then said, "You practice the craft of a kidnapper. You gather up women and children and carry them into a strange country to the weakening of my master's kingdom."

But now Great Heart replied, "I am a servant of the God of Heaven. My business is to bring Sinners to repentance. I'm commanded to do my work to turn men, women, and children from darkness to light and from the power of Satan to God.

And if this is indeed the basis of your quarrel, let us get to it as soon as you would like."

Then the Giant came up.

Mr. Great Heart went to meet him; and as he went he drew his Sword. But the Giant had a club.

Without any more ado, they went at it. And at the first blow, the Giant struck Great Heart down upon one of his knees.

With that, the women and children cried out.[23]

Recovering himself, Mr. Great Heart laid into him in a full energetic manner and gave the Giant a wound in his arm. He fought like this for the space of an hour to such a height of heat that the breath came out of the Giant's nostrils like the heat coming out of a boiling cauldron.

Then they sat down to rest themselves, but Mr. Great Heart applied himself to prayer. The women and children also did nothing except sigh and cry all the time that the battle lasted. When they had rested themselves and caught their breath, they both went at it again, and Mr. Great Heart knocked the Giant down to the ground with a full blow.

"No!" cried Maul. "Let me recover!"

In fairness, Mr. Great Heart let him get up.

At that, they went at it again, and the Giant missed only slightly from breaking Mr. Great Heart's skull with his club. Seeing that, Mr. Great Heart ran to him in the full heat of his spirit and pierced him under the fifth rib.

Thus wounded, the Giant began to faint and could not hold up his club any longer.

Mr. Great Heart seconded his blow and cropped the head of the Giant from off his shoulders.

Then the women and children rejoiced, and Mr. Great Heart also praised God for the deliverance He had worked. When this was done, they all erected a pillar and fastened the Giant's head upon it and wrote underneath it in letters that those passing by might read:

He that did wear this Head, was one
That Pilgrims did misuse;
He stopt their Way, he spared none,
But did them all abuse:

Mr. Great Heart fights with the Giant

Until that I, Great-heart arose,
The Pilgrims Guide to be;
Until that I, did him oppose,
That was their Enemy.

NOTES ON CHAPTER 26

[1] **Song of Songs 2:1.**

[2] **James 4:6; 1 Peter 5:5**; Proverbs 3:34. **Men thrive in the Valley of Humiliation.**

[3] **Philippians 4:12-13.**

[4] **Hebrews 13:5**; Deuteronomy 31:6-8.

[5] Acts 8:32-33; Philippians 2:5-8.

[6] **Hosea 12:4,5**; Genesis 32:24-30.

[7] Matthew 13:45-46.

[8] John 6:67-68; Philippians 2:14-16; 1 John 1:1-3.

[9] There is no shortage in either God's supply or methods through which He can supply the needs of Pilgrims during their journey in this life. **Matthew 11:29**; Philippians 4:19.

[10] **Song of Songs 7:4**; Numbers 21:25-26.

[11] **Psalm 84:5-7.**

[12] **Hosea 2:14-15.**

[13] Isaiah 66:2.

[14] Psalm 23.

[15] James 4:7.

[16] **1 Peter 5:8,9.**

[17] Proverbs 14:10.

[18] Psalm 107:23-28 (KJV).

[19] Jonah 2:1-6.

[20] Isaiah 50:10.

[21] 2 Samuel 22:29; Revelation 21:23,24.

[22] Sophistry is defined as "subtle or deceptive reasoning," and gets its bad name from an ancient school of Greek philosophy that was known for its "skeptical view on absolute truth and morality," and for its leanings toward egoism and gain.

[23] **Weak folks' prayers do sometimes help strong folks' cries.**

Mr. Honest

27

MR. HONEST, MR. FEARING, AND MR. SELFWILL

NOW I SAW THAT they went to the ascent, which was a little way off and was built up to be a viewpoint for Pilgrims. It was the place where Christian had the first sight of Faithful, his brother. They sat down and rested there and made merry because they had gotten away from Maul, the giant who was so dangerous. As they sat there and ate, Christiana asked the Guide if he'd been hurt in the battle.

Then Mr. Great Heart said, "No, except a little on my flesh. Yet that will also be so far from being to my detriment that it is actually proof of my love to my Master and you. And by grace it will be a means to increase my reward at last."

"But weren't you afraid, good Sir, when you saw him come out with his club?" asked Christiana.

"It's my duty," he said, "to distrust my own ability so I might rely on Him who is stronger than all." [1]

"But what did you think when he knocked you down to the ground at the first blow?" inquired Christiana.

"Why, I thought about how my Master himself was likewise assaulted," he said. "Yet it was He who was the Conqueror."

Then Matthew said, "When you've all thought what you please, I think God has been wonderfully good to us, both in bringing us out of this valley and in delivering us out of the hand of this enemy. For my part, I see no reason why we should distrust our God anymore since He has now given us such a testimony of His love in such a place as this."

Then they got up and went forward. A short distance ahead of them stood an oak, and when they came to it they found under it an old Pilgrim fast asleep. They knew he was a Pilgrim by his Clothes, his Staff, and his Belt.

So the Guide, Mr. Great Heart, woke him up, and the old Gentleman cried out as he lifted up his eyes, "What's the matter? Who are you? And what's your business here?"

"Come, Man," said Great Heart, "don't be so hot. We're only friends."

Yet the old man got up and stood at his guard,[2] and he wanted to know of them what they were.

Then the Guide said, "My name is Great Heart. I'm the Guide of these Pilgrims who are going to the Celestial Country."

Then the Old Pilgrim said, "I ask for your pardon. I feared you were of the company of those who some time ago robbed Little Faith of his money, but now that I look around me better I perceive you are more honest people."

"Why, what would you or could you have done to have helped yourself if we indeed had been of that company?" asked Great Heart.

"Done?" exclaimed the Old Pilgrim. "Why, I would've fought as long as I had breath in me. And if I'd done so, I'm sure you never could've given me the worst of it, for a Christian can never be overcome unless he himself yields."[3]

"Well said, Father," said the Guide. "By this I know you are made of the right stuff, for you've said the truth."

"And by this I know that you also know what a true Pilgrimage is," said the man, "for all others think that we are the quickest of any to be overcome."

322

"Well," said Great Heart, "now that our meeting has been happy, please let me have your name and the name of the place you came from."

"I can't say my name," said the old Gentleman, "but I came from the Town of Stupidity. It lays about four degrees beyond the City of Destruction."

"Oh!" exclaimed Great Heart. "Are you a citizen of that country then? I believe I have half a guess of you. Your name is Old Honesty, isn't it?"

So the old Gentleman blushed, and said, "Not Honesty in the abstract, but Honest is my name, and I hope that my nature will agree to what I'm called. But, Sir," he asked, "how could you guess that I am such a man since I came from that kind of a place?"

"I'd heard of you before, from my master," said Mr. Great Heart, "for He knows all things that are done on the Earth.[4] But I've often wondered that anyone could come from your place, for your town is worse than what the City of Destruction is itself."[5]

"Yes," said Mr. Honest, "we're farther away from the sun, so are more cold and senseless. But even if a man lived in a mountain of ice, if the sun of righteousness[6] arose upon him, his frozen heart would feel a thaw; and this is how it has been with me."

"I believe it, father Honest," said Great Heart. "I believe it, for I know the thing is true."

Then the old Gentleman greeted all the Pilgrims with a holy kiss of love,[7] and he asked them about their names and how they had fared since they set out on their Pilgrimage.

Then Christiana said, "I suppose you've heard of my name. Good Christian was my husband, and these four are his children."

You cannot imagine how the old Gentleman was taken back when she told him who she was. He skipped, smiled, and blessed them with a thousand good wishes, saying, "Be it spoken to your comfort that the name of your husband rings all over these parts of the world. His faith, courage, endurance, and sincerity in everything made his name famous."

Then he turned himself to the boys and asked them their names, which they told him. And then he said to them, "Matthew, you be like Matthew the tax collector, not in vice but in virtue.[8] Samuel, you be like Samuel the prophet, a man of faith and prayer.[9] Joseph, you be like Joseph in Potiphar's house, chaste and one who flees from temptation.[10] And James, you be like James the Just, like James the brother of our Lord."[11]

Then they told him about Mercy and how she had left her town and her relatives to come along with Christiana and her sons.

At that, the old honest man said, "Mercy is your name, and by mercy you'll be sustained and carried through all those difficulties that shall assault you in your way until you arrive there, where you'll look the Fountain of Mercy in the face with comfort."

All this while, the Guide, Mr. Great Heart, was very much pleased and smiled upon his companion. As they walked along together, the Guide asked the old gentleman if he knew one named Mr. Fearing, who came on Pilgrimage out of his parts.

"Yes, very well," he said. "He was a man who had the root of the matter in him, but he was one of the most troublesome Pilgrims I ever met in all my days."

"I perceive you knew him," said Great Heart, "for you've given a very accurate description of him."

"Knew him!" exclaimed Honest, "I was a great companion of his! I was with him almost to the end. When he first began to think of what would come upon us hereafter, I was with him."

Then Great Heart said, "I was his Guide from my Master's house to the Gate of Celestial city."

"Then you knew him to be a troublesome one," said Honest.

"I certainly did," replied Great Heart, "but I could bear it very well, for men of my calling are often entrusted with the conduct of such as he."

"Well then," said Mr. Honest, "please let us hear a little about him and how he behaved himself under your leadership."

Great Heart began, "Why, he was always afraid that he would come short of wherever he had a desire to go. He was frightened by everything he heard anybody say, who gave the least appearance of opposition to it. I hear he lay bellowing in the Swamp of Despondence for over a month altogether. And, seeing several go over before him, neither did he dare venture on, even though many of them offered to lend him their hand. He said he would die if he didn't get to Celestial City, and yet he was dejected at every difficulty and stumbled at every straw that anybody cast in his way."

"Well," continued Great Heart, "after he had lain in the Swamp of Despondence a great while, as I've told you, one sunshine morning he ventured on—I don't know how—and so he got over. But after he was over, he would scarcely believe it. He had, I think, a Swamp of Despondence in his mind, a swamp that he carried with him everywhere, or else he could've never been as he was. So he came up to the Gate—you know what I mean, the one standing at the head of this way—and he also stood there a good while before he would venture to knock. When the Gate was opened, he would step back and give place to others and say he was not worthy. Even though he got to the Gate before some, yet many of them went in before him. The poor man would stand there shaking and shrinking. I dare say, it would have brought pity to one's heart to have seen him; nor would he go back again.

"At last, he took in his hand the hammer that hung on the Gate and gave a small rap or two. Then One opened to him, but he shrank back as before. He who opened the Gate stepped out after him and said, 'You trembling one, what do you want?' With that, he fell to the ground. He who spoke to him wondered to see him so faint, so He said to him, 'Peace to you; come in, for you are blessed.' He then got up and went in, trembling. And when he was inside, he was ashamed to show his face. Well, after he had been entertained there awhile—as you know how the manner is—he was told to go on his way. He was also told the Path he should take, so he went until he came to our house. But as he behaved himself at the Gate, so he did at my master the Interpreter's door."

Great Heart said, "He lay there in the cold a good while before he would venture to call, and yet he would not go back; and the nights were long and cold then. Near his heart in his coat he had a Note of Necessity for my master, a note to receive him and grant him the comfort of His house and also to allow him a stout and valiant escort because he himself was such a chicken-hearted man. And yet, in spite of all that, he was afraid to call at the door. So he lay up and down thereabouts until, poor man, he was almost starved. Yes, his dejection was so great that even though he saw several others gain admittance by knocking, he was still afraid to venture on. At last, I think, I looked out the window and, seeing a man to be up and down around the door, I went out to him and asked what he was. But, the poor man, tears stood in his eyes, so I perceived what he wanted. I went in, therefore, and told it in the house, and we showed the thing to our Lord. So He sent me out again to plead with him to come in. But, I dare say, I had hard work to do it. At last he came in, and I will say that my Lord approached and treated him most lovingly."

"There were only a few good pieces at the table," continued Great Heart, "but some of it was laid upon his plate. Then he presented the note, and my Lord looked at it and said his desire would be granted. So when he had been there a good while, he seemed to get some heart and to be a little more comfortable. For, as you must know, my master is one of very tender feelings, especially for those who are afraid. He treated him, therefore, in a way that would tend most to his encouragement. Well, when he'd had a look at the things of the place and was ready to take his journey to go to the City, my Lord—as He did to Christian before—gave him a bottle of spirits and some pleasant things to eat. So we set forward, and I went in front of him; but the man was one of few words and would only sigh aloud."

"When we arrived at the place where the three fellows were hanged," Great Heart continued, "in doubt he said that hanging would likely be his end, too. But he seemed glad when he saw the Cross and the Tomb. I confess that he desired to stay there a little to look, and he seemed for a while after that to be a bit cheery. When we came to the Hill of Difficulty, he

326

didn't stop at that, nor did he much fear the lions; for you must know that his trouble was not about such things as those. His fear was about his final acceptance.

"At the house Beautiful, I got him in—before he was willing, I think—and also, when he was in, I made him acquainted with the young ladies who were of the place; but he was ashamed to enjoy their company much. He desired to be mostly alone, yet he always loved good talk and would often get behind the screen to hear it. He also loved much to see ancient things and to be pondering them in his mind. He told me afterward that he loved to be in those two houses from which he last came—that is, the one at the Gate and that of the Interpreter—but that he dared not be so bold to ask.

"When we went also from the house Beautiful down the hill into the Valley of Humiliation, he went down as well as I ever saw a man do in my life, for he didn't care how little or low he was as long as he could be happy at last. Yes, I think there was a kind of sympathy between that valley and him, for I never saw him better in all his Pilgrimage than when he was in that valley. He would lie down there, embrace the ground, and kiss the very flowers that grew in that valley.[12] He would now be up every morning at the break of day, tracing out and walking here and there in the valley."

"But," said Great Heart, "when he got to the entrance of the Valley of the Shadow of Death, I thought I was going to lose my man, not because he had any inclination to go back— he always abhorred that—but because he was ready to die from fear. 'Oh, the Hobgoblins will have me; the Hobgoblins will have me!' he cried; and I couldn't shake it from him. He made such a noise, and such an outcry there, that if they had only heard him, it would've been enough to encourage them to come and attack us. But I took very good notice of this: that the valley was as quiet while he went through it as I ever knew it to be before or since. I suppose those enemies there had then a special constraint upon them from our Lord, and had been commanded not to meddle until Mr. Fearing had passed over it.[13]

"It would take too long to tell you everything. Therefore, we'll mention only one or two more passages. When he arrived at the Vanity Fair, I thought he was going to fight with every man in the place. I feared we both would be knocked over the head because he was so hotly against their foolish acts. Upon the Enchanted Ground, he was also very alert. But when he came to the River where there was not a bridge, he was again in a sorry situation. Then he said he would be drowned forever and so never see with comfort that Face he had come so many miles to look upon."

Great Heart went on, "I also took notice of something remarkable there. The water of that river was lower at that time than I ever saw it in all my life. So he finally went over in water not much higher than his shoes. When he was approaching the Gate, I began to take my leave of him and to wish him to have a good reception above. He said, 'I shall! I shall!' Then we parted, and I saw him no more."

"Then it seems he was well at last," said Mr. Honest.

"Yes, yes," said Great Heart. "I never had doubt about him. He was a man of a choice spirit; only he was always kept very low, and that made his life so burdensome to himself and so troublesome to others. He was above many others in being tender about sin.[14] He was also so afraid of doing injuries to others that he often would deny himself of that which was permissible, so he wouldn't offend them."[15]

"But what would be the reason that such a good man should be so much in the dark all his days?" asked Honest.

"There are two sorts of reasons for it," answered Mr. Great Heart. "One is that the wise God will have it so; some must play the flute, and some must weep.[16] Now Mr. Fearing was one who played upon this bass instrument. He and his friends play the trombone, whose notes are more dark than the notes of other musical instruments—though, indeed, some say the bass is the foundation of music. For my part, I don't care at all for that profession that doesn't begin in heaviness of mind. When the musician intends to bring all the strings into tune, he usually touches the bass string first. God also plays upon this string first when he sets the soul in tune for himself. Only here

Mr. Fearing

was the imperfection of Mr. Fearing: he couldn't play any other music but this until toward his latter end."

I am bold to speak metaphorically like this for the maturing of the minds of young readers and because in the Book of Revelation the saved are compared to a company of musicians who play upon their trumpets and harps and sing their songs before the Throne.[17]

Then Honest said, "He was a very earnest man, as one may see by what you've related of him. He didn't fear difficulties, lions, or the Vanity Fair at all. It was only sin, death, and Hell that were a terror to him, and that was because he had some doubts about his share in that Celestial Country."

"You're right," said Great Heart. "Those were the things that troubled him, and as you've well observed, they arose from the weakness of his mind about that, not from weakness of spirit as to the practical part of a Pilgrim's life. I dare believe that, as the proverb says, 'He could have bitten a firebrand had it stood in his way.' But no man has been able to easily shake off the things with which he was oppressed."

Then Christiana said, "This account about Mr. Fearing has done me good. I thought no one had been like me, but I see there is some similarity between that good man and me. Only we differ in two things: His troubles were so great that they broke out, but I kept mine within. His also lay so hard upon him that they made him so that he couldn't knock at the houses provided for entertaining, but my trouble was always such as made me knock all the louder."

"If I might also speak my mind," said Mercy, "I must say that a part of him has also dwelled in me. For I've always been more afraid of the lake[18] and the loss of a place in Paradise[19] than I have been of the loss of other things. 'Oh,' I thought, 'If I may have the happiness to have a dwelling there, it will be enough even though I part with all the world to win it.'"

Then Matthew said, "Fear was one thing that made me think I was far from having within me that which accompanies Salvation, but if it was so with such a good man as he, why may it not also go well with me?"

"No fears, no grace," said James. "Although there isn't always grace where there is the fear of Hell, yet, to be sure, there is no grace where there is no fear of God."

Then Great Heart said, "Well said, James. You've hit the mark, for 'the fear of God is the beginning of Wisdom.'[20] To be sure, they who lack the beginning have neither middle nor end. But we'll conclude here our discussion of Mr. Fearing after we've sent after him this farewell:

Well, Master Fearing, thou didst fear
Thy God, and wast afraid
Of doing any thing, while here,
That would have thee betray'd.
And didst thou fear the Lake and Pit?
Would others did so too!
For, as for them that [lack] thy wit,
They do themselves undo.

Now I saw that they still went on in their talking, for after Mr. Great Heart had made an end with Mr. Fearing, Mr. Honest began to tell them of another whose name was Mr. Selfwill.

"He pretended himself to be a Pilgrim," said Mr. Honest, "but I'm persuaded he never came in at the Gate that stands at the start of the Way."

"Did you ever have any discussion with him about it?" asked Great Heart.

"Yes," answered Mr. Honest, "more than once or twice, but he would always be like himself, self-willed. He neither cared for man nor argument, nor even yet example. He did whatever his mind prompted him to do, and he couldn't be convinced to do anything else."

"Please tell me, what principles did he hold?" asked Great Heart, "for I suppose you know."

Mr. Honest answered, "He held that a man might follow the vices as well as the virtues of the Pilgrims, and that if he did both, he would certainly be saved."

"How?" the Guide asked in amazement. "If he had said, 'It's possible for the best to be guilty of the vices, as well as to partake of the virtues of Pilgrims,' he couldn't have been blamed much; for indeed, we're exempted from no vice absolutely, but on the condition that we watch and contend.[21] But I perceive this is not the case. If I understand you right, your meaning is that he was of an opinion that it was allowable not to be watching and contending."

"Yes, yes, that's what I mean," said Honest, "and that's what he believed and practiced."

"But what grounds did he have for saying so?" asked Great Heart.

"Why, he said he had Scripture for his justification," answered Mr. Honest.

"Pray tell, Mr. Honest, present us with a few particulars," said the Guide.

"So I will," said Honest. "He said that having affairs with other men's wives had been practiced by David, and therefore he could do it.[22] He said that having more women than one was a thing Solomon practiced, and therefore he could do it.[23] He said that Sarah and the godly Midwives of Egypt lied and that lying saved Rahab, and therefore he could do it.[24] He said that the Disciples went at the bidding of their Master and took away the owner's donkey, and therefore he could do so, too.[25] He said that Jacob got the inheritance of his father in a way of guile and deception, and therefore he could do so, too."[26]

"High profanity indeed!" exclaimed Mr. Great Heart. "And are you sure he was of this opinion?"

"I've heard him plead for it, quote Scripture for it, and bring arguments for it," stated Mr. Honest.

"It's an opinion that's not fit to be allowed in the world in any way," said Great Heart.

"You must understand me correctly," replied Honest. "He didn't say that just anyone might do this, but that those who had the virtues of those who did such things could also do the same things."

"But what is more false than such a conclusion?" asked Great Heart. "This is as much as to say that because good men have sinned before due to infirmity, therefore, he was permitted to do it out of a presumptuous mind. Or that if because of a blast of wind or that he stumbled at a stone a child fell down and defiled himself in mud, therefore he might willfully lie down and wallow like a pig in it. Who could have thought that anyone could've been so thoroughly blinded by the power of evil desires? But what is written must be true: 'They stumble because they disobey the message—which is also what they were destined for.'"[27]

Great Heart continued, "His supposing that such people who addict themselves to their vices may have the godly man's virtues is also a delusion as strong as the other. It's just as if the dog should say, 'I have or may have the qualities of the child because I lick up it's stinking excrements.' To eat up the sin of God's people is no sign that one possesses their virtues.[28] Nor can I believe that one who is of this opinion can presently have in him faith or love. But I know you've made strong objections against him. Pray tell, what can he say for himself?"

Mr. Honest answered, "He says to do this by way of opinion seems abundantly more honest than to do it and yet hold an opinion that is contrary to it."

"That's a very wicked answer," said Great Heart, "for although it's bad to let loose the bridle to evil desires while our opinions are against such things, yet to sin and plead a toleration toward doing so is worse. The one accidentally causes those watching to stumble, the other pleads them into the snare."

"There are many of this man's mind who don't have this man's mouth," said Honest, "and that makes going on Pilgrimage of so little esteem as it is."

"You've said the truth," said Great Heart, "and it's to be lamented; but the one who fears the King of Paradise shall come out of them all."[29]

"There are strange opinions in the world," said Christiana. "I know one who said there would be enough time to repent when they came to die."[30]

"Such are not very wise," responded Great Heart. "If that man had in his life a week to run twenty miles, he would've been unwilling to defer that journey until the last hour of that week."

"You speak the truth," said Honest, "and yet, indeed, the majority of those who count themselves Pilgrims do that. As you see, I'm an old man. I've been a traveler in this road many a day, and I've taken notice of many things. I've seen some who've set out as if they would drive all the world before them, but who yet died in a few days in the Desert and so never got sight of the Promised Land."[31]

Mr. Honest continued, "I've seen some who seemed not to be the least bit promising when they first set out to be Pilgrims, and who one wouldn't think could've lived a day, which yet proved to be very good Pilgrims. I've seen some who've run hastily forward, and who after a little time have run just as fast back again."

"I've seen some" he went on, "who spoke very well of a Pilgrim's life at first, and who after a while have spoken as much against it. I've heard some who when they first set out for Paradise, say positively there is such a place, and who when they've almost gotten there, have come back again saying there is none. I've heard some boast about what they would do in case they should be opposed, who even at a false alarm have fled faith, the Pilgrim's Way, and everything."[32]

NOTES ON CHAPTER 27

[1] **2 Corinthians 4**.

[2] **One saint sometimes takes another for his enemy.**

[3] Romans 8:35-39.

[4] Psalm 147:5; Proverbs 15:11; Isaiah 46:9-10.

[5] **Stupefied ones are worse than those merely carnal.**

[6] Malachi 4:2.

[7] Romans 16:16; 1 Corinthians 16:20; 1 Peter 5:14.

[8] Matthew 9:9-12, **10:1-4**.

[9] 1 Samuel 1:24-28, 3:19 through 4:1, 7:8-9, 8:6, 12:16-18; **Psalm 99:6**.

[10] **Genesis 39**.

[11] Matthew 13:55; Mark 6:3; Galatians 1:18-19. James, the brother of Jesus, who while not accepting his brother's

ministry before the crucifixion, became a leader in the church in Jerusalem. **Acts 1:14**, 12:17, 15:2, 6, 12-21; 1 Corinthians 15:7; Galatians 2:8-9. *The New Bible Dictionary*, ©1964 by Eerdmans, says, "according to Hegesippus, he became known as 'the Just' because of his faithful adherence to the Jewish law and his austere manner of life."

12 **Lamentations 3:27-30**.

13 1 Corinthians 10:13.

14 **Psalm 88**.

15 **Romans 14:21**; **1 Corinthians 8:13**, 9:12, 10:23-24.

16 **Matthew 11:16-18**.

17 **Revelation 8:2, 14:2-3**

18 Revelation 20:13-15.

19 Luke 23:43; 2 Corinthians 12:3-4; Revelation 2:7.

20 Proverbs 9:10.

21 Matthew 26:41; Luke 21:36; 1 Corinthians 16:13; 1 Thessalonians 5:4-9; Book of Jude, especially verse 3.

22 2 Samuel 11.

23 1 Kings 11:1-6.

24 Genesis 18:9-15; Exodus 1:19; Joshua 2, 6:22-23.

25 Luke 19:28-35; John 12:14-15.

26 Genesis 27:1-29.

27 **1 Peter 2:8**.

28 **Hosea 4:8**.

29 2 Corinthians 6:17-18; Revelation 18:4; Ezra 10:11.

30 Luke 12:20; 2 Corinthians 6:2; James 4:13-14.

31 Joshua 5:6.

32 Mark 14:29-31, 66-72.

28

THE PILGRIMS ARE ENTERTAINED BY GAIUS

NOW WHEN THEY WERE thus in their way, an individual came running to meet them and said, "Gentlemen, and you of the weaker sort, if you love life, prepare yourselves, for the Robbers are ahead of you!"

Then Mr. Great Heart said, "They're the three who attacked Little Faith some time ago. Well, we're ready for them."

So they went on their way.

They looked at every turning where they might have met with the villains, but whether they had heard of Mr. Great Heart or whether they had some other prey, they did not come up to the Pilgrims.

Christiana then wished for an Inn for herself and her children because they were weary.

Mr. Honest said, "There is one a short distance ahead of us where a very honorable disciple named Gaius lives."[1]

So they all decided to turn in there, mainly because the old gentleman gave such a good recommendation of him. When they came to the door, they went in without knocking, for folks did not used to knock at the door of an Inn. Then they called for the owner of the house, and he came to them. So they asked if they might stay there that night.

"Yes, if you are true believers," said Gaius, "for my house is for no one but Pilgrims."

Then Christiana, Mercy, and the boys were even more glad because the Innkeeper loved Pilgrims. So they called for rooms, and he showed them one for Christiana, her children, and Mercy, and another one for Mr. Great Heart and the old gentleman.

Then Mr. Great Heart said, "Good Gaius, what do you have for supper? These Pilgrims have come far today and are weary."

"It's late," said Gaius, "so we can't conveniently go out to seek food, but you'll be welcome to such as we have, if that will suffice."

"We'll be content with what you have in the house," said Great Heart, "because I have examined you. You're never destitute of that which is agreeable."

Then Gaius went down and spoke to the cook, whose name was Tastethat Whichisgood,[2] telling her to get supper ready for the number of Pilgrims. This done, he came up again, saying, "Come my good Friends, you're welcome here. I'm glad I have a house in which to entertain you. While supper is being prepared, if you please, let's entertain one another with some good conversation."

They all were contented to do so.

Then Gaius said, "Whose wife is this older matron? And whose daughter is this young lady?"

"The woman," said Mr. Great Heart, "is the wife of one named Christian, a Pilgrim of former times, and these are his four children. The girl is one of her acquaintances, one whom she persuaded to come with her on Pilgrimage. All the boys take after their father and desire to walk in his steps.[3] If they see any place where the old Pilgrim laid down or any print of his foot, it ministers joy to their hearts, and they desire to lay or walk in the same place."

Then Gaius said, "Is this Christian's wife, and are these Christian's children? I knew your husband's father...yes, and also his father's father. Many of this stock have been good. Their ancestors lived first at Antioch.[4] Christian's forefathers were very worthy men. I suppose you've heard your husband talk of them. Above any I know, they've shown themselves to be people of great virtue and courage in behalf of the Lord of the Pilgrims, His ways, and those who loved Him. I've heard of many of your husband's relatives who have endured all trials for the sake of the Truth.

"Stephen, who was one of the first of your husband's family, was knocked on the head with stones.[5] James, another of that generation, was slain with the edge of the sword.[6] To say nothing of Paul and Peter,[7] men anciently of the Family your husband came from: there was Ignatius who was cast to the lions,[8] Romanus whose flesh was cut by pieces from his bones,[9] and Polycarp who stood bravely in the fire;[10] there was the one who was hanged up in a basket in the sun for the wasps to eat, and the one they put in a sack and cast into the sea to be drowned. It would be impossible to utterly count up all of that Family who have suffered injuries and death because of their love for a Pilgrim's life. Nor can I be anything but glad to see your husband has left behind him four boys such as these. I hope they'll hold up their father's name, walk in their father's steps, and come to their father's end."

"Indeed, Sir," said Great Heart, "they are promising lads. They seem to heartily choose their father's ways."

"That's what I said," commented Gaius. "Christian's family, therefore, is likely to continue spreading abroad and be numerous upon the face of the earth. Let Christiana, therefore, search out for her sons some girls to whom they may be engaged, so the name of their father and the house of his ancestors may never be forgotten in the world."

"It would be a pity for this family to fall and become extinct," said Honest.

"It can't fall, but it may be diminished," said Gaius. "But let Christiana take my advice. That's the way to uphold it."

"And, Christiana," said this Innkeeper, "I'm glad to see you and your friend Mercy together here—such suitable friends. And if I may advise, take Mercy into a nearer relationship to you. If she will, let her be given to Matthew, your oldest son. It's the way to preserve you a posterity in the earth." So this match was agreed to, and in the process of time they were married...but more of that later.

Gaius proceeded and said, "I'll now speak on behalf of women to take away their reproach. For as death and the Curse came into the world by a woman,[11] so also did life and health. 'God sent his Son, born of a woman.'[12] Yes, to show how much those who came after her hated the act of their mother Eve, this gender in the Old Testament desired children in order that this or that woman might be so fortunate as to become the mother of the Savior of the world. Furthermore, when the Savior came, women rejoiced over Him before either man or angel.[13] I haven't read that any man ever gave to Christ so much as one penny, but the women followed Him and helped support Him out of their own means.[14] It was a woman who washed His feet with tears,[15] and a woman who anointed His body for burial.[16] They were women who wept when He was going to the Cross,[17] and women who followed Him from the cross and who sat by His Sepulcher when He was buried.[18] They were women who were with Him first at His Resurrection Morning,[19] and women who first brought to His disciples word that He had risen from the dead.[20] Women, therefore, are highly favored, and by these things they show that they are sharers with us in the Grace of Life."[21]

Now the cook sent up to announce that supper was almost ready, and she sent one to lay the cloth and plates and to set the salt and bread in place.

Then Matthew said, "The sight of this cloth and of this forerunner of supper causes a greater appetite in me for my food than I had before."

"So let all doctrines ministering to you in this life cause you to have within you a greater desire to sit at the Supper of the Great King in His Kingdom," said Gaius, "for all preaching, books, and ordinances here are just like the laying of the plates and the setting of the salt upon the dinner table when compared to the feast our Lord will make for us when we come to His House."[22]

So supper came up, and first, a heave shoulder and a wave breast were set on the table before them to show they must begin their meal with prayer and praise to God.[23] David lifted up his heart to God with the heave shoulder,[24] and when he played his harp, he used to lean upon it with the wave breast, where his heart lay. These two dishes were very fresh and good, and they all ate very well of them.

The next thing they brought up was a bottle of wine, red as blood. So Gaius said to them, "Drink freely! This is the juice of the True Vine,[25] which makes glad the heart of God and man."[26] So they drank and were merry.

The next thing was a dish of milk well crumbed with bread.[27] Gaius said, "Let the boys have that so they may grow from it."[28]

Then in course they brought up a dish of butter and honey. Then Gaius said, "Eat freely of this, for this is good to cheer up and strengthen your judgments and understandings. This was our Lord's dish when He was a child. 'Butter and honey shall he eat, that he may know to refuse the evil and choose the good.'"[29]

Then they brought them up a dish of apples, and they were very good tasting fruit. Then Matthew said, "May we eat apples since they were such as the Serpent beguiled our first mother with?"[30]

Then Gaius said,

Apples were they with which we were beguiled,
Yet Sin, not Apples, hath our Souls defiled;
Apples forbid, if eat, corrupt the blood:
To eat such, when commanded, does us good;
Drink of his Flagons then, thou Church, his Dove,
And eat his Apples, who are sick of Love"

Supper is served at the house of Gaius

Then Matthew said, "I made the hesitation because a while back I was sick from the eating of fruit."

"Forbidden fruit will make you sick, but not what our Lord has tolerated," said Gaius.

While they were thus talking, they were presented with a dish of Nuts.[31] Then some at the table said, "Nuts spoil tender teeth, especially the teeth of the children."

When Gaius heard that, he said,

Hard Texts are Nuts, (I will not call them Cheaters)
Whose Shells do keep their Kernels from the Eaters.
Ope then the shells, and you shall have the Meat,
They here are brought, for you to crack and eat.[32]

Then they were very merry and sat at the table a long time talking of many things.

Then the old Gentleman said, "My good Innkeeper, while you're here shelling Nuts, open this riddle if you please:"

A man there was, tho' some did count him mad,
The more he cast away, the more he had.

Then they all listened closely, wondering what good Gaius would say. So he sat still for a while and then thus replied:

He that bestows his Goods upon the Poor,
Shall have as much again, and ten times more.

Then Joseph said, "I dare say, Sir, I didn't think you could've figured it out."

"Oh," exclaimed Gaius, "I've been trained up in this way a great while. Nothing teaches like experience. I've learned from my Lord to be kind, and I've found by experience that I've gained from it. 'One man gives freely, yet gains even more; another withholds unduly, but comes to poverty.'[33] 'One man pretends to be rich, yet has nothing; another pretends to be poor, yet has great wealth.'"[34]

Then Samuel whispered to his mother, Christiana, "Mother, this is a very good man's house. Let's stay here a good while, and let my brother Matthew be married to Mercy here before we go any farther."

Overhearing the exchange, Gaius said, "With a willing heart, my Child."

(So they stayed there more than a month, and Mercy became Matthew's wife. And, as her custom was, while they stayed there Mercy made coats and garments to give to the poor. By this, she brought a very good reputation to the Pilgrims.)

But to return to our story:

After supper, the lads desired a bed, for they were weary with traveling. Then Gaius called to show them their room, but Mercy said, "I'll take them to bed." So she took them to their beds, and they slept well. But the rest sat up all night, for Gaius and they were such suitable company that they did not know how to part. Then after much talk about their Lord, themselves, and their journey, old Mr. Honest (he who posed the riddle to Gaius) began to nod.

Then Great Heart said, "Say, Sir, you're beginning to be drowsy. Come, shake it off! Now here's a riddle for you."

Then Mr. Honest said, "Let's hear it."

Then Mr. Great Heart said,

He that will kill, must first be overcome:
Who live abroad would, first must die at home.

"Ha!" exclaimed Mr. Honest, "It's a hard one—hard to explain and harder to practice. But come, Innkeeper," he said. "I will, if you please, give it to you. You explain it, and I'll hear what you say."

"No," said Gaius, "it was given to you, and it is expected that you should answer it."

Then the old Gentleman said:

He first by Grace must conquer'd be,
That Sin would mortify:

And who, that lives, would convince me,
Unto himself must die.

"That's right," said Gaius. "Good doctrine and experience teach this. First—until grace displays itself and overcomes the soul with its glory, it's entirely without strength to oppose sin. Besides, if sin is Satan's cords, by which the soul lies bound, how can it make resistance before it's loosed from that infirmity? Second—nor will any who understands either reason or grace believe that such a man can be a monument to grace when he is a slave to his own corruptions."

"And now that it comes to mind," said Gaius, "I'll tell you a story worth hearing. There were two men who went on Pilgrimage. One began when he was young and the other when he was old. The young man had strong corruptions to struggle with; but the old man's were decayed with the decays of nature. The young man took his steps as evenly as the old one and was every way as light as he. Who now, or which of them, had their graces shining clearest since both seemed to be alike?"

"The young man's, doubtless," said Honest, "for that which goes against the greatest opposition gives the best demonstration that it is the strongest, especially when it also maintains pace with that which doesn't meet with half so much as, to be sure, old age does not. Besides, I've observed that old men have blessed themselves with this mistake: namely, taking the decays of nature for a gracious conquest over corruptions, and so have been apt to beguile themselves. Indeed, old men who are gracious are best able to give advice to them who are young because they've seen most of the emptiness of things. Yet when an old man and a young man set out together, the young one has the advantage of the fairest discovery of a work of grace within him, even though the old man's corruptions are naturally the weakest."

They sat talking like this until the break of day.

Now when the family was up, Christiana told her son James that he should read a chapter, so he read the fifty-third chapter of Isaiah. When he was done, Mr. Honest asked why the Savior is said to have come out of a dry ground, and also that He had no beauty or majesty in Him.[35]

Then Mr. Great Heart said, "To the first, I answer: Because the Church of the Jews, of which Christ came, had lost by then almost all the sap and spirit of religion. To the second I say: The words are spoken in the person of the unbelievers. And because they lack that eye that can see into our Prince's heart, they therefore judge Him by the lowliness of His exterior. It's just like those who don't know that precious stones are covered over with a homely crust. When they've found one, they throw it away again, as men do with a common stone, because they don't know what they've found."[36]

"Well," said Gaius, "now that you are here, and since, as I know, Mr. Great Heart is good with his weapons, if you would like, after we've refreshed ourselves we'll walk into the fields to see if we can do any good. About a mile from here there is a giant named Slay Good. He greatly annoys the King's Highway in these parts, and I know where his haunt is. He's the leader of a number of thieves, it would be good if we could clear these parts of him."

So they consented and went—Mr. Great Heart with his Sword, Helmet, and Shield and the rest with spears and clubs. When they came to the place where the Giant was, they found the Giant with an individual in his hand named Feeblemind,[37] whom his servants had brought to him after taking him from the Way. Now the Giant was plundering him with an intention of picking his bones afterward, for he was of the nature of cannibals.

Well, as soon as he saw Mr. Great Heart and his friends at the mouth of his cave with their weapons, he demanded to know what they wanted.

"We want you," said Mr. Great Heart, "for we've come to revenge the quarrel of all those whom you've dragged out of the King's Highway. Therefore, come out of your cave."

So the Giant armed himself and came out, and they went to battle. They fought for over an hour, and then they stood still to catch their breath.

Then the Giant asked, "Why are you here on my ground?"

"To revenge the blood of Pilgrims, as I've already told you," answered Great Heart.

So they went at it again, and the Giant forced Mr. Great Heart to go back. But he came forward again, and in the greatness of his mind, he let fly with such strength at the Giant's head and sides that he made him let his weapon fall out of his hand. So he struck and killed him, then cut off his head and brought it back to the Inn. He also brought Feeblemind the Pilgrim with him to his lodgings. When they had gotten home, they showed the Giant's head to the Family and, as before, they hung it up for a warning to those in the future who would attempt to do as he.

Then they asked Mr. Feeblemind how he fell into the Giant's hands.

The poor man then said, "I'm a sickly man, as you see, and because death usually knocked at my door once a day, I thought I would never be well at home. So I took upon myself a Pilgrim's life, and I've traveled here from the Town of Uncertain, where I and my father were born. I'm a man of no strength at all, of body or yet of mind. But though I can only crawl, if I could I would spend my life in the Pilgrim's Way."

"When I came to the Gate at the start of the Path," continued Mr. Feeblemind, "the Lord of that place entertained me freely. He didn't object against my weakly looks or my feeble mind, but He gave me such things as were necessary for my journey and told me to hope to the end.[38] When I came to the House of the Interpreter, I received much kindness; and because the Hill of Difficulty was judged to be too hard for me, I was carried up it by one of His servants. Indeed, I've found much relief from Pilgrims, although none of them were willing to go so softly as I am forced to do. Yet still, as they went on, they encouraged me to be of good cheer and said it was the will of their Lord that encouragement should be given to the feebleminded.[39] And so they went at their own pace."

"When I came to Assault Lane," said Mr. Feeblemind, "this Giant then met with me and told me to prepare for an encounter. But—alas!—feeble one that I was, I had a need of a more cordial meeting. So he came up and took me. I fancied he wouldn't kill me. Also, when he had taken me into his den, I believed I would come out alive again since I didn't go with

347

him willingly. For I've heard that by the laws of providence, no Pilgrim who is taken by violent hands is to die by the hand of the enemy if he remains sincere toward his Master.[40] I expected to be robbed, and, to be sure, I was robbed. But as you see, I escaped with life, and for that I thank my King as Author and you as the means. I expect more onslaughts, too, but this I've resolved to do—to run when I can, to walk when I can't run, and to crawl when I can't walk. As to the heart of the matter, I'm steadfast. My way is before me, and my thoughts are beyond the River that has no bridge, even though, as you see, I'm of a feeble mind."[41]

Then old Mr. Honest said, "Haven't you been acquainted some time ago with a Pilgrim named Mr. Fearing?"

"Yes," said Mr. Feeblemind. "He came from the Town of Stupidity, which lies four degrees northward of the City of Destruction and just as far from where I was born. Yet we were well acquainted, for he was my uncle, my father's brother. He and I have been much of the same general disposition. He was a little shorter than I, yet we were of much the same complexion."

"I perceived you knew him," said Honest. "I'm also apt to believe you are related to one another, for you have his pale look, a squint like his with your eye, and your speech is much alike."

"Most who have known us have said so," agreed Feeblemind. "Besides, what I've seen in him I have for the most part seen in myself."

"Come, Sir," said good Gaius, "be of good cheer. You're welcome to me and to my house, and you can freely ask for what you have a mind to. What you would like my servants to do for you, they'll gladly do it."

Then Mr. Feeblemind said, "This is an unexpected favor, and it's like the sun shining out of a very dark cloud. Did Giant Slay Good intend me to have this favor when he stopped me and resolved to let me go no farther? Did he intend for me to go to my host Gaius after he had looted my pocket? Yet, it is so."

Mr. Feeblemind

Now just as Mr. Feeblemind and Gaius were talking, someone came running and called at the door, saying that about a mile and a half away was one named Mr. Not Right, a pilgrim, who had been struck dead by a thunderbolt upon the place where he was.

"Alas!" exclaimed Mr. Feeblemind. "Is he dead? He passed me some days before I came this far, and he wanted to be my traveling companion. He also was with me when Slay Good, the Giant, took me, but he was nimble on his feet and escaped. But it seems that he escaped to die, and I was taken to live.

What, one would think, doth seek to slay outright,
Oft-times delivers from the saddest plight.
That very Providence, whose Face is Death,
Doth oft-times to the lowly, Life bequeath:
I was taken, he did escape and flee;
Hands crost, give Death to him, and Life to me.

NOTES ON CHAPTER 28

1   **Romans 16:23.**
2   Psalm 34:8.
3   **Mark this.**
4   **Acts 11:26.**
5   **Acts 7:54-60.**
6   **Acts 12:1-2.**
7   **Acts 12:3-8**, 14:19-20, 16:22-24.
8   Ignatius was the bishop of Antioch. He was condemned to death by wild beasts during the reign of the Roman emperor Trajan. He died about 110 AD.
9   According to the writings of Eusebius Pamphilus, Bishop of Caesarea in Palestine during a period in the third century A.D., Romanus was a deacon in the church at Caesarea. This Romanus had a ministry of casting out devils. He is said to have undergone several tortures before his death.
10   Polycarp was the bishop of Smyrna during the first half of the second century. He was possibly a disciple of John.

Polycarp was martyred at Smyrna at the age of 86.

[11] **Genesis 3.**

[12] **Galatians 4:4; Luke 2.**

[13] Luke 1:39-56.

[14] **Luke 8:1-3.**

[15] **Luke 7:37-38, 50; John 11:2.**

[16] **John 12:1-8.**

[17] **Luke 23:27.**

[18] **Matthew 27:55-61.**

[19] Matthew 28:1; Luke 24:1.

[20] Matthew 28:5-8; Luke 24:9-10, **22-23.**

[21] Galatians 3:26-29.

[22] Revelation 19:6-9.

[23] **Leviticus 7:32-34, 10:14-15; Hebrews 13:15.**

[24] **Psalm 25:1.**

[25] **John 15:1.**

[26] **Judges 9:13** (KJV).

[27] **Deuteronomy 32:14.**

[28] **1 Peter 2:2.**

[29] **Isaiah 7:15** (KJV).

[30] Genesis 3:1-6.

[31] **Song of Songs 6:11.**

[32] 2 Peter 3:14-18.

[33] **Proverbs 11:24.**

[34] **Proverbs 13:7.**

[35] Isaiah 53:2.

[36] Psalm 118:22; Matthew 21:33-46; Mark 12:1-12; Luke 20:9-19; Acts 4:8-12; 1 Peter 2:4-8.

[37] Although "feeblemind(ed)" is considered an offensive expression today, in Bunyan's day it meant "irresolute and weak-willed"—a meaning that is now obsolete. The word has been retained because the obsolete meaning best expresses the spiritual nature of the character.

[38] 1 Peter 1:13 (KJV).

[39] **1 Thessalonians 5:14** (KJV).

[40] **Mark this.**

[41] Psalm 112:7-8. **Mark this.**

29

CHRISTIANA AND MERCY AT THE VANITY FAIR

ABOUT THIS TIME, MATTHEW and Mercy were married. Also, Gaius gave his daughter Phebe[1] to James, Matthew's brother, for his wife. After this, they stayed more than ten days at Gaius' house, spending their time and the seasons as Pilgrims used to do. When they were to depart, Gaius made them a feast; and they ate, and drank, and were merry.

When the hour had come for them to leave, Mr. Great Heart asked for a bill; but Gaius told him that it was not the custom for Pilgrims to pay for their entertainment at his house. He lodged them on a yearly basis, but he looked for his payment to come from the Good Samaritan, who had promised to faithfully repay him upon his return for whatever charge had accumulated for their care.[2]

Then Mr. Great Heart said to him, "Dear friend, you are faithful in what you are doing for the brothers, even though they are strangers to you. They have told the church about your love. You will do well to send them on their way in a manner worthy of God."[3]

Then Gaius bid farewell to all of them, and he paid particular attention of Mr. Feeblemind and gave him something to drink in his journey. As they were going out the door, Mr. Feeblemind acted as if he intended to linger. When Mr. Great Heart noticed it, he said, "Please, go along with us. I'll be your guide, and you will do as well as the others."

"Alas!" responded Mr. Feeblemind. "I lack a suitable companion. You're all energetic and strong, but as you see I'm weak. I rather choose to come along behind, lest by reason of my many infirmities I would be both a burden to myself and to you. I am, as I said, a man with a weak and feeble mind, and I'll be offended and made weak at that which others can hold up under. I won't like laughing; I won't like showy clothing; I won't like unprofitable questions. No, I'm so weak a man that I'm likely to be offended by that which others have the freedom to do.[4] I don't know all the truth; I'm a very ignorant Christian man. Sometimes, if I hear some people rejoice in the Lord, it troubles me because I can't do the same thing. With me, it's like it is with a weak man among the strong, or as it is with a sick man among the healthy, or as misfortune despised—'Men at ease have contempt for misfortune as the fate of those whose feet are slipping'[5]—so that I don't know what to do."

"But, brother," said Mr. Great Heart, "I've been commissioned to 'encourage the feebleminded, and to help the weak.'[6] You must go along with us. We'll wait for you, we'll lend you our help, and for your sake we'll deny ourselves some of the things both biased and practical. We won't pass judgment on disputable matters,[7] and, rather than allow you to be left behind, we'll become all things for you rather than have you left behind."[8]

All this happened while they were at Gaius' door. And as they were in the heat of their discussion about this, Mr. About Tofall came by with his Crutches in his hand, and he, too, was going on Pilgrimage.[9]

Then Mr. Feeblemind said to him, "Man! How did you get here? I was just now complaining that I didn't have a suitable companion, but you're according to my wish. Welcome, welcome, good Mr. About Tofall. I hope you and I may be of some help to one another."

"I'll be glad to have your company," said Mr. About Tofall, "and rather than part, since we have so happily met, I'll lend you one of my crutches, good Mr. Feeblemind."

"No," said Feeblemind. "Although I thank you for your goodwill, I'm not inclined to limp before I'm lame. However, if the occasion arises, it may be that it will help me against a dog."

"If either myself or my crutches can do you good, we're both at your command, good Mr. Feeblemind," said Mr. About Tofall.

So they went on their way. Mr. Great Heart and Mr. Honest went in front, Christiana and her family went next, and Mr. Feeblemind and Mr. About Tofall came behind with the crutches.

Then Mr. Honest said to Great Heart, "Please, Sir, now that we're on the road, tell us some profitable things about some of those who've gone on Pilgrimage before us."

"Gladly," said Mr. Great Heart. "I suppose you've heard how Christian of old met with Apollyon in the Valley of Humiliation, and also what hard work he had going through the Valley of the Shadow of Death. I think you also couldn't have kept from hearing how Faithful was confronted by Madam Wanton, with Adam the First, with one Discontent, and Shame. These four are as deceitful of villains as a man can meet with upon the Road."

"Yes," answered Honest, "I've heard of all this, but good Faithful was indeed most severely challenged by Shame. He was an unwearied one."

"Yes," agreed Great Heart, "for, as the Pilgrim correctly said, he of all men had the wrong name."

"But tell me, Sir," said Honest, "where was it that Christian and Faithful met Talkative? He was also a notable individual."

"He was a confident fool," said Great Heart, "but many follow his ways."

"He just about had Faithful beguiled," said Mr. Honest.

355

"Yes," said Mr. Great Heart, "but Christian quickly put him in his place by revealing what he was like."

They continued on until they came to the place where Evangelist met with Christian and Faithful and told them what would happen to them at the Vanity Fair.

Then their Guide said, "Christian and Faithful met with Evangelist hereabouts. He's the one who prophesied to them about what troubles they would meet with at the Vanity Fair."

"You don't say," said Honest. "I dare say it was a hard chapter he then read to them."

"That it was," agreed Mr. Great Heart, "but he gave them encouragement along with it. But what can we say of them? They were a couple of lionlike men. They had set their faces like flint.[10] Don't you remember how undaunted they were when they stood before the judge?"

"I remember it well," said Mr. Honest "Faithful suffered bravely."

"So he did," said Great Heart, "and just as brave things came from it. As the story relates it, Hopeful and some others were converted by his death."

"That's good," said Honest, "but please go on, for you're well acquainted with things."

"Above all of those whom Christian met after he had passed through the Vanity Fair," said Great Heart, "that individual named ByEnds was the most notorious one."

"What was he?" asked Mr. Honest.

"A very notorious fellow, a downright hypocrite," said Great Heart. "He was one who would be religious whichever way the world went. But he was so cunning that he would be sure never to lose anything or suffer for it. He had a style of religion for every fresh occasion, and his wife was as good at it as he was. He would turn and change from opinion to opinion— yes, and justify himself for doing it, too. But as far as I could learn, he came to a bad end because of his by-ends, nor did I ever hear that any of his children were ever held in any esteem by any who truly feared God."

By this time they had come within sight of the Town of

Vanity, where the Vanity Fair is kept. So when they saw that they were so near the town, they consulted with each other about how they should pass through it.

Some said one thing and some another, but at last Mr. Great Heart said, "As you may understand, I've often been a leader of Pilgrims through this town. I'm acquainted with an individual, Mr. Mnason, a Cyprusian by nationality, an old disciple, and at whose house we may lodge.[11] If you think it good," he said, "we'll turn in there."

"Agreed," said old Honest.

"Agreed," said Christiana.

"Agreed," said Mr. Feeblemind.

The others all said the same thing.[12]

You must understand, it was evening by the time they got to the outskirts of the town, but Mr. Great Heart knew the way to the old man's house. So they went there, and he called at the door. The old man inside recognized his voice as soon as he heard it; so he opened, and they all went in.

Then Mr. Mnason, their host, asked, "How far have you come today?"

"From the house of Gaius, our friend," they said.

"I promise you," said Mr. Mnason, "you've come a good distance. You must be weary. Sit down."

Then their Guide said, "Come, such cheer, Sirs. It appears you are welcome with my friend."

"I do welcome you," said Mr. Mnason, "and whatever you want, just ask, and we'll do what we can to get it for you."

"Our great need for a while has been for refuge and good company, and now I hope we have both," said Honest.

"As far as refuge goes, you see what it is," said Mnason, "but as for good company, that will appear in the trying."

"Well," said Mr. Great Heart, "will you lead the Pilgrims up into their rooms?"

"I will," said Mr. Mnason.

So he took them to their respective places and also showed them a very nice dining room where they might go together and eat a little until the time had come to go to bed. Now when they were in their places and had cheered up a little after the journey, Mr. Honest asked his landlord if there were any collections of good people in the town.

"We have a few," said Mnason, "for indeed they are only a few when compared with those on the other side."

"But how shall we go about seeing some of them?" asked Honest. "For the sight of good men to those who are going on Pilgrimage is like the appearing of the moon and stars to those who are sailing upon the seas."

Then Mr. Mnason stamped with his foot, and his daughter, Grace, came up. So he said to her, "Grace, you go and tell my friends, Mr. Contrite, Mr. Holy Man, Mr. Love Saint, Mr. Darenot Lie, and Mr. Penitent that I have in my house a friend or two who have a mind to see them this evening." So Grace went to call them, and they came. After opening salutations, they sat down together at the table.

Then Mr. Mnason, their landlord, said, "My Neighbors, as you see, I have a company of strangers who have come to my house. They're Pilgrims who have come from far off and are going to Mount Zion.[13] But who do you think this is?" he asked, pointing with his finger to Christiana. "It's Christiana, the wife of Christian, that famous Pilgrim who with Faithful, his brother, was so shamefully treated in our town."

At that, they stood up amazed, saying, "We hardly thought we'd see Christiana when Grace came to call us. This is a very pleasing surprise." Then they asked her about her welfare and if these young men were her husband's sons. When she told them they were, they said to them, "May the King whom you love and serve make you like your father and lead you in peace to where he is."

When they had all sat down again, Mr. Honest asked Mr. Contrite and the rest what condition their town was presently in.

Mr. Contrite answered, "You can be sure that we're full of hurry at fair time. It's hard keeping our hearts and spirits in any good order when we're in a challenged condition. He who lives in such a place as this and has to put up with what we do has need of an item to remind him to take heed every moment of the day."

"But how are your neighbors now as for peacefulness?" asked Honest.

"They're much more moderate now than before," answered Mr. Contrite. "You know how Christian and Faithful were abused in our town, but lately I say they've been far more moderate. I think the blood of Faithful weighs heavily upon them to this day, for since they burned him they've been ashamed to burn anyone else. In those days, we were afraid to walk the streets, but now we can show our heads. Then, the name of a professor of faith was detestable; but now, especially in some parts of our town—for you know our town is large—religion is accounted honorable."

Then Mr. Contrite asked them, "Please tell me, how does it go with you in your Pilgrimage? How is the country treating you?"

"What's happened to us is what happens to wayfaring people," answered Mr. Honest. "Sometimes our way is clean, sometimes foul, sometimes uphill, sometimes downhill. We're seldom at a fixed place. The wind is not always at our backs, nor is everyone we meet with in the Way a friend. We've already met with some notable difficulties, and we don't know what are still lurking. But for the most part, we find to be true what's been said of old: 'A good man must suffer trouble.'"

"You speak of difficulties," said Mr. Contrite. "What kind of difficulties have you met with?"

"No," said Honest, "ask Mr. Great Heart, our Guide, for he can give the best account of that."

"We've been harassed three or four times already," said Great Heart. "First, Christiana and her children were attacked by two ruffians, whom they feared would take away their lives. We were attacked by Giant Bloody Man, Giant Maul, and Giant Slay Good. Actually, we accosted the last one rather than being attacked by him, and this is the way it was:

"After we'd been some time at the house of Gaius, my host and that of the whole Church, we were of a mind at one time to take our weapons with us and to go see if we could battle any of those who were enemies of Pilgrims, for we'd heard there was a notorious one thereabouts. Now Gaius, since he lived around there, knew better than I where he hung out; so we looked and looked until we finally spotted the mouth of his cave. Then we were glad and stirred up our spirits. We advanced up to his den, and when we got there we saw that by mere force he had dragged this man, Mr. Feeblemind, into his net and was about to bring him to his end."

Great Heart went on speaking, "But when he saw us—supposing, as we thought, that he had another victim—he left the poor man in his hole and came out. So we went at it with everything we had, and he prepared himself forcefully. But at the conclusion, he was brought down to the ground, and his head was cut off and set up by the wayside for a warning to those who would practice such ungodliness. To show I'm telling you the truth, here is the man himself to affirm it, the man who was like a lamb taken out of the mouth of the lion."[14]

Then Mr. Feeblemind said, "I found this true, to both my cost and comfort—to my cost when he threatened to pick my bones every moment, and to my comfort when I saw Mr. Great Heart and his friends approach so near with their weapons for my deliverance."

Then Mr. Holy Man said, "There are two things that those who go on Pilgrimage need to have with them—courage and an unpolluted life.[15] If they don't have courage, they can never stay on their path, and if their lives are corrupt, they'll make the very name of a Pilgrim stink."

Then Mr. Love Saint said, "I hope this warning is not needful among you, but there really are many who go upon the road who show themselves to be strangers to pilgrimage rather than strangers and pilgrims on the earth.[16]

Then Mr. Darenot Lie said, "It's true, they have neither the Pilgrim's garment nor the Pilgrim's courage. They don't go uprightly but go all astray with their feet. One shoe goes inward, and one shoe goes outward; and their pants are ripped out behind them—here a rag, and there a rent, to the slighting of their Lord."

Mercy works hard for the poor

"They ought to be troubled over these things," said Mr.
Penitent, "and the Pilgrims aren't likely to have that grace
upon them and their Pilgrim's Progress until their way is cleared
of such spots and blemishes."

They sat talking and spending the time like that until supper
was set upon the table. They ate it and refreshed their weary
bodies, and then they went to rest. They stayed in the Fair a
great while at the house of Mr. Mnason, who in the process of
time gave his daughter Grace to Samuel, Christian's son, for
his wife, and his daughter Martha to Joseph.

As I said, the time they stayed there was long (for it was
not now as in former times).[17] The Pilgrims grew acquainted,
therefore, with many of the good people of the town and did
what service they could for them. As she was likely to do,
Mercy worked hard for the Poor (for which their bellies and
backs blessed her), and she was an ornament to her profession
there. And to tell you the truth about Grace, Phebe, and Martha,
they were all of a very good nature and did much good in their
positions. All of the sons' wives were also very fruitful, so
Christian's name, as was said before, was likely to live on in
the world.

While they were staying there, a Monster came out of the
woods and killed many of the people of the town. It would also
carry away their children and teach them to suck its whelps.
Now no man in the town dared so much as to face this Monster,
but instead, everyone fled when they heard the noise of its
coming.

The Monster was like no other beast upon the earth. Its
body was like that of a dragon, and it had seven heads and ten
horns. It made great havoc of children, and yet it was governed
by a woman.[18] This Monster set forth conditions to men, and
men who loved their lives more than their souls accepted those
conditions. So they came under its control.[19]

Now Mr. Great Heart, together with these who came to
visit the Pilgrims at Mr. Mnason's house, entered into a
covenant to go and engage this Beast if perhaps they might
deliver the people of this town from the paw and mouths of
this devouring serpent. Then Mr. Great Heart, Mr. Contrite,

Confronting the devouring serpent

Mr. Holy Man, Mr. Darenot Lie, and Mr. Penitent went to meet him with their weapons. At first, the Monster was very rampant and looked upon these enemies with great contempt; but, being sturdy men with weapons, they beat it so soundly that they made it retreat. So they came home to Mr. Mnason's house again.

You must know, the Monster had its certain times in which to come out and make its attempts upon the children of the people of this town. Also, these valiant, worthy men watched it in those times and continually assaulted it, so much so that in the process of time it became not only wounded but lame. Also, it was not able to make the havoc of the townspeople's children as it formerly had done, and it is truly believed by some that this Beast will certainly die of its wounds.

This, therefore, brought Mr. Great Heart and his friends great fame in this town, so that many of the people who still wanted their taste of things yet also had a revered estimation and respect for them. It was for this reason, therefore, that these Pilgrims did not receive much harm there. True, there were some of the lower sort who could see no more than a mole nor understand more than an animal. Those had no reverence for these people, nor did they take notice of their valor and adventures.

Well, the time grew close that the Pilgrims must go on their way, so they prepared for their journey. They sent for their friends, conferred with them, and had some time set aside to commit each other to the protection of their Prince. Again, there were those who brought them such things that they had and that were fit for the weak and the strong, for women and men, and so loaded them up with such things as were necessary.[20]

They then set forward on their way; and, accompanying them as far as was convenient, their friends again committed each other to the protection of their King and departed. They who were of the Pilgrim's company went on, therefore; and Mr. Great Heart went in front of them. Now the weaker women and children were forced to go as they could bear, and by this means Mr. About Tofall and Mr. Feeblemind had more to sympathize with their condition.

When they had gone from the townspeople and their friends had told them good-bye, they quickly came to the place where Faithful was put to death. They stood still there and thanked Him who had enabled him to bear his cross so well, and rather because they had found they received a benefit by such a manly suffering as his.

They went on, therefore, talking about Christian and Faithful, and how Hopeful joined himself to Christian after Faithful was dead.

NOTES ON CHAPTER 29

[1] Romans 16:1-2.
[2] **Luke 10:25-37.**
[3] **3 John 5-6.**
[4] **1 Corinthians 8.**
[5] **Job 12:5.**
[6] **1 Thessalonians 5:14** (KJV).
[7] **Romans 14:1.**
[8] **1 Corinthians 9:22.**
[9] **Psalm 38:17.** Bunyan called the man *Ready-to-halt*, which is from the same verse in the KJV.
[10] Isaiah 50:7.
[11] This name comes from the disciple from Cyprus who gave lodging to Paul and his traveling companions. Acts 21:16.
[12] Psalm 133:1
[13] Hebrews 12:22; Revelation 14:1.
[14] 1 Samuel 17:34-35.
[15] James 1:27.
[16] Hebrews 11:13 (KJV).
[17] Acts 9:31.
[18] **Revelation 17:1-6.**
[19] Revelation 13.
[20] **Acts 28:10.**

The Pillar of Salt

30

DOUBTING CASTLE IS DEMOLISHED

NOW THEY CAME UP to the Hill Lucre, where the silver mine was that took Demas away from his Pilgrimage and into which some think Mr. ByEnds fell and perished. They considered that, but when they came to the old monument which stood over by the Hill Lucre—that is, the Pillar of Salt, which stood within view of Sodom and its stinking lake[1]—they marveled, as Christian had before, that men with the knowledge and seasoned wit that they had could be so blinded as to turn aside there. But they considered again that nature is not affected with the inflictions that others have met with, especially if that thing upon which they look has an attracting quality to the foolish eye.

I saw that they went on until they came to the river that was on this side of the Delightful Mountains. This is the river where the fine trees grow on both sides, trees whose leaves, if taken internally, are good against problems of excess and overindulgence. This is where the meadows are green all year long and where people might lie down safely.[2]

In the meadow beside this river there were shelters and folds for sheep and a house built for the nourishing and raising of those lambs, the babes of the women who go on Pilgrimage. There was also an individual there who was entrusted with their care, one who could have compassion[3] and who gathers the lambs with His arms and carries them close to His heart, and who gently leads those who have young.[4] Now Christiana admonished her four daughters-in-law to commit their little ones to the care of this Man, so they might be housed, protected, helped, and nourished by these waters, and so that none of them might be missing in time to come.[5]

"If any of them go astray or are lost, He will bring them again," she said. "He will also bind up the injured and strengthen the weak.[6] They will never lack meat, drink, and clothing here. They will be protected from thieves and robbers, for this Man will die before one of those committed to His trust should be lost.[7] Besides that, they shall be sure to have good training and instruction here and shall be taught to walk in right paths; and you know that is no small favor.[8] Also, as you see, here there are delicate waters, pleasant meadows, dainty flowers, a variety of trees, and such trees that bear wholesome fruit. This is not fruit like that which Matthew ate, that which fell over the wall out of Beelzebub's garden, but fruit that brings health where there is none, and that continues and increases where it is."

So they were content to commit their little ones to Him, and that which also encouraged them to do so was that it was to be at the expense of the King, and so, it was a place of refuge, education, and care for young children and Orphans.

Then they went on, and when they had come to By-path Meadow—to the steps over which Christian went with his friend Hopeful and where they had been taken by Giant Despair and put into Doubting Castle— they sat down and talked about what would be best to do. Now that they were so strong and had such a man as Mr. Great Heart for their Guide, they wondered whether it would be best for them, before they went any farther, to attempt to defeat the Giant, demolish his castle, and set free any Pilgrims who might be in it.

So one said one thing, and another said the contrary. One questioned if it was lawful to go on unconsecrated ground; another said they could, provided the end result was just. But Mr. Great Heart said, "Although that assertion offered last can't be universally true, yet I've been commanded to resist sin, to overcome evil,[9] and to fight the good fight of the faith.[10] And I ask, with whom should I fight this good fight if not with Giant Despair? Therefore, I'll attempt to take away his life and demolish Doubting Castle. Who, then, will go with me?"

Then old Honest said, "I will."

"And so too will we," said Christian's four sons—Matthew, Samuel, James, and Joseph—for they were young men and strong.[11]

Then they left the women in the road, and with them Mr. Feeblemind and Mr. About Tofall, with his crutches, to be their guard until they came back; for in that place that was so near to where Giant Despair lived, if they stayed in the Road, a little child could lead them.[12]

So Mr. Great Heart, old Honest, and the four young men left to go up to Doubting Castle to look for Giant Despair. When they came to the castle gate, they knocked for entrance with an unusually loud noise.

At that, the old Giant came to the gate, and his wife Diffidence followed. Then the Giant said, "Who and what is he who is so bold as to molest Despair, the Giant, like this?"

Mr. Great Heart replied, "It is I, Great Heart, one of the King of the Celestial Country's leaders of Pilgrims to their place. And I demand of you that you open your gates for my entrance. Prepare yourself also to fight, for I've come to take away your head and to demolish Doubting Castle."

Now because he was such a giant, Giant Despair thought no man could overcome him. Again he thought, "Since I've made a conquest before of angels, shall Great Heart make me afraid?"

"So he furnished himself with what was necessary and went out. He had a cap of steel upon his head, a breastplate of fire was attached to him,[13] and he came out in iron shoes and with a great club in his hand.

369

Then these six men approached him and encircled him behind and before.

When Diffidence, the Giantess, came up to help him, old Mr. Honest cut her down with one blow.

Then they all fought for their lives, and Giant Despair was brought down to the ground. But he was very hesitant to die. He struggled hard and had, as they say, as many lives as a cat; but Great Heart was his death, for he did not leave him until he had severed his head from his shoulders.

Then they started to demolish Doubting Castle.

As you might know, it was easily done once Giant Despair was dead. They destroyed Doubting Castle in seven days, and in it they found some Pilgrims—one Mr. Despondency, who was almost starved to death, and his daughter Much Afraid. These two they saved alive. But it would have made you wonder to have seen the dead bodies that lay here and there in the castle yard and at how full of dead men's bones the dungeon was.

When Mr. Great Heart and his companions had performed this exploit, they took Mr. Despondency and his daughter Much Afraid into their protection, for they were honest people even though they were prisoners of that tyrant, Giant Despair, in Doubting Castle.

They took with them the head of the Giant (for they had buried his body under a heap of stones), and they went down to the road and to their companions and showed them what they had done. Now when Feeblemind and About Tofall saw that it was indeed the head of Giant Despair, they were very cheerful and merry.

If there was a need, Christiana could play upon the viol, and her daughter-in-law Mercy upon the lute. Since everyone was disposed to merriment, she played them a piece. About Tofall wanted to dance, so he took Despondency's daughter Much Afraid by the hand, and they began dancing in the road. True, he could not dance without one crutch in his hand, but I promise you he stepped it well. Also, the girl was to be commended, for she answered the music elegantly.

Giant Despair is killed

As for Mr. Despondency, the music was not much to him. He was in favor of eating rather than dancing because he was almost starved. So Christiana gave him some of her bottle of spirits for his present relief and then prepared him something to eat, and in little time the old gentleman came to himself and began to be finely revived.

I saw in my dream that when all these things were finished, Mr. Great Heart took the head of Giant Despair and set it upon a pole by the highway side, right over next to the pillar that Christian erected for Pilgrims who came later to warn them to take heed of entering into his grounds. Then under it, upon a marble stone, he wrote the following verses:

This is the Head of him, whose Name only
In former times did Pilgrims terrify.
His Castle's down, and Diffidence his wife
Brave [Mister Honest] has bereft of life.
Despondency, his daughter Much-afraid,
Great-heart, for them also the Man has play'd.
Who hereof doubts, if he'll but cast his eye,
Up hither, may his scruples satisfy.
This head also, when doubting cripples dance,
Does show from Fears they have Deliverance.

NOTES ON CHAPTER 30

[1] Genesis 13:10, 14:1-3.
[2] **Psalm 23**.
[3] Hebrews 4:15 - **5:2**.
[4] **Isaiah 40:11**.
[5] **Jeremiah 23:4**.
[6] Ezekiel 34:16, **Ezekiel 34:11-16**.
[7] **John 10:14-15**.
[8] Proverbs 4:10-11; Ephesians 6:4.
[9] Romans 12:21.
[10] 1 Timothy 6:12.

[11] **1 John 2:13-14**.
[12] **Isaiah 11:6**.
[13] Revelation 9:17 (KJV).

31

CHRISTIANA AND MERCY IN THE DELIGHTFUL MOUNTAINS

WHEN THESE MEN HAD thus shown themselves bravely against Doubting Castle and had slain Giant Despair, they continued on until they came to the Delightful Mountains, where Christian and Hopeful refreshed themselves with the variety of things in the place. They also acquainted themselves with the Shepherds there, who welcomed them to the Delightful Mountains as they had Christian before.

Now seeing so great a line of individuals following Mr. Great Heart (for they were well acquainted with him), the Shepherds said to him, "Good Sir, you have a good sized company here. Tell us, where did you find all these?"

Then Mr. Great Heart replied:

First, here's Christiana and her train,
Her Sons, and her Sons wives, who, like the wain,
Keep by the Pole, and do by Compass steer,
From Sin to Grace, else they had not been here:

Next here's old Honest come on Pilgrimage,
About-to-fall too, who I dare engage,
True-hearted is, and so is Feeble-mind,
Who willing was, not to be left behind.
Despondency, good man, is coming after,
And so also is Much-afraid his daughter,
May we have entertainment here, or must
We further go? Let's know whereon to trust?

Then the Shepherds said, "This is an appropriate company. You're welcome to us, for we share with the feeble as well as the strong. Our Prince has an eye for what is done to the least of these.[1] Infirmity, therefore, must not be a barrier to our entertainment."

So they took them to the palace door and said to them, "Come in, Mr. Feeblemind. Come in, Mr. About Tofall. Come in Mr. Despondency and Mrs. Much Afraid, his daughter." The Shepherds then turned to the Guide, and said, "We call these by name, Mr. Great Heart, for they're most subject to drawing back. But as for you and the rest who are strong, we leave you to your customary liberty."

Then Mr. Great Heart said, "I see this day that grace shines in your faces and that you are indeed my Lord's Shepherds, for you haven't shoved these weak ones with either flank or shoulder, but have rather strewn their way into the palace with flowers as you should."[2]

So the feeble and the weak went in, and Mr. Great Heart and the rest followed. When they had sat down, the Shepherds said to those of the weakest sort, "What is it that you would like? For," said they, "all things must be managed here for the helping of the weak as well as the warning of the idle."[3]

So they made them a feast of things that were easy to digest, pleasant to the taste, and nourishing. After they had received it, they went to their rest, each one respectively to his proper place. When morning came, because the mountains were high and the day was clear, and since it was the custom of the Shepherds to show Pilgrims some rarities before their departure, when they were ready and had refreshed themselves, they took them out into the fields and showed them first what they had shown to Christian before.

Then they took them to some new places. The first was Mount Marvel, where they looked and saw in the distance a man who moved the hills with Words. Then they asked the Shepherds what that should mean. So they told them the man was the son of one Mr. Great Grace, of whom you read in the First Part of the records of *The Pilgrim's Progress*. They said he is placed there to teach Pilgrims how to believe down, or to move out of their way by Faith, the difficulties they meet with.[4]

Then they led them to another place called Mount Innocent, and there they saw a man clothed all in white. And two men, Prejudice and Illwill, were continually casting dirt upon him. Now whatever dirt there was that was cast at him would fall off in a short time, and his garment would look as clean as if no dirt had been cast on it.

Then the Pilgrims asked, "What does this mean?"

The Shepherds answered, "This man is named Godlyman, and the garment is to show the innocence of his life. Now those who throw dirt at him are such as hate his goodness, but as you see, the dirt will not stick upon his clothes; and so it will be with anyone who truly lives innocently in the world. Whoever they be that would make such men dirty, they labor all in vain, for in time, God will cause their innocence to shine like the dawn and their righteousness as the noonday."[5]

Then they led them to Mount Charity, where they showed them a man who had a bundle of cloth lying in front of him. Out of the cloth he cut coats and garments for the Poor who stood about him, yet his bundle or roll of cloth never dwindled.

Then they said, "What should this be?"

"This is to show you that he who has a heart to give of his labor to the Poor shall never lack the ability to give," said the Shepherds. "'He who refreshes others will himself be refreshed.'[6] And the cake that the Widow gave to the prophet didn't cause her to have any less in her barrel."[7]

They also took them to a place where they saw an individual named Fool and one named Lackwit washing an Ethiopian with the intention of making him white. But the more they washed him, the blacker he was. They then asked the Shepherds what that should mean.

So they told them, saying, "Thus shall it be with the vile person. All means used to get such an individual a good name shall end up making him more abominable. This is the way it was with the Pharisees, and so shall it be with all hypocrites.

Then Mercy, the wife of Matthew, said to Christiana her mother-in-law, "If possible, I'd like to see the hole in the hill, or that which is commonly called the Byway to Hell."

When her mother-in-law told her desire to the Shepherds, they took her to the door that was in the side of a hill. They opened it and invited Mercy to listen for a while. So she listened and heard a person saying, "Cursed be my father for holding my feet back from the way of peace and life!" And another one said, "Oh, I wish I'd been torn in pieces before I had lost my soul to save my life!" And another one said, "If I were to live again, how I would deny myself rather than come to this place!" Then it was as if the actual earth groaned and quaked for fear under the feet of this young woman; so she looked white and came away trembling, saying, "Blessed be he and she who are delivered from this place."

Now when the Shepherds had shown them all these things, they took them back to the palace and entertained them with what the house had to offer. Mercy, being young and expecting a child, longed for something she saw there, but she was ashamed to ask. Her mother-in-law then asked her what ailed her, for she looked like an individual not well.

Then Mercy said, "I can't take my mind off a Mirror that hangs in the dining room. If I can't have it, I think I'll miscarry."

Then her mother-in-law said, "I'll mention your desire to the Shepherds, and they won't deny you of it."

"But I'm ashamed that these men should know how I longed," said Mercy.

"No, my Daughter," said Christiana. "It's no shame but a virtue to long for such a thing as that."

So Mercy said, "Then, Mother, if you please, ask the Shepherds if they're willing to sell it."

Now the Mirror was one in a thousand. It would present a person one way with one's own features exactly,[8] but turn it another way and it would show the actual face and similitude of the Prince of Pilgrims himself.[9] Yes, I have talked with them who know, and they have said that by looking through the Mirror they have seen the actual Crown of Thorns upon His head. They have also seen in it the holes in His hands, in His feet, and in His side. Certainly, there is such an excellency in that Mirror that it will show Him to an individual wherever the person would like to see Him, whether living or dead, whether in earth or Heaven, whether in a state of humiliation or in His exaltation, and whether coming to suffer or coming to reign.[10]

Christiana, therefore, went along to the Shepherds, whose names were Knowledge, Experience, Watchfulness, and Sincerity, and said to them, "There is one of my daughters, an expectant mother, who I believe longs for something she's seen in this house, and she thinks she'll miscarry if she should be denied it by you."

Then Experience said, "Call her, call her! She shall certainly have what we can help her to."

So they called her and said to her, "Mercy, what is that thing you want to have?"

Then she blushed and said, "The great Mirror that hangs up in the dining room."

So Sincerity ran and fetched it, and it was given to her with a joyful agreement. Then she bowed her head and gave thanks, and said, "I know by this that I've obtained favor in your eyes."

They also gave to the other young women such things as they desired, and to their husbands they gave great commendations for joining with Mr. Great Heart to slay Giant Despair and demolish Doubting Castle. The Shepherds put a necklace around Christiana's neck, and they did the same to the necks of her four daughters. They also put earrings in their ears and jewels on their foreheads.[11]

When they were planning to go on, they let them go in peace, but they did not give to them those same warnings that were given before to Christian and his companion. The reason for that was that these had Great Heart for their Guide, and he was one who was well acquainted with things. He could give them warnings more opportunely at the time the danger was near to come.

The warnings Christian and his companion had received from the Shepherds had also been lost by them by the time it had come for them to put them in practice. Here, therefore, was the advantage that this company had over the other.

From there, they went on singing, and they said:

Behold, how fitly are the Stages set!
For their Relief that Pilgrims are become,
And how they us receive without one let,
That make the other Life the mark and Home.
What Novelties they have, to us they give,
That we, tho' Pilgrims, joyful lives may live.
They do upon us too, such Things bestow,
That show we Pilgrims are, where-e'er we go.

NOTES ON CHAPTER 31

1   **Matthew 25:40-46.**
2   **Ezekiel 34:20-24.**
3   1 Thessalonians 5:14-15.
4   **Mark 11:22-24.**
5   Compare Psalm 37:6. See Isaiah 58:10.
6   Proverbs 11:25.
7   1 Kings 17:7-16.
8   **1 Corinthians 13:12; James 1:23-24.**
9   **2 Corinthians 3:18.**
10 **It was the Word of God.**
11 Ezekiel 16:8-12.

32

THE PILGRIMS MEET VALIANT FORTRUTH

AFTER THEY LEFT THE Shepherds, they quickly came to the place where Christian had met with one named Turn Away, who lived in the Town of Apostasy. Mr. Great Heart, their Guide, put them in mind of him, therefore, saying, "This is the place where Christian met with one named Turn Away, who carried with him on his back the character of his rebellion. I have this to say concerning this man: He would not listen to any advice, and once he was falling, persuasion could not stop him."

Great Heart continued, "When he came to the place where the Cross and Tomb were, he met with one who invited him to look there; but he gnashed with his teeth and stomped and said that he was resolved to go back to his own town. Before he came to the Gate, he met with Evangelist, who offered to lay hands on him to turn him into the Way again. But this Turn Away resisted him, and having done much in defiance of him, he got away over the Wall and so escaped his hand."[1]

Valiant Fortruth

Then they went on, and just at the place where Little Faith was formerly robbed, there stood a man with his Sword drawn and his face all bloody. Then Mr. Great Heart asked, "Who are you?"

"I'm one whose name is Valiant Fortruth," he said. "I'm a Pilgrim, and I'm going to Celestial City. Now, as I was in my way, three men assaulted me and offered me three things— one—to become one of them, two—to go back from where I came, or, three—to die on the spot. To the first, I answered that I had been a true man for a long time, and therefore, it could not be expected that I should now cast in my lot with thieves.[2] When they demanded what I would respond to the second, I told them I wouldn't have forsaken the place from where I came at all if I hadn't found discomfort there; but finding it altogether unsuitable and unprofitable for me, I forsook it for this Way. Then they asked me what I said to the third, and I told them my Life cost more dearly by far than that I should lightly give it away. 'Besides,' I said, 'you have no right to demand me to choose anything. It will be at your peril, therefore, if you meddle.' Then these three—named Wildhead, Inconsiderate, and Pragmatic—drew their weapons upon me, and I also drew mine upon them."

Valiant Fortruth continued, "So we went at it, one against three, for the space of above three hours. As you see, they've left upon me some of the marks of their valor, and they've also carried away with them some of mine. They just now left. I suppose they might, as the saying goes, 'hear your horse dash,' and so they took to flight."

"But those were great odds, three against one," said Great Heart.

"That's true," said Valiant, "but little and more are nothing to him who has the truth on his side. 'Though an army besiege me, my heart will not fear; though war break out against me, even then will I be confident.'[3] Besides," he said, "I've read in some records that one man has fought an army.[4] And how many did Samson slay with the jaw bone of a donkey?"[5]

Then the Guide said, "Why didn't you cry out, so that some might have come to your assistance?"

383

"That's what I did, to my King," answered Valiant. "I knew He could hear and provide invisible help, and that was sufficient for me."

Then Mr. Great Heart said to Mr. Valiant Fortruth, "You've behaved yourself worthily. Let me see your Sword."

So he showed it to him, and when he had taken it in his hand and looked at it awhile, he exclaimed, "Ha! It's a genuine Jerusalem Blade."[6]

"That it is," said Valiant. "Let a man have one of these blades, with a hand to exercise it and skill to use it, and he may confront an angel with it.[7] He need not fear holding it if he can only know how to apply it. Its edges will never dull; it will cut flesh, bones, soul, spirit, and all."[8]

"But you fought a great while! I'm amazed you weren't worn out," commented Great Heart.

Valiant said, "I fought until my hand froze to my Sword,[9] and when they were joined together—as if a sword grew out of my arm—and when the blood ran through my fingers, I then fought with the most courage."

"You've done well," said Great Heart. "You've resisted to the point of shedding your blood in your struggle against sin.[10] You'll live by us. Come in and go out with us, for we're your companions."

They then took him, washed his wounds, and gave him of what they had to refresh him. And so, they went on together. Now because Mr. Great Heart was delighted in him (for he greatly loved an individual whom he found to be a man of his hands), and because there was with his company those who were feeble and weak, as they went therefore, he questioned the man about many things, such as what country he was from.

"I'm from Darkland," said Valiant, "for I was born there, and my father and mother are still there."

"Darkland," said the Guide. "Doesn't that lie along the same coast with the City of Destruction?"

"Yes, it does," answered Valiant. "Now this is what caused me to come on Pilgrimage: We had an individual named Mr. Telltrue come into our parts, and he told about what Christian, who had left the City of Destruction, had done—namely, how he had forsaken his wife and children and taken upon himself a Pilgrim's life. It was also confidently reported how he had killed a serpent that came out to resist him in his journey, and how he got through to where he intended to go."

"It was also told what welcome he had at all his Lord's lodgings, especially when he came to the Gates of Celestial City. For there," said the man, "he was received with the sound of trumpets by a company of Shining Ones. Along with many other things that I'll forbear relating now, he also told how all the bells in the city rang for joy at his reception and what golden garments he was clothed with. In a word, that man told the story of Christian and his travels in such a way that my heart fell into a burning haste to go after him. Nor could father or mother stop me, so I left them and have come this far on my way."

"You came in at the Gate, didn't you?" asked Great Heart.

"Yes, yes," answered Valiant. "The same man also told us that all would be for nothing if we didn't begin to enter this Way at the Gate."

The Guide said to Christiana, "Look at what people have received from the Pilgrimage of your husband, and how it has spread abroad far and near."

"Why," said Valiant with surprise, "is this Christian's wife?"

"Yes, so it is," responded Great Heart, "and these are also her four sons."

"What!" exclaimed Valiant, "and going on Pilgrimage, too?"

"Yes, truly," said Great Heart. "They're following after."

"It makes my heart glad!" exclaimed Valiant yet again. "Good man! How joyful he'll be when he sees those who wouldn't go with him and who yet enter after him in at the gates into the City."

"Without doubt, it'll be a comfort to him," said Great Heart, "for next to the joy of seeing himself there, it will be a joy to meet his wife and his children there."

"But now that you're on that," said Valiant, "please let me hear your opinion about it. Some question whether we'll know one another when we're there."

Mr. Great Heart then said, "Do they think they'll know themselves then, or that they'll rejoice to see themselves in that bliss? And if they think they'll know and do these things, why not know others and rejoice in their welfare also? Again, since marriage partners are our second self, and though that state will be dissolved there,[11] yet why may it not be rationally concluded that we'll be more glad to see them there than to see they were left wanting?"

"Well, I understand what you're getting at there," said Valiant. "Do you have any more things to ask me about concerning my beginning to come on Pilgrimage?"

"Yes," answered Great Heart. "Were your father and mother willing for you to become a Pilgrim?"

"Oh, no!" he answered. "They used all the means imaginable to persuade me to stay at home."

"What could they say against it?" asked Great Heart.

"They said it was an idle life," answered Valiant, "and if I myself weren't inclined to idleness and laziness, I'd never favor a Pilgrim's condition."

"And what else did they say?" inquired Great Heart.

"Why, they told me it was a dangerous way," said Valiant. "According to them, the most dangerous way in the world is that which the Pilgrims travel."

"Did they show how this way is so dangerous?" asked Great Heart.

"Yes," answered Valiant, "and they did so in many particulars."

"Name some of them," requested Mr. Great Heart.

Valiant then began his listing: "They told me about the Swamp of Despondence, where Christian was nearly smothered. They told me there were archers standing ready in Beelzebub's Castle to shoot those who would knock at the Narrow Gate for entrance. They also told me about the woods and dark Mountains, about the Hill of Difficulty, about the lions, and also about the three giants, Bloody Man, Maul, and Slay Good. Moreover, they said there was a foul Fiend that haunted the Valley of Humiliation, and that Christian was almost robbed of life by them."

"Besides these," continued Valiant, "they said one must go over the Valley of the Shadow of Death where the Hobgoblins are, where the light is darkness, and where the Path is full of snares, pits, traps, and tricks. They also told me about Giant Despair, of Doubting Castle, and about the ruin the Pilgrims met with there. Furthermore, they said I must go over the Enchanted Ground, which was dangerous, and after all this, that I would find a River over which I would find no bridge, and that the River lay between me and the Celestial Country."

"And was this all?" asked Great Heart.

"No," said Valiant, "they also told me this way was full of deceivers and persons who laid in wait there to turn good men out of the Path."

"But how did they explain that?" inquired Great Heart.

"They told me that Mr. Worldly Wiseman would lay there in wait to deceive," said Valiant Fortruth. "They also said Formality and Hypocrisy were continually there on the road. They also said that ByEnds, Talkative, or Demas would draw near to gather me up, that the Flatterer would catch me in his net, or that with green headed Ignorance I would presume to go on to the gate—from where he was always sent back to the hole that was in the side of the hill—and I would be made to go on the Byway to Hell."

"I promise you, this was enough to discourage a person," said Great Heart, "but did they end there?"

"There was no end," said Valiant. "They also told me about many who had tried that Way of old and who had gone a great distance in it to see if they could find something of the glory there which so many talked of from time to time, and how that to the satisfaction of all the country, they came back again and made themselves fools for setting a foot out of doors in that Path. And they named several who did so, such as Obstinate, Pliable, Mistrust, and Fearful, Turnback, and old Atheist, with several more, some of whom, they said, had gone far to see if they could find it, but not one of them found so much advantage as amounted to the weight of a feather by going."

"Did they say anything more to discourage you?" asked Great Heart.

"Yes," said Valiant, "they told me of one named Mr. Fearing, who was a Pilgrim, and how he found this way so lonely that he never had a comfortable hour in it. Also, they said Mr. Despondency like to have been starved in it. Yes, and also, which I had almost forgotten, after all his ventures for a celestial crown, they said that Christian himself—about whom there has been such a stir—was certainly drowned in the Black River and never went a foot farther; however it was smothered up."

"And didn't any of these things discourage you?" asked Great Heart.

"No," he answered, "they seemed only so many nothings to me."

"And how did that happen," inquired Great Heart.

"Why, I still believed what Mr. Telltrue had said," responded Valiant, "and that carried me beyond them all."

"Then this was your victory, even your Faith,"[12] said Mr. Great Heart.

"That it was," agreed Valiant Fortruth. "I believed, and therefore came out, got into the Way, fought everything that set itself against me, and by believing I've come to this place."

Who would true Valour see,
Let him come hither;
One here will constant be,
Come wind, come weather:
There's no Discouragement
Shall make him once relent,
His first avow'd intent
   To be a Pilgrim.

Whoso beset him round
With dismal stories,
Do but themselves confound,
His Strength the more is.
No Lion can him fright;

He'll with a Giant fight,
But he will have a right
     To be a Pilgrim.

Hobgoblin, nor foul Fiend
Can daunt his spirit;
He knows, he at the End
Shall Life inherit.
Then Fancies fly away,
He'll fear not what men say,
He'll labour Night and Day
     To be a Pilgrim.

NOTES ON CHAPTER 32

[1] **Hebrews 10:26-29.**

[2] **Proverbs 1:10-19.**

[3] **Psalm 27:3.**

[4] 1 Samuel 14:1-14; 2 Samuel 23:8-12.

[5] Judges 15:15-16.

[6] **Isaiah 2:3**; **Ephesians 6:12-17**; Ephesians 6:17; Revelation 19:11-15.

[7] Ephesians 6:12.

[8] **Hebrews 4:12.**

[9] **2 Samuel 23:10.**

[10] Hebrews 12:4.

[11] Matthew 22:23-33.

[12] 1 John 5:4.

33

THE PILGRIMS GO THROUGH THE ENCHANTED GROUND

BY THIS TIME, THEY had gotten to the Enchanted Ground, where the air naturally tended to make one drowsy. And that place was all grown over with briars and thorns, except here and there where there was an Enchanted Arbor. Some say it is a question whether a person will rise or waken again in this world if he sits or sleeps in them.

Each one and then another went, therefore, through this forest. Mr. Great Heart went in front of them because he was the Guide, and Mr. Valiant Fortruth came behind them, being there for a guard for fear, in case some Fiend, or Dragon, or Giant, or Thief would attack the rear and do mischief. They went on here, each man with his Sword drawn in his hand, for they knew it was a dangerous place. They also cheered up one another as well as they could. Mr. Great Heart commanded that Feeblemind should go behind him, and Mr. Despondency was under the eye of Mr. Valiant.

Now they had not gone far until a great mist and darkness fell upon them all, so that for a great while they could scarcely see one another. For some time, therefore, they were forced to feel for one another by words, for they did not walk by sight.[1]

Anyone must think that it was sorry going for the best of them all, but how much worse it was for the women and children, who were tender of feet and heart. Yet it was that the encouraging words of him who led in the front and of him who brought them up behind made a pretty good means for them to wag along.

The Way was also very wearisome here through dirt and rockiness. Nor was there on all this ground so much as one inn or boarding house in which to refresh the more feeble sort. Here, therefore, there was grunting, puffing, and sighing. While one tumbled over a bush, another stuck fast in the mud, and some of the children lost their shoes in the mire.[2] One would cry out, "I'm down!" Another would exclaim, "Hey, where are you?" And a third would shout, "The bushes have gotten a firm hold on me! I think I can't get away from them!"

Then they came to an arbor that was warm and which promised much refreshing to the Pilgrims, for it was finely furnished overhead, beautified with greenery. It was provided with benches and seats. It also had a soft couch in it upon which the weary might lean. All things considered, you must think this was tempting, for the Pilgrims already began to be frustrated with the poorness of the path. But there was not one of them who made so much as a motion to stop there. Yes, for what I could see, they continually paid so good attention to the advice of their Guide, and he so faithfully told them of dangers and of the nature of dangers when they were at them, that when they were nearest to them, they usually picked up their spirits better and encouraged one another to deny the flesh.[3] This arbor was called the Slothful's Friend on purpose to allure if it could some of the Pilgrims there to take up their rest when weary.

I then saw in my dream that they went on in their solitary ground until they came to a place where people would be apt to loose their way. Although when it was light, their Guide could tell well enough how to miss those ways that led wrong, yet now in the dark he was challenged. But in his pocket he had a Map of all ways leading to or from Celestial City; therefore, he struck a light (for he also never goes anywhere without his tinderbox) and took a look at his Book, or Map, which advised him to be careful in that place to turn to the Right-hand Way. And if he had not been careful to look in his Map, in all probability they would have been smothered in the mud; for just a little in front of them, and at the end of the cleanest way, too, there was a pit. No one knows how deep it is, but it is filled with mud, and it was put there on purpose to destroy Pilgrims.

Then I thought to myself, "Who that goes on Pilgrimage wouldn't have one of these Maps with him, so he may look in it when he is at a place of difficulty to see which is the way he must take?"[4]

They then went on in this Enchanted Ground until they came to where there was another arbor, and it was built by the highway side. And in that arbor there lay two men whose names were Heedless and Toobold. These two went this far on Pilgrimage, but here, being wearied with their journey, they sat down to rest themselves and so fell fast asleep. When the Pilgrims saw them, they stood still and shook their heads, for they knew that the Sleepers were in a pitiful situation. Then they discussed what to do, whether to go on and leave them in their sleep or approach them and try to wake them up. So they concluded to go to them and wake them—that is, if they could. But they decided to use caution, namely to take heed that they themselves did not sit down or embrace the offered benefit of that arbor.[5]

So they went in and spoke to the men and called each by his name (for it seems the Guide knew them); but there was no reply or answer. Then the Guide shook them and did what he could to disturb them. Then one of them said, "I'll pay you when I get my money." At that, the Guide shook his head.

The other one said, "I'll fight as long as I can hold my Sword in my hand."

At that, one of the children laughed.

Christiana then asked, "What's the meaning of this?"

The Guide replied, "They talk in their sleep. If you strike them, beat them, or whatever else you do to them, they'll answer you in this way. Or, as one of them said in old time when the waves of the sea beat upon him and he slept as one in the rigging of a ship, 'When will I wake up so I can find another drink?'[6] You know, when men talk in their sleep, they say anything; their words are not governed by either faith or reason. There is an incoherence in their words now as there was before between their going on Pilgrimage and sitting down here. This then is the mischief of it; when heedless individuals go on Pilgrimage, it's twenty to one but what this will happen to them, for this Enchanted Ground is one of the last refuges that the enemy of Pilgrims has. As you see, therefore, it's placed almost at the end of the Way, and so it stands against us with more advantage. For the enemy thinks, 'When will these fools be so desirous of sitting down as when they are weary, and when will they be more weary than at their journey's end?' That's why, I say, that the Enchanted Ground is placed so close to the Land of Beulah[7] and so near the end of their race.[8] Let Pilgrims watch themselves, therefore, lest it happen to them as it has to these who, as you see, have fallen asleep, and whom no one can waken."

Then with trembling the Pilgrims desired to go forward, only they asked their Guide to strike a light so they could go the rest of their way with the help of the light of a lantern. So he struck a light, and they went by the help of that through the rest of this way, although the darkness was very great.[9]

But the children began to be very weary, and they cried out to Him who loves Pilgrims to make their way more comfortable. So when they had gone a little farther there arose a wind that drove away the fog, so that the air became more clear. They were not far off the Enchanted Ground by much, but they could see one another better and also see better the Way in which they should walk.

When they were almost to the end of this ground, they heard a short distance before them a solemn noise of an individual who was much concerned. So they went on and

Standfast upon his knees in the Enchanted Ground

looked before them, and they saw there, as they thought, a man upon his knees with hands and eyes lifted up. And as they thought, he was speaking to One who was above. They came near but could not tell what he said, so they went quietly until he was finished. When he was done, he got up and began to run towards Celestial City.

Then Mr. Great Heart called after him, saying, "Hey there, Friend, let us have your company if you're going to Celestial City, as I suppose you are!"

So the man stopped, and they came up to him.

As soon as Mr. Honest saw him, he said, "I know this man!"

Then Mr. Valiant Fortruth said, "Please tell me, who is he?"

"He's one who came from around where I lived," said Honest. "His name is Standfast and is certainly a very good Pilgrim."

So they came up to one another, and Standfast said to old Honest, "Say, Father Honest, is that you?"

"Yes," said Honest, "it's me as sure as you live."

"I'm so very glad I've found you on this road," said Mr. Standfast.

"And I'm just as glad that I saw you upon your knees," responded Mr. Honest.

Then Mr. Standfast blushed and asked, , "Why...did you see me?"

"Yes, that I did," said Honest, "and I was glad with all my heart at the sight."

"What did you think?" asked Standfast.

"Think?" questioned old Honest. "What should I think? I thought we had an honest man upon the road and, therefore, that we should now have his company."

"If your thinking wasn't wrong, then I'm so happy," said Mr. Standfast, "but if I'm not as I should be, I alone must bear it."

"That's true," said Honest, "but your fear further confirms to me that things are right between the Prince of Pilgrims and your soul, for He says, 'Blessed is the man who always fears the Lord.'"[10]

"Very good," said Valiant, "but, Brother, I ask you to please tell us: What was it that caused you to be upon your knees just now? Was it because of some special mercy that obligated you to do so, or what?"

"Why, as you see, we're now upon the Enchanted Ground," answered Mr. Standfast. "As I was going along, I was reflecting about what a dangerous road the Road in this place was, and how many there were who had come this far on Pilgrimage and had been stopped here and destroyed. I also thought about the manner of the death with which this place destroys men. Those who die here don't die of a violent disorder; the death that such die is not grievous to them. For he who goes away in sleep begins that journey with desire and pleasure. Yes, such people as these are contented with the will of this disease."[11]

Then, interrupting him, Mr. Honest asked, "Did you see the two men asleep in the arbor?"

"Yes, yes!" said Standfast. "I saw Heedless and Toobold there, and for all I know, they'll lay there until they rot.[12] But let me go on with my tale: As I was thus reflecting, as I said, there was a woman in pleasant but old clothing who presented herself to me and offered me three things—her body, her purse, and her bed. Now the truth is that I was both weary and sleepy. I'm also as poor as a baby owl, and perhaps the witch knew that. Well, I repulsed her once and twice, but she put aside my refusals and smiled. Then I began to be angry, but it didn't matter at all to her. Then she made offers again and said she would make me great and happy if I would be ruled by her."

"Then I asked her for her name," continued Standfast, "and she told me it was Madam Delusive.[13] This caused me to distance myself farther from her, but she still followed me with enticements. Then I took myself to my knees, as you saw, and with hands lifted up and with cries I prayed to Him who said He would help.[14] So, just as you came up, the woman went her way. Then I continued to give thanks for this, my great deliverance, for I truly believe she intended no good but to make me stop in my journey."

"Without doubt, her intentions were bad," agreed Mr. Honest, "but stop. Now that you speak of her, I think I've either seen her or have read some story about her."

"Perhaps you've done both," said Standfast.

"Madam Delusive," said Honest. "Isn't she a tall, nice looking woman with something of a dark complexion?"

"Right!" agreed Standfast. "You hit it! She is just such a woman."

"Doesn't she speak very smoothly, and give you a smile at the end of a sentence?" asked Honest.

"You're right again," said Standfast, "for these are her exact actions."

"Doesn't she carry a great purse at her side?" inquired Honest. "And isn't her hand often in it, fingering her money as if that were her heart's delight?"

"It's just like that," agreed Standfast, "and had she stood here all this while you couldn't have more aptly set her before me nor better described her features."

"Then he who drew her picture was a good painter, and he who wrote of her said the truth," said Mr. Honest.[15]

"This woman is a witch," said Mr. Great Heart, "and it is by virtue of her sorceries that this ground is enchanted. Whoever lays his head down in her lap might just as well lay it down upon the block over which the ax hangs. And whoever lays his eyes upon her beauty is accounted an enemy of God.[16] This is she who maintains in splendor all those who are the enemies of Pilgrims. Yes, this is she who has bought off many a man from a Pilgrim's life. She's a great gossiper. Both she and her daughters are always at the heels of one Pilgrim or another, first commending and then preferring the excellencies of this life. She's a bold and impudent slut, and she'll talk with any man. She always laughs poor Pilgrims to scorn but highly commends the rich. If there is one who is cunning to get money in a place, she'll speak well of him from house to house. She greatly loves banqueting and feasting and is always at one full table or another."

Great Heart continued, "In some places, she has claimed to be a goddess, and therefore some actually worship her. She has her times and open places of cheating, and she will say and declare openly that no one is as good as she. She promises to live with children's children if they'll just love and make over her. In some places and to some people she'll cast out of her purse gold like dust. She loves to be sought after, spoken well of, and to inhabit the hearts of men. She's never weary of commending her goods, and she loves those most who think best of her. To some she'll promise crowns and kingdoms if they'll just take her advice, yet she's brought many to the hangman's rope and ten thousand times more to Hell."[17]

"Oh!" exclaimed Standfast. "What a mercy it is that I resisted her, for where might she have drawn me?"

"Where?" said Great Heart. "No one but God knows where. But to be sure, in general, she would've drawn you into many foolish and harmful desires that plunge men into ruin and destruction.[18] She was the one who set Absalom against his father[19] and Jeroboam against his master.[20] She was the one who persuaded Judas to sell his Lord[21] and who prevailed with Demas to forsake the godly Pilgrim's life.[22] No one can tell of the mischief that she does. She causes disputations between rulers and subjects, between parents and children, between neighbor and neighbor, between a man and his wife, between a man and himself, and between flesh and the heart."

"Therefore, good Mister Standfast," said Great Heart, "be as your name is, and when you've done all, stand."[23]

At this discussion there was a mixture of joy and trembling among the Pilgrims, and in time they broke out and sang:

What danger is the Pilgrim in?
How many are his Foes?
How many ways there are to Sin,
No living mortal knows.
Some in the ditch shy are, yet can
Lie tumbling on the mire.
Some, though they shun the frying-pan,
Do leap into the fire.

NOTES ON CHAPTER 33

[1] 2 Corinthians 5:7.

[2] Ephesians 6:15.

[3] Matthew 16:24; Mark 8:34; Luke 9:23; Titus 2:11-14.

[4] **God's Book.**

[5] 1 Corinthians 9:27.

[6] **Proverbs 23:34-35.**

[7] Isaiah 62:4.

[8] 1 Corinthians 9:24; 2 Timothy 4:7-8; Hebrews 12:1-3.

[9] **2 Peter 1:9. The Light of the Word.**

[10] Proverbs 28:14.

[11] Many go into eternity with a deceptive feeling of their well-being.

[12] **Proverbs 10:7.**

[13] The original was **"Madam Bubble: Or this vain World."** The use of 'bubble" to refer to something meaningless, vaporlike, or delusive was somewhat common in Bunyan's day.

[14] Isaiah 41:10.

[15] Proverbs 9:13-18.

[16] **James 4:4; 1 John 2:15.**

[17] Proverbs 7:6-27, 9:13-18.

[18] **1 Timothy 6:9.**

[19] 2 Samuel 15.

[20] 1 Kings 11:26-12:24.

[21] Matthew 26:14-16.

[22] 2 Timothy 4:10.

[23] Ephesians 6:13.

34

THE PILGRIMS CROSS THE RIVER

AFTER THIS, I WATCHED until they had come to the Land of Beulah,[1] where the sun shines night and day. They allowed themselves to rest here for a while because they were weary. This country was common for Pilgrims and the orchards and vineyards there belonged to the King of the Celestial Country; therefore they were allowed to use freely any of His things. But a little while here soon refreshed them, for the bells rang so and the trumpets continually sounded so melodious that they could not sleep. Yet they received as much refreshing as if they had never slept more soundly.

Also, all the discussion of those who walked in the streets here was about more Pilgrims coming to town, and another would talk about how many went over the water today and were let in at the Golden Gates. They would cry again, "There is now a legion of Shining Ones coming to town. By this we know that there are more Pilgrims upon the road, for they come here to wait for them and to comfort them after all their sorrow."

Resting in the Land of Beulah

Then the Pilgrims got up and walked here and there, and their ears were now filled with heavenly noises and their eyes delighted with celestial visions! In this land they heard nothing, saw nothing, felt nothing, smelled nothing, and tasted nothing that was offensive to their stomach or mind. But when they tasted of the water of the River over which they were to go, they thought it tasted a little bitter to the liking and yet proved sweeter when it was down.[2]

In this place there was a record kept of the names of those who had been Pilgrims of old, along with a history of all the famous acts they had done. Also, many talked about how the River flowed for some who had gone over, while it ebbed for others. In a manner, it was dry for some while it overflowed its banks for others.[3]

In this place, the children of the town would go into the King's Gardens and gather bouquets of flowers for the Pilgrims and bring them to them with much affection. Camphor also grew here, with spikenard, saffron, calamus, and cinnamon, with all its trees of frankincense, myrrh, and aloes, and with all the most popular spices. The Pilgrims' rooms were perfumed with these while they stayed here, and their bodies were anointed with these to prepare them to go over the River when the appointed time came.[4]

Christiana Crosses the River

Now while they lay here waiting for the good hour, there was word in the town that a Postman[5] had arrived from Celestial City with a matter of great importance to a certain Christiana, the wife of Christian the Pilgrim. So she was searched for, and the house was found where she was. The Postman presented her with a letter, and the contents of it were as follows:

Greetings, Good Woman! I bring you word that the Master calls for you and expects that within ten days you should stand in His presence clothed with immortality.[6]

403

Christiana's time to cross the River

When he had read this letter to her, with it he gave to her a token that he was a true messenger and had come to tell her to make haste to leave. The token, let easily into her heart, was an arrow with a point sharpened with love, which by degrees worked so effectually in her that at the time appointed she must be gone.[7]

When Christiana saw that her time had come and that she was the first of this group to go over, she called for Mr. Great Heart, her Guide, and told him how things were. So he told her he was very glad of the news, and that he could have been glad if the Postman had come for him. Then she asked that he would give her advice about how everything should be prepared for her journey.

So he told her, saying this and that must happen, and then said, "We who survive will accompany you to the riverside."

Then she called for her children and gave them her blessing, and she told them she still read with comfort the mark that was set in their foreheads and was glad to see them with her there and that she was glad they had kept their garments so white. Lastly, she bequeathed to the poor what little she had and commanded her sons and daughters-in-law to be ready for the messenger, should he come for them.

When she had spoken these words to her Guide and to her children, she called for Mr. Valiant Fortruth and said to him, "Sir, you've shown yourself in all places to be true hearted. Be faithful, even to the point of death, and my King will give you the crown of life.[8] I would also implore you to keep an eye on my children, and if at any time you see them faint, speak appropriately to them. As for my daughters, my sons' wives, they have been faithful, and a fulfilling of the promise upon them will be their end."

She gave a ring to Mr. Standfast and then called for old Mr. Honest and said of him, "'Here is a true Israelite, in whom there is nothing false.'"[9]

Mr. Honest replied, "I wish you a pleasant day when you set out for Mount Zion, and I'll be glad to see that you go over the River with dry feet."

But she answered, "Come wet, come dry, I long to be gone; for however the weather is in my journey, when I arrive there I'll have time enough to sit down to rest and dry myself."

Then that good man, Mr. About Tofall, came in to see her. So she said to him, "Your travel here has been with difficulty, but that will make your rest all the sweeter. But watch and be ready, for the messenger may come at an hour when you think not."[10]

After him, Mr. Despondency came in with his daughter Much Afraid to whom she said, "You ought to remember forever with thankfulness your deliverance from the hand of Giant Despair and from out of Doubting Castle. The effect of that mercy is that you were brought safely here. Be watchful, and cast away fear; be sober, and hope to the end."[11]

Then she said to Mr. Feeblemind, "You were delivered from the mouth of Giant Slay Good so that you might live in the Light of the Living forever and see the King with comfort. Only, I advise you to repent of your tendency to fear and doubt His goodness before He sends for you, lest when He comes you should be forced to stand before him for that fault with blushing."

Now the day drew near that Christiana must be gone, so the Road was full of people to see her take her journey. But even more exciting was that the banks beyond the River were lined all along with horses and chariots that came down from above to accompany her to the City Gate. So she went forward and entered the River with a gesture of farewell to those who followed her to the riverside. The last word she was heard to say here was, "I come, Lord, to be with you and worship you."

Soon those who waited for Christiana had carried her out of their sight.

Christiana went to the Gate and called, and she entered with all the ceremonies of joy that her husband Christian had received when he went in before her. At her departure, her children wept, but Mr. Great Heart and Mr. Valiant played joyfully upon the well tuned cymbal and harp. So everyone departed to their respective places.

Mr. About Tofall Crosses the River

In the process of time, a Postman came to the town again, and this time his business was with Mr. About Tofall. So he searched him out and said to him, "I've come to you in the name of Him whom you have loved and followed, though upon crutches. And my message is to tell you that He expects you at His table to dine with Him in His Kingdom the day after Easter. Prepare yourself, therefore, for your journey."

Then he also gave him a token that he was a true messenger, saying, "I have broken your golden bowl and severed your silver cord."[12]

After this, Mr. About Tofall called for his fellow Pilgrims and told them, saying, "I've been sent for, and God shall surely visit you too." And because he had nothing except his crutches and his good wishes to bequeath to those who would survive him, he said therefore, "To my son, who will follow in my steps, I bequeath these crutches along with an hundred warm wishes that he may walk them better than I have."

Then he thanked Mr. Great Heart for his guidance and kindness, and so addressed himself to his journey.

When Mr. About Tofall came to the brink of the River, he said, "Now I'll have no more need of these crutches since yonder are chariots and horses for me to ride on." The last words he was heard to say were, "Welcome, life!" So he went his way.

Mr. Feeblemind Crosses the River

After this, Mr. Feeblemind had word brought to him that the Postman sounded his horn at his bedroom door. Then he came in and told him, saying, "I've come to tell you that your Master has need of you, and that in a very short time you must look upon His face in brightness. Take this as a token of the truth of my message; 'those looking through the windows grow dim.'"[13]

407

Then Mr. Feeblemind called for his friends and told them what errand had been brought to him and what token he had received of the truth of the message. Then he said, "Since I have nothing to bequeath to anyone, what would be the purpose of making out a will? As for my feeble mind, I'll leave that behind me, for I'll have no need of that in the place where I'm going; nor is it worth giving to the poorest Pilgrims. When I'm gone, therefore, I desire that you, Mr. Valiant, would bury it in a dunghill."

With this done, and the day in which he was to depart having arrived, he entered the River like the rest. His last words were, "Hold out, Faith and Patience!" So, he went over to the other side.

Mr. Despondency Crosses the River

When many days had passed, Mr. Despondency was sought out, for a Postman had come and brought this message to him: "Trembling Man, these are to summon you to be ready with your King by the next Lord's Day to shout for joy because of your deliverance from all your doubtings. And," said the messenger, "take this for a proof that my message is true." So he gave him a grasshopper dragging himself along.[14]

Now when she heard what had happened, Mr. Despondency's daughter, whose name was Much Afraid, said she would go with her father. Then Mr. Despondency said to his friends, "As for myself and my daughter, you know what we've been and how troublesomely we have behaved ourselves in every company. My and my daughter's will is that our despondencies and slavish fears should never be received by anyone from the day of our departure forever. I know that after my death they will offer themselves to others, for to be plain with you, they are ghosts that we entertained when we first began to be Pilgrims and that we could never shake off thereafter. And they will walk about and seek entertainment of the Pilgrims. But for our sakes, shut the doors upon them."

When the time came for them to depart, they went to the brink of the River. The last words of Mr. Despondency were, "Farewell, Night! Welcome, Day!" His daughter went through the River singing, but no one could understand what she said.

Mr. Honest Crosses the River

Then a while thereafter, it came to pass that there was a Postman in the town who inquired for Mr. Honest. So he came to the house where he was and delivered into his hands these lines: "You are commanded to be ready against a week from today to present yourself before your Lord at His Father's house. And for a token that my message is true, all the birds' songs grow faint."[15]

Then Mr. Honest called for his friends and said to them, "I'm going to die, but I'll make no will. As for my honesty, it will go with me. Let him who comes after me be told of this."

When the day came in which he was to go over the River, he addressed himself to go over it. Now the River at that time overflowed its banks in some places. But in his lifetime, Mr. Honest had spoken to Good Conscience to meet him there; and doing so, he lent him his hand and helped him over. The last words of Mr. Honest were, "Grace reigns!" So, he left the world.

Mr. Valiant Fortruth Crosses the River

After this, the word spread that Mr. Valiant Fortruth received a summons by the same Postman as the other, and he had this for a token that the summons was true, that his "pitcher is shattered at the spring."[16]

When he understood it, he called for his friends and told them about it. "Then I'm going to my Father's House," he said, " and although I've gotten there with great difficulty, yet I don't regret all the trouble I've had to deal with to arrive where I am. I give my Sword to him who shall succeed me in my Pilgrimage, and my courage and skill to him who can get

Good Conscience helps Mr. Honest over the River

it. I'll carry my marks and scars with me to be a witness that I've fought the battles of Him who is now my Rewarder."

When the day arrived that he must go there, many accompanied him to the riverside, into which as he went he said, "Where, O death, is your sting?"[17] And as he went down deeper, he said, "Where, O death, is your victory?" So he passed over, and all the trumpets sounded for him on the other side.

Mr. Standfast Crosses the River

Then there came a summons for Mr. Standfast (this Mr. Standfast was he whom the rest of the Pilgrims found upon his knees in the Enchanted Ground), and the Postman brought it to him open in his hands. The contents of it was that he must prepare for a change of life, for his Master was not willing that he should be so far from Him any longer.

At this, Mr. Standfast was caused to contemplate. "No," said the messenger, "you needn't doubt the truth of my message, for here is a token of the truth of it: Your wheel is broken at the well."[18]

Then he called to him Mr. Great Heart, who was their Guide, and said to him, "Sir, although it wasn't my privilege to be in your good company much in the days of my Pilgrimage, yet since the time I knew you, you've been profitable to me. When I came from home, I left behind me a wife and five small children. Upon your return—for I know you will go and return to your Master's house in hopes that you may still be a Guide to more of the Holy Pilgrims—let me ask you that you send to my family and let them be acquainted with all that has and shall happen to me. Tell them, moreover, of my happy arrival to this place and of the present blessed condition that I'm in of late. Tell them also about Christian and Christiana, his wife, and how she and her children came after her husband. Tell them also about what a happy end she had and where she has gone. I have little to send to my family except it be prayers and tears for them. If you acquaint them with those, that will be enough if they prevail with them."

When Mr. Standfast had thus set things in order, and the

time having arrived for him to haste away, he also went down to the River. Now there was a great calm at that time in the River. When he was about halfway in, therefore, Mr. Standfast stood for a while and talked to his companions who had waited upon him there.

And he said, "This River has been a terror to many. Yes, also the thoughts of it have often frightened me. But now I think I stand easy. My foot is fixed upon that which the feet of the Priests who carried the Ark of the Covenant stood upon while Israel went over this Jordan.[19] The waters are indeed bitter to the taste and cold to the stomach, yet the thoughts of where I'm going and of the escort that awaits me on the other side lay as a glowing coal in my heart."

Mr. Standfast continued, "I see myself now at the end of my journey. My toilsome days have ended. I'm now going to see that Head that was crowned with thorns and that Face that was spit upon for me.[20] I have formerly lived by hearsay and faith, but now I'm going where I'll live by sight; and I'll be with Him in whose company I delight myself.[21] I've loved to hear my Lord spoken of, and wherever I've seen the print of His shoe in the earth, there I have desired to set my foot also"[22]

"His name has been to me as a civet box,[23] yes, sweeter than all perfumes," said Mr. Standfast. "His voice to me has been most sweet, and I've desired His countenance more than they who have most desired the light of the sun.[24] I used to gather His Word for my food and for antidotes against my faintings.[25] He has held me, and I've kept myself from my iniquities. Yes, He has strengthened my steps in His Way."

Now, while he was talking like this, his countenance changed. His strong man bowed under him, and after he had said, "Take me, for I come to You!" he ceased to be seen of them.

But it was a glorious thing to see how the open region was filled with horses and chariots, with trumpeters and pipers, with singers, and with players on stringed instruments, which welcomed the Pilgrims as they went up and followed one another in at the Beautiful Gate of the City.

As for Christian's children—the four boys whom Christiana

brought with her, along with their wives and children—I did not stay where I was until they went over. Also, since I came away, I heard one say that they were still alive, and so for a time they would be there for the increase of the Church in that place where they were.

If it is my lot to go that way again, I may give those who desire it an account about which I am here silent. In the meantime, I bid you farewell.

The End

NOTES ON CHAPTER 34

1 Isaiah 62:4.
2 **Death bitter to the flesh, but sweet to the soul.**
3 **Death has its ebbings and flowings like the tide.**
4 Matthew 26:7-12; Mark 14:3-8.
5 **A messenger of death sent to Christiana.**
6 1 Corinthians 15:53-54.
7 **How welcome is death to them who are willing to die.**
8 Revelation 2:10.
9 John 1:47.
10 Matthew 24:44; Luke 12:40; Revelation 3:3.
11 Hebrews 6:11; 1 Peter 1:13.
12 **Ecclesiastes 12:6-7.**
13 Ecclesiastes 12:3.
14 **Ecclesiastes 12:5.**
15 **Ecclesiastes 12:4.**
16 **Ecclesiastes 12:6.**
17 1 Corinthians 15:55.
18 **Ecclesiastes 12:6.**
19 **Joshua 3:17.**
20 Matthew 27:27-31; Mark 15:16-20.
21 1 Corinthians 13:12.
22 John 10:4.
23 A "civet cat" is a catlike animal about the size of a fox, native to Africa, which secretes a yellowish substance with a musky odor used in the manufacture of perfumes.
24 Psalm 42:1-2.
25 Psalm 111:5; 1 Peter 2:2-3.

Bunyan's birthplace, Elstow

The Life of John Bunyan

John Bunyan, author of *The Pilgrim's Progress*, was born in November, 1628, to a poor family in the village of Elstow, about a mile from Bedford, England. His father was a tinker—a mender of pots and other household utensils—and John followed his father in the tinker's trade. His parents could not afford an extensive education for him, but they did manage to scrape together enough of their meager earnings to send John to school to learn to read and write. But by his own admission, he lost most of what he had learned long before his Christian conversion.

Through his literary work and the testimonies of others, we know that John Bunyan was an intuitive and highly creative man, capable of deeply serious contemplation and blessed with a flare for symbolism. Even as a child, he was prone to somber thought, which at times brought him terror. He admitted, "[I] so offended the Lord, that even in my childhood He did scare and affrighten me with fearful dreams, and did terrify me with fearful visions."

In his first major published work, *Grace Abounding To The Chief of Sinners,* he testified of the various stages of the awakening to his own spiritual condition and to future judgment. He described himself as having had few equals for "cursing, swearing, lying, and blaspheming the holy name of God." He said that until his marriage he "was the very ringleader of all the youth that kept [him] company, in all manner of vice and ungodliness."

After serving in the army, at about the age of twenty he married Margaret Bentley; and to this union were born four children—Mary (born blind), Elisabeth, John, and Thomas. John's wife Margaret was a woman of devout religious upbringing, and her life became a great influence on her husband, who eventually began reading again and seeking a religious solution for his troubled soul. He joined the village church; but his early attempts to find peace proved unsuccessful as he struggled with a strong and vile nature that was not abated by his increased religious activity.

Much like the "Pilgrim" of whom he was to write, John Bunyan experienced a long pilgrimage before he felt free from condemnation and found peace in his relationship with God. His search for salvation led in time to his leaving the parish church and joining a group of believers of Puritan persuasion who met apart from the official Church of England. The Puritans baptized him by immersion, and he became a member of the Bedford Separatist congregation. As his pilgrimage continued, he matured in his Christian experience and eventually became a lay preacher.

His wife Margaret died at a young age in 1655, and four years later John married his second wife Elizabeth. By this time, he had become a popular lay preacher, holding house worship services and speaking wherever he was welcome. But his growing popularity and separatist teachings were far from welcome among the leaders of the state church. After a twenty-year period in which nonconforming religious groups had been allowed freedom of worship, the rule over England changed and with it came new power and authority for the official church hierarchy.

In 1660, under the restoration of Charles II, freedom of worship was taken away from the Puritans, and the conduct of religious services except for those in accordance with the Church of England was outlawed. Bunyan refused to stop preaching and was soon arrested. He was convicted of holding a service not in conformance with those of the state church and confined in the Bedford County Jail. A short time after his arrest he was offered a release if he would return to attending services in the state church and stop preaching, but he would not recant. He remained in prison for twelve years, all the while holding to his convictions. It was during this imprisonment that he wrote *Grace Abounding To The Chief of Sinners*, published in 1666.

Bunyan's second wife, Elizabeth, was a brave Christian woman who stood by his side through his persecution and campaigned for his release. He finally gained that release in 1672 and enjoyed a period of freedom—during which time he began serving as pastor of the congregation in Bedford—but in a time of renewed persecution in 1677 he was again arrested and detained in jail for six months.

There is some disagreement concerning during which of these imprisonments he wrote his most famous and popular work, *The Pilgrim's Progress From This World To That Which Is To Come*. Some believe he wrote the first half of the book (the experiences of Christian, Faithful, and Hopeful) during his first imprisonment and held it for a time before publishing it. Others believe he wrote it during the second imprisonment. Whichever the case, it does appear—based on his own notations and contemporary sources—that he did in fact write the first half of the book while in prison. The book's first edition was published in 1678. The second half of the book, in which he told the story of the pilgrimage of Christiana and her children and friends, was written later and added to his 1684 edition.

The prison on Bedford Bridge

The Pilgrim's Progress has been translated into many languages and is held in high regard around the world. There was a time when there was hardly an English-speaking Christian household without a copy. Next to the Bible, this classic allegory has been the best-selling Christian book and the leading allegory in all of English literature. Its influence can be seen in Christian writing, preaching, literary criticism, commentary, and song lyrics spanning the centuries since its writing. Bunyan's other major works include The Life and Death of Mr. Badman (1680), and The Holy War (1682).

John Bunyan, who without a doubt became the leading Puritan clergyman of his time, died on August 31, 1688, and is buried in Bunhill Fields, a London burial ground for nonconformists. His own pilgrimage—paralleled by that of Christian in Bunyan's timeless classic The Pilgrim's Progress— at last brought the author to the gates he so eloquently and vividly exalted.

EVENT OUTLINE AND TWO-PART COMPARISON OF THE EXPERIENCES OF THE PRINCIPLE CHARACTERS

421

Part One Ch.	**Event**	**Part Two** Ch.
2	Christian and Pliable fall into the swamp.	
	Christiana and her group use the steps to get across the swamp.	22
2	Pliable is discouraged and goes back from where he came.	
2	One named Help assists Christian to get out of the swamp and explains its existence and about the steps.	
3	Christian follows the wrong advice and is nearly brought to ruin by his failed attempt to find deliverance through Legality.	
3	Christian is once again ministered to and encouraged by Evangelist, who explains to him the deceptive nature of Legality.	
4	Christian, and Christiana's group, reach the Gate.	22
4	The enemy is near the Gate to interfere with the Pilgrims.	22
	Christiana's group experiences some difficulty actually entering through the Gate once they have arrived	22
	Christiana, who has already gained admittance, intercedes for Mercy, who remains outside the Gate.	22
4	Christian is told his burden will be carried on his journey until he reaches the place of deliverance.	
	Christiana's sons eat the dangerous fruit of the enemy's garden.	23
	Christiana and Mercy are accosted by ill-intentioned individuals.	23
	Those of the House hear the women's cries and come to their rescue.	23
	Christiana's group are told they should have asked for a Guide.	23
5	Christian, and Christiana's group, are entertained in the Interpreter's house.	23

Part One Ch.	**Event**	**Part Two** Ch.

Part One Ch.	Event	Part Two Ch.
	Christiana's group sees the platform and discusses the end of Mistrust and Fearful.	24
7	Christian laments his loss and returns to retrieve his Document.	
8	Christian, and Christiana's group, meet with Lions in the path.	24
	Christiana's group is confronted by Grim, the giant who supports the work of the Lions.	24
	Great Heart brings down the giant.	24
8	Christian, and Christiana's group, reach the palace (house) named Beautiful and are met by the Porter.	25
	Great Heart leaves the Pilgrims with the Family and returns to his former place.	25
8	Christian, and Christiana's group, are welcomed into the house by members and leaders of the Family	25
8	Christian has a long discussion with the Family about his pilgrim experiences.	
8	Christian, and Christiana's group, eat and sleep in the House.	25
	One Pilgrim, Mercy, has a pleasant dream.	25
	Christiana's sons are taught doctrine.	25
	Mercy receives romantic advances from Mr. Brisk, who is turned away by her compassion for others.	25
	Mathew, one of the young pilgrims who ate the enemy's fruit becomes very ill.	25
	Mr. Skill, the Physician, prepares a cure for Mathew, and he is restored to health.	25
	Mathew inquires further into the meaning of things.	25

Part One Ch.	Event	Part Two Ch.
8	Christiana's group is shown records and items of historical value to the Family.	25
8	Christian is shown the lineage and acts of the Lord of the Hill.	
8	Christian is shown the records of those in His service and many of their acts. (There is no expansion on them, so they are not listed here separately.)	
	Christiana's group is shown the fruit that Eve ate.	25
	Christiana's group is shown angels ascending on Jacob's Stairway.	25
	Christiana's group is shown a golden anchor.	25
	Christiana's group is led up the mountain where Abraham offered his son to God.	25
8	Christian is shown the Delightful Mountains standing in the distance.	
8	Before leaving, Christian is outfitted with items from the armory.	
	Great Heart returns to lead the Pilgrims farther.	25
8	Christian, and Christiana's group, are accompanied down the hill by members of the Family.	26
9	Christian, and Christiana's group, descend into the Valley of Humiliation.	26
9	Christian battles Apollyon.	
	Great Heart instructs the Pilgrims in the character of the Valley of Humiliation.	26
9	Christian, and Christiana's group, reach the Valley of the Shadow of Death.	26
9	Christian meets two more men who are going back and who warn him to also return.	

427

Part One Ch.	**Event**	**Part Two** Ch.
12	Christian and Faithful are arrested, mistreated, subjected to public humiliation, and led in chains to court.	
12	Judge Hate Good presides and hears the testimony of Envy, Superstition, and Gainglory.	
12	The judge instructs the jury in the law he upholds.	
12	The jury finds Faithful guilty.	
12	Faithful is put to death in a cruel fashion.	
12	Christian escapes after spending time in prison.	
	Great Heart leads the Pilgrims to the house of Mnason, an old disciple.	29
	Mr. Mnason invites other godly friends and residents of the town to meet the Pilgrims.	29
	Christiana's group recounts their journey and Mnason's friends share their wisdom.	29
	Two of Christian's sons are married to Mnason's daughters.	29
	Christiana's group and their friends do battle with a peculiar monster.	29
	Christiana's group comes to the place where Faithful was put to death, and they worship God there.	29
13	Another Pilgrim named Hopeful joins Christian in his pilgrimage.	
13	Christian and Hopeful meet an individual named ByEnds and debate his doctrine of error.	
13	ByEnds meets with others of similar persuasion, and they embolden themselves with their materialistic beliefs.	
13	ByEnds and his friends confront Christian and Hopeful, who refute their beliefs.	

Part One Ch.	Event	Part Two Ch.
13	Christian, and Christiana's group, arrive at the Hill Lucre.	30
13	Demas calls Christian and Hopeful to come look into a silver mine in the hill; they refuse the temptation.	
13	At the first call, ByEnds and his friends go to the mine and are never again seen in the Way.	
13	Christian, and Christiana's group, see a monument on the side of the road, the pillar of salt which was once Lot's wife.	30
13	Christian's, and Christiana's group's path leads them beside the river of the water of life.	30
13	Christian, and Christiana's group, find rest and sustenance in the meadow by the river.	30
14	Christian, and Christiana's group, come to another meadow called By-path Meadow.	30
14	Christian and Hopeful walk on an adjacent path, and it proves to be a dreadful mistake.	
14	Christian and Hopeful are taken captive by Giant Despair.	
14	Christian and Hopeful are terrorized by the Giant, who, following his wife's recommendations, threatens them and advises them to take their own lives.	
14	After serious consideration of suicide, Christian remembers his Key called Promise; Christian and Hopeful escape from the Giant's dungeon.	
	Christiana's group and their friends decide to attack Giant Despair and destroy his castle.	30
	Mr. Honest strikes down Diffidence, the Giant's wife.	30
	Great Heart kills Giant Despair.	30
	While demolishing the castle, they free two captives, Mr. Despondency and his daughter Much Afraid.	30

Part One Ch.	**Event**	**Part Two** Ch.
15	Christian, and Christiana's group, reach the Delightful Mountains and are welcomed by the Shepherds.	
30		
15	Christian and Hopeful are shown the hill called Error.	
15	Christian and Hopeful are taken to the top of a mountain called Caution.	
	Christiana's group is taken to Mount Marvel.	30
	Christiana's group is taken to Mount Innocent.	30
	Christiana's group is taken to Mount Charity	30
	Christiana's group is shown the deeds of Fool and Lackwit.	30
15	Christian, and Christiana's group, are shown a door in the side of a hill.	30
	The Shepherds give Mercy a mirror and also give items to others of the pilgrim party.	30
15	Christian and Hopeful are shown Celestial City in the distance from the top of a high hill called Clear.	
16	Christian and Hopeful encounter a young man named Ignorance, who is attempting to reach Celestial City from another path.	
16	Christian and Hopeful see one named Turn Away being carried back to the door in the side of the hill.	
	Great Heart tells the Pilgrims the story of Turn Away.	32
16	Christian and Hopeful discuss the experiences of one named Little Faith.	
16	Little Faith is robbed of everything but his Jewels.	
16	A difference is made between Little Faith and Esau.	
16	Christian and Hopeful talk about an individual named Great Grace.	

431

Part One Ch.	Event	Part Two Ch.
	Christiana's group meets Valiant Fortruth where Little Faith was earlier robbed.	32
	Valiant tells of his recent battle with those who assaulted him.	32
	Great Heart and Valiant talk about his sword.	32
	Valiant recounts the opposition of his parents to his going on pilgrimage.	32
17	Christian and Hopeful meet and succumb to Flatterer, a False Apostle.	
17	Christian and Hopeful are rescued and punished by a Shining One.	
17	One named Atheist challenges and ridicules Christian and Hopeful.	
18	Christian, and Christiana's group, come to the Enchanted Ground.	33
18	Christian and Hopeful enter into a discussion to stay alert.	
18	Hopeful tells of his conversion.	
18	Hopeful reveals he was influenced to become a pilgrim by Faithful at the Vanity Fair.	
18	Faithful gave to Hopeful a Book of the words of Jesus.	
	Christiana's group travels through darkness upon muddy, thorny ground.	33
	Being weary, Christiana's group is tempted to stop and rest in an arbor called the Slothful's Friend.	33
	Great Heart Strikes a light and looks to his Book for directions.	33
	Christiana's group comes to another arbor in which two pilgrims are asleep.	33

| **Part One** | **Event** | **Part Two** |
Ch.		Ch.
	The Pilgrims cannot wake them; the Guide explains the reasons.	33
	Near the end of the Enchanted Ground, Christiana's group comes upon Mr. Standfast, who is in prayer.	33
	Mr. Standfast tells of his experience of meeting Madam Delusive.	33
19	In an attempt to help Ignorance, Christian and Hopeful slow down and talk with him.	
19	Ignorance is confronted with the truth about his deceptive heart and his thoughts about his own condition.	
19	Ignorance is proven to be completely devoid of understanding about the righteousness by which pilgrims are saved.	
19	Ignorance cannot keep pace with Christian and Hopeful.	
19	Christian and Hopeful discuss how many people are in the same condition and how the ignorant deal with conviction.	
19	Christian and Hopeful discuss backsliding, why people go back, and how they do it.	
20	Christian, and Christiana's group, reach the Land of Beulah, where they are allowed to rest for a while.	34
20	Christian and Hopeful find between them and Celestial City a River over which there is no bridge.	
20	Christian and Hopeful enter the River.	
20	Hopeful must encourage and help Christian as they cross the river.	
20	Christian finally is encouraged, and Christian and Hopeful get to the other side.	
20	With much excitement, Christian and Hopeful are led to the City gate by the heavenly host.	

INDEX

A

Abiram 142
About Tofall, Mr. 355, 364, 369, 370, 376, 406, 407
Abraham 136, 141, 207, 302
Absalom 399
Adam the First 92, 93, 355
Alexander 160
All-Prayer 84
Altar 302
Ananias 160
Ancient of Days 70
Anything, Mr. 132
Apollyon 77, 78, 79, 80, 81, 82, 83, 84, 97, 117, 153, 234, 307, 311, 355
Apostle 109
Armory 70
Arrogance 94
Art of Getting 135
Assault Lane 347
Atheist 175, 176, 177
avenger of blood 89, 200

B

barking dog 251
Bath 266, 267
Beautiful 327
Beautiful Gate of the City 412
Beautiful, house called 267
Beautiful, palace called 59
Bedford County Jail 417
Bedford, England 415
Bedford Gaol 7
Bedford Separatist 416
Beelzebub 31, 82, 117, 118, 123, 124
Beelzebub's Castle 386
Beelzebub's garden 368
Beelzebub's Orchard 296
Belt 322
Bentley, Margaret 416
Best of Books 37
Beulah 201
Black River 388
Blessed One 118

C

I

Ignorance 163, 189, 190, 191, 192, 193, 194, 195, 196,
        210, 211
Illwill 377
Immanuel's Land 71, 72, 157
Inconsiderate 383
Inconsiderate, Mrs. 236
Innkeeper 340
Interpreter 33, 35, 37, 38, 39, 40, 42, 43, 44, 45, 65, 257, 259
        260, 261, 262, 263, 264, 265, 266, 267, 301, 315, 325
Iron Cage of Despair 42, 43
Isaac 207, 302
Israel 59
Italian Avenue 118

J

Jacob 138, 207, 332
Jacob's Stairway 301
Jael 71
James 291, 301, 324, 339, 345, 369
James the Just 324
Japheth 63
Jeroboam 399
Jerusalem Blade 384
Jewel 166, 167
Job 7, 136, 145, 172, 200
Joseph 91, 106, 292, 313, 324, 343, 362, 369
Judas 139, 160, 399
Judge Hate Good 122, 124

K

Keeper 242, 243, 244, 245, 247
Key called Promise 154
King 207, 227, 238
King David 84
King of Glory 24, 38, 207
King of Paradise 333
King of Princes 78
King of the Abyss 169
King of the Celestial Country 155, 401
King of the Country 234
King, The 171
Kingdom of Heaven 96, 102
King's Champion 169
King's Gardens 403

Salvation 330
Salvation, wall called 49
Samson 71, 383
Samuel 293, 296, 311, 324, 344, 362, 369
Sapphira 160
Sarah 332
Satan 65
Satyrs 83, 86
Saveall, Mr. 135, 136
Saveself 197
Saving Faith 168
Saywell, man named 102
Seal 267
Secret 231
Self Conceit 94
Selfwill, Mr. 331
Sepulchre 50
Seraphim 10
Serpent 341
Shadow of Death 83, 234
Shame 95, 96, 97, 355
Shamgar 71
Shechem 138
Shepherd 158
Shepherd Boy 309, 310
Shepherds 71, 157, 158, 159, 160, 161, 174, 179, 375, 376,
        377, 378, 379, 380, 381
Shield 70, 80, 267, 346
Shining Men 206
Shining Ones 50, 53, 174, 201, 206, 207, 208, 227, 385, 401
Shoes 70
Simon the sorcerer 139
Simple 50, 66, 275
Sincerity 158, 379
Sisera 71
Skill, Mr. 296, 297, 299, 313
Slaughter House 260
Slay Good, the Giant 350
Sleepers 393
Sleepy Head 276
Sloth 50, 66, 275
Slothful's Friend, an arbor called 392
Slow Pace 276
Smooth Man, Mr. 132
Sodom 142, 143, 367
Solomon 97, 332
Sophistry 316

CHRISTIAN CLASSICS
IN MODERN ENGLISH

In-depth topical & scriptural indexes
Full-color 2000-year historical timeline
Hundreds of scriptural references & notes
Comprehensive author biography & photographs
Many other features

THE NEW FOXE'S BOOK OF MARTYRS

to include
recent
accounts
from the
160,000
martyred
in

Classic

JOHN FOXE

REWRITTEN AND UPDATED BY HAROLD J. CHADWICK

ISBN: 0-88270-875-9

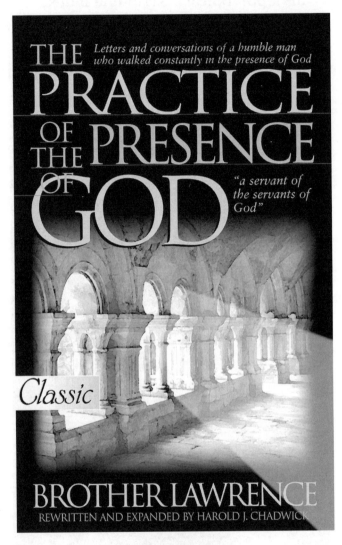

THE
Letters and conversations of a humble man who walked constantly in the presence of God

PRACTICE
OF PRESENCE
THE
OF GOD

"a servant of the servants of God"

Classic

BROTHER LAWRENCE
REWRITTEN AND EXPANDED BY HAROLD J. CHADWICK

ISBN: 0-88270-793-0

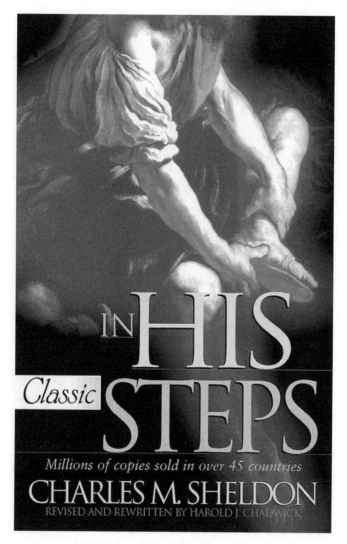

IN HIS

Classic STEPS

Millions of copies sold in over 45 countries

CHARLES M. SHELDON

REVISED AND REWRITTEN BY HAROLD J. CHADWICK

ISBN: 0-88270-782-5

THE
IMITATION
OF
CHRIST

After the Bible, this is probably the best loved book
of Christianity

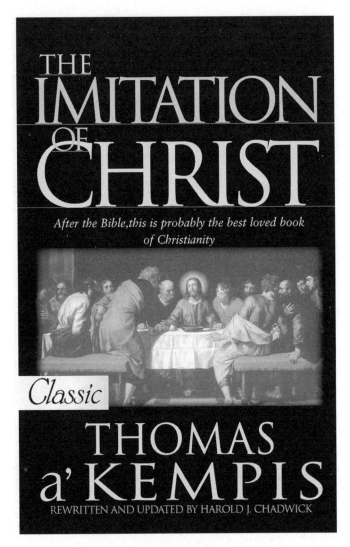

Classic

THOMAS
a'KEMPIS
REWRITTEN AND UPDATED BY HAROLD J. CHADWICK

ISBN: 0-88270-766-3

HUMILITY

The deepest humility is the secret of the truest happiness, of a joy that nothing can destroy. Andrew Murray

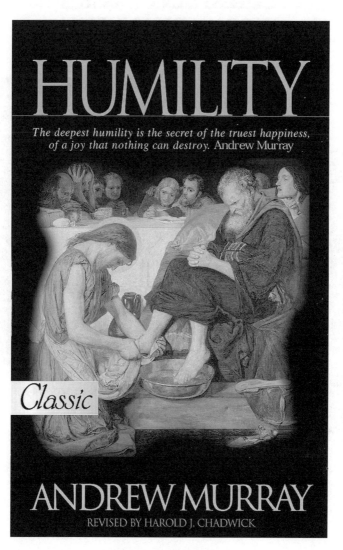

Classic

ANDREW MURRAY

REVISED BY HAROLD J. CHADWICK

ISBN: 0-88270-854-6

CHRISTIAN CLASSICS
IN MODERN ENGLISH

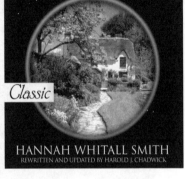

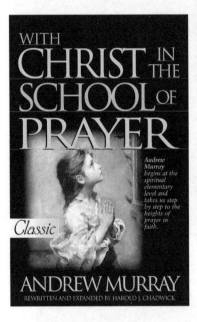

ISBN: 0-88270-754-X

ISBN: 0-88270-779-5

CHRISTIAN CLASSICS
IN MODERN ENGLISH

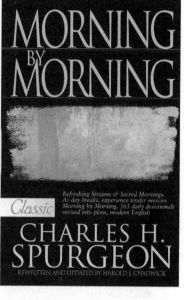

ISBN: 0-88270-821-X

ISBN: 0-88270-763-9

MADAME JEANNE GUYON

Classic

EXPERIENCING UNION WITH GOD
THROUGH INNER PRAYER
&THE WAY AND RESULTS OF
UNION WITH GOD

REVISED IN MODERN ENGLISH BY HAROLD J. CHADWICK

ISBN: 0-88270-873-2